Socialism in Galicia:
The Emergence of Polish Social Democracy and Ukrainian Radicalism (1860–1890)

John-Paul Himka

Socialism in Galicia

*The Emergence of Polish Social Democracy
and Ukrainian Radicalism (1860-1890)*

Distributed by Harvard University Press
for the
Harvard Ukrainian Research Institute

Publication of this book was made possible by a grant from the
Ukrainian Studies Fund

The Harvard Ukrainian Research Institute was established in 1973 as an integral part of Harvard University. It supports research associates and visiting scholars who are engaged in projects concerned with all aspects of Ukrainian studies. The Institute also works in close cooperation with the Committee on Ukrainian Studies, which supervises and coordinates the teaching of Ukrainian history, language, and literature at Harvard University.

Dedicated to the Memory of my Grandmother,
EVA HIMKA (1886–1974),
and to the other heroes of this narrative,
named and unnamed,
who struggled for human dignity.

Vichnaia im pamiat'

Contents

Preface

Austrian Poles and Ukrainians had for many things three names: a German, Polish and Ukrainian name. The viceroy of Galicia, for instance, was called *Statthalter, namiestnik* and *namisnyk*. A district was called *Bezirk, powiat* and *povit*. Cracow was called Krakau, Kraków and Krakiv. In general, I have used English equivalents for all administrative offices and divisions to avoid favoring the language of one nationality over that of another. For geographical names, I have favored common English usage where such exists: Vienna, Kiev, Cracow and Warsaw, for example. Otherwise, I have given Galician place names in their modern Polish or Ukrainian spelling, depending on whether the places are now in Poland or Soviet Ukraine. The only exception is Ivano-Frankivsk, for which I use the old name Stanyslaviv. Since Ivan Franko is a leading *dramatis persona* of this study, it would have been ludicrous to use the modern name.

I have not tampered at all with Polish words and names: all diacritical marks remain. In the case of Ukrainian and Russian, I have transliterated from Cyrillic according to the Library of Congress system, with some simplifications. Except in bibliographical references, Ia, Ie, Io and Iu are rendered as Ya, Ye, Yo and Yu when they are found at the beginning of proper nouns; the endings -yi and -ii in Ukrainian and Russian surnames are replaced by -y; and all apostrophes indicating soft signs are omitted. Since Ukrainian was not standardized in the nineteenth century, some letters that Ukrainians then used are not to be found in the modern Ukrainian alphabet (and hence in the LC system). In these cases, I have phonetically transliterated the old into the modern alphabet and then used the LC system. In the case of writings in *iazychiie* and "attempted Russian" emanating from Galicia, I have transliterated them as though they were in Ukrainian. This follows the actual phonetic practice of nineteenth-century Galicia.

In some cases it has been difficult to decide how to refer to certain individuals. Some ethnic Ukrainians, for example, were almost totally assimilated into Polish society. In the end, I decided to call them by their Polish names (Józef Daniluk instead of Osyp Danyliuk). There were some borderline cases, however, whom I ended up calling by their Ukrainian names (Mykhailo Drabyk instead of Michał Drabik, Stanyslav Kozlovsky instead of Stanisław Kozłowski). Many Austrian Ukrainians considered themselves Russians, but I have consistently used the Ukrainian version of their names. I have used the current standard version of almost all Ukrainian first names except in bibliographical references where the author's name is given in the publication itself and in regularly used peasant diminutives.

I am grateful to the International Research and Exchanges Board, to both the East European and Soviet divisions, for arranging and funding two years of research in Poland and the USSR; to the Department of Health, Education and Welfare (Fulbright-Hays Doctoral Dissertation Research Abroad Program) for supporting research in Poland and Austria; to the Department of History of The University of Michigan for a Rackham Predoctoral Fellowship enabling me to spend an academic year writing; and to the Ukrainian Academy of Arts and Sciences in the U.S. for a stipend to prepare an earlier draft of this study.

I would also like to thank the staffs of the following archives and libraries for their great generosity: Archiwum Państwowe M. Krakowa i Woj. Krakowskiego (Cracow); Centralne Archiwum Komitetu Centralnego PZPR (Warsaw); Haus-, Hof- und Staatsarchiv (Vienna); Verein für Geschichte der Arbeiterbewegung (Vienna); Instytut literatury Akademii nauk URSR, Viddil rukopysiv (Kiev); L'vivs'kyi oblasnyi derzhavnyi arkhiv (Lviv); Tsentral'nyi derzhavnyi istorychnyi arkhiv URSR u L'vovi (Lviv); the university libraries of Vienna, Warsaw, Leningrad, Lviv and Kiev; Biblioteka Jagiellońska (Cracow); Biblioteka Narodowa (Warsaw); Österreichische Nationalbibliothek (Vienna); Glavnaia publichnaia biblioteka im. Saltykova-Shchedrina (Leningrad); and Tsentral'na naukova biblioteka Akademii nauk URSR (Kiev). Thanks are also due to my hosts in Europe: Jagellonian University (Cracow), Leningrad University, Lviv University and Kiev University.

I am especially indebted to those who acted as my advisors in an official capacity: Professor Roman Szporluk at The University of Michigan; Prorector Józef Buszko at Jagellonian University; Professor Stanislav Mikhailovich Stetskevich at Leningrad University; and Professor Antin Petrovych Kalynovsky at Lviv University. I wish to thank, too, for their guidance: Dr. Roman Solchanyk (Radio Liberty); Edward Kasinec (Harvard Ukrainian Research Institute); Academicians Krzysztof Dunin-Wąsowicz, Stefan Kozak and Walentyna Najdus (Polska Akademia Nauk, Warsaw); Professor Elżbieta Hornowa (Wyższa Szkoła Pedagogiczna w Opole); the late Professor Jan Kozik (Jagellonian University); Professor Marian Tyrowicz (emeritus, WSP w Krakowie); and Professor Vladimir Vasilevich Mavrodin (Leningrad University). For comments on earlier drafts and suggestions for revision, I am also grateful to Professors John V. A. Fine, Arthur P. Mendel and Horace W. Dewey (The University of Michigan); Professor Taras Hunczak (Rutgers University); Professor Martha Bohachevsky-Chomiak (Manhattanville College); and Andrij Makuch (The University of Alberta). David Marples (Canadian Institute of Ukrainian Studies, The University of Alberta) was kind enough to help me with proofreading.

Introduction

In this study of socialist movements in the Austrian crownland of Galicia, the term "socialist" is used to denote people and groups that described themselves as such and were so described by their contemporaries. It is necessary to stress this formal criterion, because Galician "socialism" did not always correspond to what is now understood by that term. Indeed, in Soviet historiography the movements here investigated are generally defined as "revolutionary democratic" rather than socialist. The terminological difference goes beyond semantics to imply a value judgment. Soviet scholarship infers from the deficiencies of the Galician movements and their ideologies that these movements were not authentically socialist, but languished instead in the purgatory of "revolutionary democracy." This study proceeds from different assumptions: that the movements in question *were* the equivalents of the socialist movements elsewhere in Europe, that whatever peculiarities or deficiencies marked them had deep roots in the East European realities of the time, that — however confused about their goals and methods — these were the social *isms* of nineteenth-century Galicia.

Older studies had not shunned the word "socialism." Mykhailo Hrushevsky's monograph concerned "the origins of the Ukrainian socialist movement" and Emil Haecker published one volume of his uncompleted "history of socialism in Galicia." Soviet historiography, however, has not produced a single history of the Ukrainian socialist movement or Ukrainian socialist thought. In the 1920s, Matvii Yavorsky wrote an (unfortunately, very confused) history of "the revolutionary struggle in Ukraine" that dealt in part with the history of Ukrainian socialism in Galicia. Since that time, Soviet historians have studied individual "revolutionary democrats" — Ivan Franko continually, but Mykhailo Drahomanov, Mykhailo Pavlyk and Serhii Podolynsky only in moments of relative "thaw." Occasionally more synthetic studies have appeared, such as Oleksandr Dei's detailed monograph on the revolutionary democratic press of the late 1870s and early 1880s. Although much of Soviet historiography is useful, it still leaves many gaps in our understanding of Ukrainian socialism/revolutionary democracy.

Polish scholars have done far more work on the history of their socialist movement. They have published letters and memoirs of socialists active in Galicia as well as collections of other primary source material. To name only a few Polish scholars and their achievements: Marian Żychowski wrote a study of Bolesław Limanowski, Leon Baumgarten — a massive history of Proletariat, Józef Buszko — a synthetic account of the origins of Polish socialism and a monograph on the Galician Social Democratic Party, Walentyna Najdus — numerous studies on Galician social history, the workers' movement and socialism. Recently Western scholars have also become interested in Polish socialism, as evidenced by Kazimiera Cottam's biography of Limanowski, Norman Naimark's analysis of Proletariat and William Harwood's dissertation on Ignacy Daszyński.

Of the many Polish works dealing with some aspect of Galicia and its socialist movements, the one closest in theme to the present study is Elżbieta Hornowa's monograph on "the Ukrainian progressive camp and its collaboration with the Polish social left wing in Galicia, 1876–1895." If this excellent work is only infrequently cited in the pages that follow, it is because it has served as a point of departure. And the present work has departed from it both in emphasizing a comparison of the two movements rather than the history of their mutual relations and in moving the chronological limits back to encompass a wider problem.

Like Hornowa's monograph, the present study deals with neither Ukrainian nor Polish society in isolation, but is a comparative study of the two socialist movements. Because the geographic focus, Galicia, is the same for both movements, a difference in the political, socioeconomic and administrative units does not distort the comparison; instead, the differences in political development, social structure and culture of the two national groups are highlighted. This is, then, a study of Polish society in terms of Ukrainian society and vice versa.

To readers already acquainted with the historical framework of Galician socialism, the chronological limits — 1860 to 1890 — may seem inappropriate, because it was only in 1890 that socialist political parties appeared in Galicia. The study starts, however, with the dawn of the constitutional era, when the extension of civil liberties and the restructuring of the empire stimulated political activity among the many nations of the Habsburg realm. In this way it is possible to trace the origin of the socialist movements, their organic procession from the democratic nationalisms of the 1860s. The study ends in 1890 with the founding of socialist political parties, a sign that the movements had "taken off."

To have treated the period beyond 1890 would have shifted the focus to a different problem. The present study shows how socialist movements developed out of national movements, how nations turned into classes. In the period 1860–90, the Polish and Ukrainian intelligentsia, in organizing and politicizing the working classes for *national* purposes, had inadvertently mobilized the artisans (in the Polish case) and the peasants (in the Ukrainian case) for *class* politics as well. In the period 1890–1920, however, the converse occurred: the socialist movements evolved into national movements. Socialists were the first to put forward programs calling for independent Ukrainian statehood in the 1890s. Among the Poles, socialists were the first to revive the struggle for the restoration of Polish independence, also in the 1890s. Both Polish and Ukrainian socialist parties eventually became involved in paramilitary preparation for the establishment of national states and, however reluctantly, they fought one another in the Polish-Ukrainian war of 1918–19.

Galicia: Poles and Ukrainians

Before its annexation by Austria in 1772, the territory later known as Galicia was part of the Polish-Lithuanian Commonwealth. Today, what was once Galicia is divided, roughly along ethnic boundaries, between the Polish People's Republic and the Ukrainian SSR. Western Galicia, with its center in Cracow, is now part of Poland, while Eastern Galicia, with its center in Lviv (Lwów, Lvov, Lemberg), is now in Soviet Ukraine.

From 1867 to 1918, Galicia was the largest crownland of Austria, accounting for over a quarter of Austria's total area and — with a population of six and a half million in 1890 — over a quarter of Austria's total population.[1] Although in square kilometers and countable souls, Galicia stood first among the Lands and Kingdoms represented in the Reichsrat, in economic development Galicia lagged far behind. There was almost no factory industry in the region. What industry did exist was extractive (oil, ozocerite, salt), intimately connected with forestry or agriculture (breweries, mills) or else was artisanal, craftsman-based. The Galician population was primarily agricultural (77 percent in 1900) and the countryside overpopulated. Since the emancipation from serfdom in 1848, peasant holdings continually shrank. Many peasants, indeed, became landless and, because native industry could not employ them, they hired themselves out as agricultural laborers or emigrated from Galicia, primarily to North America.

Urbanization, in the sense of a large demographic shift from countryside to city and the corresponding rapid growth of urban centers, bypassed the crownland. Neither of Galicia's two large cities, Lviv and Cracow, functioned as an industrial center, so neither city attracted the surplus labor of the overpopulated countryside. Rivalry between the two cities and the existence outside of Austria of traditional national capitals (Warsaw for the Poles, Kiev for the Ukrainians) prevented the emergence of a "primate city."

Galicia was the uncomfortable home of three nationalities: Poles, Ukrainians and Jews. Poles and Ukrainians each accounted for over 40 percent of Galicia's population, Jews for over 10 percent. The Jewish population will not be treated in depth in this study, because Jewish socialism emerged late in Galicia. The first socialist periodicals in Polish and Ukrainian appeared in 1878; in Yiddish — in 1891. The Poles and Ukrainians founded socialist political parties in 1890; the Jews — in 1905.[2] Hence discussion here will be confined to the Poles and Ukrainians. The Poles in Galicia were a minority of the Polish nation; the majority lived in the Russian empire (in the Congress Kingdom and Western Russia) and in Prussia. The majority of the Ukrainians also lived outside of Galicia, in the Russian empire, though close to a million also inhabited parts of Hungary and Bukovyna. The Polish and Ukrainian minorities in Austria, however, were significant culturally and politically, since the Austrian constitution afforded Galicia's Poles and Ukrainians much greater freedom than their conationals enjoyed in Russia, Prussia or Hungary.

The Poles and Ukrainians represented two distinct types of nation. Students of East Central European national movements generally agree on the existence of two types of nation and national formation in that region, though they do not agree on how to express this distinction.[3] The terms "historical nation" and "nonhistorical people," used by Engels and before him by Hegel, are the oldest expressions of the difference between the two models of the nation. In East Central Europe, certain nations — Russians, Poles, Germans and Magyars — were considered "historical," because they had their own tradition of national life in the form of a state. "Nonhistorical peoples" — Czechs,

Slovaks, Belorussians, Ukrainians and others — "appeared" in the nineteenth century and before that were without "history," i.e., without a state tradition.

Owing to the central role of statehood in this distinction, the historical nations were also referred to as "state nations" (even when, as in the case of the Poles, they were temporarily without a state) and the nonhistorical peoples as "stateless peoples." This distinction had an effect on the ideologies of the national and socialist movements of the two types of nation, but, more than that, the heritage of historicity/statehood and nonhistoricity/statelessness left differing social structures in these two categories of nation. In the nineteenth century, historical nations retained and nonhistorical peoples lacked a nobility of the same nationality (more precisely, of the same faith and language) as the mass of the nation. The historical nations dominated the cities, even in areas whose hinterland was inhabited almost exclusively by peasants of the nonhistorical peoples, and therefore artisans and merchants tended to be members by birth or assimilation of the historical nations. The nonhistorical peoples were formed predominantly of peasants and have therefore been referred to also as "peasant" or "plebeian" peoples.

The historical nation in Austrian Galicia was the Polish nation, historical thanks to a long tradition of independent statehood, armed insurrections for the restoration of that statehood after the partitioning of Poland in the late eighteenth century, and the survival of a Polish ruling class, the *szlachta* or nobility. The nonhistorical people was the Ukrainian (or Ruthenian) people, whose nonhistoricity is well summed up in a Polish saying: "There is no Ruthenia, just priests and peasants." The Ukrainian boyars and nobles were Polonized by the seventeenth century, when a series of cossack rebellions failed to create a Ukrainian state. Only the peasantry and lower clergy inertly retained their ethnicity until the Ukrainian nation "awoke," along with other Slavic nations, in the middle of the last century. The class structure of the two nationalities reflected their historicity and nonhistoricity. While the Poles exhibited a differentiated structure, the overwhelming majority of the Ukrainians were peasants. In 1900, only 6 percent of the Ukrainian-speakers, but one third of the Polish-speakers, worked outside agriculture. Table 1 shows the occupational distribution of the Polish and Ukrainian populations of Galicia in 1900.

The Poles were not only the more socially differentiated, they were also better educated. The Ukrainians, as a predominantly peasant

Table 1
Occupational Distribution by Language and Nationality, 1900

Occupational Sector	Total Population	By Language		By Nationality	
		Polish	Ukrainian	Polish	Ukrainian
Agriculture and Forestry	76.6	66.8	93.7	76.5	94.8
Industry, Trade and Transportation	14.2	20.9	2.9	13.1	2.1
Bureaucracy and Free Professions	2.3	3.3	0.8	2.9	0.7
Other	6.9	9.0	2.6	7.5	2.4
	100.0	100.0	100.0	100.0	100.0

SOURCE: Józef Buzek, *Stosunki zawodowe i socyalne ludności w Galicyi według wyznania i narodowości, na podstawie spisu ludności z 31. grudnia 1900 r.* (Lviv, 1905), "Tablice."

NOTE: Poles and Ukrainians by language include Polish- and Ukrainian-speaking Jews. Poles and Ukrainians by nationality do not. The Austrian census-takers did not offer the choice of Yiddish as an *Umgangssprache*. In the 1900 census, 76.6 percent of the Jews gave Polish as their language of intercourse, 5.0 percent Ukrainian.

people, had less access to higher education. In the early 1890s, Poles comprised over 65 percent of the students of Galicia's two universities (Lviv and Cracow), while Ukrainians made up less than 20 percent. Similar proportions obtained in the secondary schools. Poles and Ukrainians also studied different subjects in the universities. Over half the Ukrainian students in the period 1861–1901 studied theology, while only 9 percent of the Polish students did the same. In Lviv Polytechnic in this period, 83 percent of the students were Polish, 11 percent Jewish and only 6 percent Ukrainian.[4]

The comparisons of the social structures and educational tendencies of the Poles and Ukrainians show that the Poles were in a much better position to accomplish the transition to a modern society than were the Ukrainians. This was the difference between a legacy of historicity/statehood and one of nonhistoricity/statelessness. In this connection, a final point remains to be raised: about the degree of maturity of national consciousness in the Polish and Ukrainian nations.

The Poles, as a historical nation, had few doubts about who they were. They were Poles, claimants to the heritage of the old Polish Commonwealth. The Galician people referred to as "Ukrainian," however, did not, during the period under investigation, refer to themselves by that term. They used the designation "Ukrainian" until 1900 to refer exclusively to the Ukrainian people in the Russian empire. East Slavic Galicians of the Greek Catholic faith called themselves "Ruthenians" (*rusyny, Ruthenen*), and even Galicians who cherished the concept of a single Ukrainian nation from the San to Don rivers consistently employed the distinction "Ruthenian" and "Ukrainian" when referring to Austrian or Russian citizens. The use of the term "Ukrainian" in reference to nineteenth-century Galician Ruthenians is a commonly accepted anachronism in historical scholarship, but it permits hindsight to settle a question that at that time was by no means settled. Many Galician "Ukrainians," that is, of those who even reached the point of consciously identifying themselves with a nation, did not consider themselves part of a separate Ukrainian nation, but either a separate Ruthenian nation or part of the Polish or Russian nation. In the last third of the nineteenth century, the "Ukrainian" nation in Galicia was still undergoing an identity crisis.

For this reason, the remainder of this book will use the nineteenth-century term "Ruthenians" to refer to the Galician Ukrainians. By retaining the old term, the text can operate with the same vocabulary as the quotations from sources that are frequently introduced. In an attempt to compromise between an overly strict historicism and an anachronism, the term "Ukrainian" remains in the title of the work and in the chapter titles. Since the word "Ruthenian" came to have a negative connotation in the twentieth century (especially in interwar Poland), it seemed better not to enshrine it in a title. Such enshrinement, moreover, might have disguised the fact that the study concerns the history of the Ukrainian nation. The text uses the term "Ukrainian" not only in reference to the inhabitants of Russian Ukraine, but also in reference to the language of the Ruthenians. To distinguish between Ruthenians who felt they were Russians and Ruthenians who felt they were Ukrainians, the terms "Russophile" and "Ukrainophile" are used. (Chapter two also uses the word "Ruthene" in a very specific sense, to translate the derogatory *rutenets'*. Generally, of course, "Ruthene" is synonymous with "Ruthenian," and the distinction made here is merely an *ad hoc* convention.)

Galician Autonomy

In light of the preceding, it should come as no surprise that the Ruthenians were also politically disadvantaged in Galicia. They lacked both a noble estate and an urban working class, elements that proved crucial in the establishment of Polish sovereignty in autonomous Galicia. From the late 1860s until the collapse of the monarchy, i.e., during the whole period of Galician autonomy, Ruthenians were cut off from positions of political power.

This was one major result of the struggle for Galician autonomy in the 1860s. Although aspects of the autonomy struggle will be discussed in more detail in the next chapter, some more general points about its effects will be made here to establish the contours of the political situation in late-nineteenth-century Galicia. The issue of autonomy flared up at several junctures in the 1860s: in 1860–61, when the emperor wavered between reorganizing Austria on a centralist or federalist basis; in 1863, when the Poles in the Russian partition rose in revolt and received support from the Poles in Austria; and in the two years following the Compromise of 1867, when this volatile issue was at last settled.

The most uncompromising proponents of autonomy were the Polish

Democrats, who viewed autonomy as the first step to the restoration of Polish independence. In their efforts to achieve autonomy, they organized a series of street demonstrations, especially in 1868–69, that brought the struggle to a climax. The Democrats were an urban party, more a Lviv than Cracovian party; their leadership came primarily from the *declassé* nobility and free professions, though other urban groups, particularly artisans and shopkeepers, were conspicuous in their support. Significantly, even though nearly 80 percent of the ethnic Poles in Galicia were peasants, the Democrats did not trouble themselves with an agrarian program and had no qualms about allying themselves with *szlachta* autonomists in 1861 and 1868–69.

The Democrats' *szlachta* allies were the Podolians. The Podolian *szlachta,* the landed nobility of Eastern Galicia, was the most socially conservative element in the crownland. The Podolians were doubly vulnerable to any peasant awakening; they feared not only social consciousness on the part of the peasantry, but national consciousness as well, since the peasants of Eastern Galicia were Ruthenian. The Podolians consequently entered the campaign for autonomy with motivations quite distinct from those of the Democrats: to achieve dominion, unbridled by the central government, over local Galician affairs, that is, over their own peasantry. In comparing the Democrats' and Podolians' motives for championing autonomy, one might note that the Democrats sought to redress the wrongs of a century of Poland's subjugation, while the Podolians sought to insure that centuries of subjugation be undisturbed by outside forces, indeed, that the subjugation of the Ruthenian peasantry be made the more secure.

In Western Galicia, the counterpart of the Podolians was the group of conservative Cracow *szlachta* headed by Paweł Popiel (this group only later fused with the young Cracow conservatives known as the Stańczyks). But the Cracow conservatives opposed the campaign for autonomy; instead, they urged reaching an understanding with the emperor. Already in 1851, Popiel and sixty other West Galician nobles had presented a declaration of loyalty to the emperor in which they made clear that the *szlachta,* "the prevailing social element of the land," was eager to collaborate with the dynasty.[5] Cracow conservatives renounced insurrection altogether. Soon after the 1863 insurrection was quelled, Popiel outraged his countrymen by writing: "We must decisively repudiate the recent movement, we must recognize and condemn it as pernicious, we must spurn those people who led it or assented to it."[6] The

Podolian *szlachta* sought preservation of their class privileges in autonomy, the Cracovian *szlachta* in a pact of mutual loyalty with the
emperor.

The most energetic opponents of formal autonomy were a group
dubbed the "utilitarians" or Mamelukes. These were members of the
bureaucracy led by Florian Ziemiałkowski and Agenor Gołuchowski.
Since the 1850s Gołuchowski had served the emperor faithfully as
viceroy of Galicia, suppressing Polish dissent when necessary and sacri-
ficing Poland's particular interests for those of Austria as a whole. His
absolute loyalty gradually accumulated sufficient capital of good will in
Vienna so that Gołuchowski could cautiously insinuate a number of
pro-Polish reforms, such as the replacement of retired or deceased civil
servants of German or Czech nationality with Poles. The Mamelukes
advocated total submission to Vienna and abandonment of the campaign for formal autonomy. They made their argument with the carrot
and stick. The carrot was the promise of a pro-Polish orientation in
Vienna and the pledge to carry through a series of Polonizing reforms.
The stick was the threat to dissolve the Galician Diet and incite the
peasantry against the recalcitrant autonomist nobility.

Forces pro and con were so balanced during the autonomy campaign
and the counterpoise of the Mamelukes' threats and the autonomists'
street agitation so tense that the entrance of the Stańczyks into the fray
in 1869 decided the issue. At the start of the confrontation, the Stańczyks, a group of young *szlachta* conservatives in Cracow, had kept
aloof and had, if anything, favored autonomy. But as the autonomist
agitation mounted and as the Democrats made more frequent use of the
streets as a political forum, the Stańczyks initiated their campaign to
win public opinion to their views. The Stańczyks promoted renunciation of demonstrations, of the autonomy resolution passed by the Diet,
of any formal guarantee of autonomy, of further attempts to restore
Polish independence. They urged renunciation in exchange for an
informal autonomy in which the Polish *szlachta* would dominate the
government of the crownland. The Stańczyk solution to the crisis won
enough support with the emperor and Austrian government and enough
support in Galicia to carry the day.

As a result of the autonomy campaign and the Stańczyk victory, the
Poles, though Galicia was awarded no formal privileges of autonomy,
enjoyed greater national sovereignty than any non-German nationality
in Austria. From the 1860s it became the custom to appoint only Poles

as viceroys of Galicia, in 1869 Polish was made the official language of the land, by 1871 the universities in Cracow and Lviv were Polonized (the elementary and secondary schools had been put under Polish control in 1867), from the early 1870s a minister without portfolio — always a Pole — represented Galician interests in Vienna, and Poles were favored for high government posts. Autonomy gave the Stańczyks predominance in the Galician government and restructured internal political life. Once the Stańczyks had consolidated their power, peasants were excluded from the political process. In the 1861 Diet, peasants had been active and numerous enough to alarm the other classes represented. From 1877 to 1889, however, not a single Polish peasant sat in the Diet (in 1877–83 there were two Ruthenian peasant deputies).[7]

The Stańczyk program's close resemblance to the program of the Mamelukes and, more especially, to that of the older Cracow conservatives accounted for the disappearance of the latter groups as separate entities in political life, for their absorption into a single (Stańczyk) party. The Stańczyk accession to power had a more complex effect on the Democrats. To begin with, the Democrats were thoroughly routed when the Stańczyks turned opinion against the demonstrations and quashed the Democrat-sponsored resolution for autonomy. More telling a blow, however, was the loss of *raison d'être* occasioned by some aspects of the Stańczyk program. The Democrats wanted autonomy; the Stańczyks stole their thunder and delivered *de facto* autonomy. Stańczyk autonomy opened up more government careers to the urban intelligentsia, thus luring members away from the Democratic party. Both the Democrats (after 1864) and the Stańczyks, moreover, advocated renunciation, at least temporarily, of insurrection, and concentration instead on the organic work of making the Polish people into an institutionally and economically developed nation. The Stańczyk conquest of Galicia left the Democrats numerically weakened and, with no issue around which to rally, politically ineffective. Defection from the Democratic party was particularly acute in Cracow, seat of the Stańczyks' court. Here the Democratic newspaper *Kraj* (Homeland) ceased publication in 1874 and the handful of Cracow Democrats were without an organ until 1882 when *Reforma* (Reform) began to appear. Its editor, Tadeusz Romanowicz, was imported from Lviv. The Democrats survived better in Lviv, perhaps, among other reasons, because here the aggregate number of the urban intelligentsia was higher. But even in the capital the Democrats lacked vigor; Lviv's Polish Progressive Club, a Democratic organization founded in 1871, was no longer active by 1874.[8] The party never returned to the prominence it had enjoyed in the 1860s.

The Democrats' close ties with the Podolian *szlachta* ended, too, as a result of the Stańczyks' success. The Podolians, in any case, had been uneasy with the Democrats and their methods of agitation. The Podolians were not fussy whether autonomy came *de jure* or *de facto*; the Stańczyk version more than satisfied them. To maintain control over Galicia, the Stańczyks had to insure that their own class, the *szlachta,* dominated the Diet. This meant, like it or not, that the nobility of Western Galicia, the Stańczyks, had to share power with the nobility of Eastern Galicia, the Podolians. The effect on Galicia was catastrophic.

The Stańczyks were what might be called a "modernizing nobility." Their program espoused a number of reforms aimed at easing Galicia's transition to capitalism without jeopardizing the nobility's political and economic advantages. The Stańczyks sought to liquidate vestiges of feudalism (such as the manor's right of propination, the exclusive monopoly on the production and sale of alcoholic beverages), to force peasants more into a market economy by abolishing restrictions on interest and the sale of land, and to check the development of national antagonisms by emancipation of the Jews and concessions to the Ruthenians in the schools, courts and government. The Stańczyks, as Konstanty Grzybowski has noted, represented the "Prussian road" to modernization: economic and, to a limited degree, political liberalization unaccompanied by a democratic extension of suffrage.[9]

The Stańczyks, however, could realize no part of their program without the consent of the Podolians, who were necessary to the Stańczyks to obtain a majority in the Diet. The Podolians exercised their veto to torpedo almost all progressive points in the Stańczyk program, especially the liquidation of feudal vestiges and concessions to the Ruthenians. The Stańczyks ruled Galicia, but they in turn were in thrall to the Podolians, who sabotaged the reformist aspect of the Stańczyk program.

Galicia, then, became a pashaluk of the Polish nobility, who excluded the Ruthenians, and the peasantry and working classes of both nations, from a share in power and also rendered Polish Democracy impotent. It was in this political context that the socialist movements of Galicia were formed.

Chapter One

Polish Artisans, 1860–1877

The Polish socialist movement developed out of a pre-existing artisan movement. When guilds were abolished in 1860, Galician journeymen replaced them with associations for mutual aid and self education. The associations were patronized by the Polish Democrats, who provided them with leadership and financial support. The Democrats also used the artisan associations in the 1860s as the basis for a series of demonstrations to win autonomy for Galicia. This politicized the artisans, especially in Galicia's capital, Lviv, where most of the demonstrations took place. By the early 1870s, Lviv journeymen were turning the political and organizational skills they had acquired over the previous decade to a purpose that the Democrats disapproved of: struggle with their employers for better wages and working conditions. A wave of strikes radicalized the artisan movement and made it interested in the socialist ideas that reached it from Western Europe.

There were about 73,000 artisans in Galicia in the late 1860s.[1] In this figure are included all practitioners of trades regulated or formerly regulated by a guild: furriers, farriers, cobblers, coopers, carpenters, bakers, locksmiths and the like. Included, too, are typesetters and other printery workers, because they played so active a part in artisan voluntary associations. Most craftsmen worked in small shops — a master with a journeyman and apprentice to help him.[2] The 1869 census records that the average Galician "industrial" entrepreneur hired only 1.7 workers. Only rarely were craftsmen employed in larger enterprises such as the machine shop of the Karl Ludwig railroad in Lviv, which in 1870 hired 350 blacksmiths, coppersmiths, locksmiths, carpenters, saddlers and turners.[3] Factories were growing very slowly, despite a tendency for some workshops to expand and introduce steam-powered machinery.[4]

Galician craftsmen were often unemployed, nearly always both underemployed and underpaid. Craftsmen employed by the construction industry were an exception, since the mid-1870s was a period of

large-scale construction in Lviv.[5] Also among the highest-paid artisans
was the typesetter, who could earn about 15 gulden a week.[6] Typically,
however, a journeyman in Lviv or Cracow made from a gulden to a
gulden and a half for every day he worked. A good working year came
to about 250 days.[7] An artisan's daily wage was twice that of an
agricultural laborer, but it was still very far from providing a comfortable standard of living. Underemployment became chronic in the 1860s
when foreign factory production began to dispossess the Galician artisan.

The Dissolution of the Guilds and the Emergence
of Voluntary Artisan Associations

Austria's defeat at the hands of the Sardinians and French in 1859
convinced Emperor Franz Joseph of the need to rebuild his empire on
more modern foundations. He inaugurated a new era in Austrian
history on 15 July 1859, when he announced the armistice at Villafranca
and the loss of Lombardy and coupled this announcement with a
promise of reform. Historians have often viewed the October Diploma
of 1860 as the first of the great reforms, but between it and Villafranca
had come another reform of consequence: an imperial patent of 20 December 1859, which aimed at stimulating industrial development.
Among the provisions of this comprehensive industrial law was the
abolition of guilds.[8]

The abolition of guilds went into effect on 1 May 1860. It perhaps
benefited the already industrialized regions of the monarchy, particularly Bohemia and Vienna, but its effect on more traditional economies,
such as that of Galicia, was painful. From 1860 on the Galician market
became ever more dominated by Viennese and Bohemian factory
imports. Galician artisans felt threatened by the growing influx of
factory wares and many viewed the abolition of guilds as the source of
this threat. In fact, the abolition of guilds probably had less to do with
the penetration of factory imports than did the completion of the
Lviv-Cracow railway in 1861 and its extension in subsequent years; the
guilds had already lost legal control over imports in 1807.[9] Nonetheless,
rightly or wrongly, a great many artisans were convinced that the
disappearance of the guilds had precipitated their impoverishment.
Thus, at the 1865–66 session of the Galician Diet, the craftsmen of

Rzeszów introduced a petition for the restitution of the guilds. They argued that "facilitated competition can only bring disadvantage to the crownland's craft manufacture, which, because of a lack of financial resources, cannot cope with the rivalry of foreign industry."[10]

Although the abolition of the guild may not have accelerated the import of factory goods, it still had a deleterious effect on Galician craft industry because it abolished the organizational framework of artisanal production. Guilds had served useful functions in the past by restricting the number of workshops to limit competition and regulating relations between master craftsmen and their journeymen and apprentices. The 1859 industrial law did urge the establishment of compulsory corporations (*Genossenschaften*), which were to assume some of the old guild functions. The provisions on corporations, however, remained a dead letter; very few were set up and the obligation to join them was not generally enforced. In effect, then, the 1859 industrial law left Galician artisans completely disorganized at a time of intense foreign competition.[11]

In these circumstances, many Polish intellectuals, and some artisans as well, began to agitate for the establishment of some form of institutional framework to replace the guilds. An anonymous master craftsman in Lviv published a booklet in 1864 "on the need for industrial or artisan associations."[12] He proposed setting up corporations such as the 1859 industrial law had recommended. He felt artisans should join together in associations that not only would assume some of the former guild functions — organizing and coordinating production within each trade — but also would transcend the aims of the guilds to provide education for the artisans, links with the intelligentsia, craftsmen's reading halls and lecture series, even an artisan press. The brochure, well received and reprinted in several newspapers,[13] generated enthusiasm, but it had no immediate effect.

More influential, it seems, were two brochures published in 1867 and written by two prominent Polish Democrats, Alfred Szczepański of Cracow and Tadeusz Romanowicz of Lviv. Both lamented that Galician industry was not keeping pace with that of the rest of Europe; raw Galician wool was exported and returned as finished cloth, rags exported returned as paper, lumber as matches. Szczepański and Romanowicz both proposed the same solution to the crisis of Galician craft industry: organization into voluntary associations. Small capital, they argued, cannot survive the competition of large capital, but an association can combine many small sources of capital, thus enabling small capital to withstand competition. Associations would facilitate access to credit, provide a basis for establishing consumer cooperatives and otherwise enhance the chances for Galicia's craftsmen to withstand the pressure of foreign capital.[14] Their belief in the need for voluntary artisan associations was shared by many other Polish Democrats of the time,[15] concerned with the organic work of nation-building in the wake of the defeated insurrection.

The extension of civil liberties in Austria made it possible to establish the artisan associations. In particular, a liberal law on associations, promulgated on 15 November 1867 and confirmed by the constitution of 21 December 1867, facilitated the formation of various public societies,[16] including artisan associations. The late 1860s and early 1870s witnessed a proliferation of voluntary artisan associations throughout Galicia — in Stanyslaviv, Przemyśl, Stryi, Ternopil, Tarnów, Drohobych, Jarosław, Pidhaitsi, Zbarazh, Pomoriany, Hlyniany, Skalat, Cracow and, above all, in Lviv, Galicia's capital. In Lviv alone some fifteen artisan associations were active in this period, including distinct associations for master craftsmen, journeymen and Catholic journeymen, for Ruthenians[17] and Jews,[18] for women, for cartwrights, tailors, cobblers, glovers and printers. Some of these associations concentrated on education, others on economic mutual aid; some were embryonic trade unions, yet others cooperatives.[19] The largest of these organizations was the journeymen's association Gwiazda (Star), founded in Lviv in 1868. Its membership exceeded a thousand in the 1870s and it published its own newspaper. Branches of Gwiazda were founded elsewhere in Galicia, notably in Cracow, but none rivalled the Lviv original in either membership or activity.

In sum, the industrial law of 1859 had abolished the ancient form of artisan organization, the guild, thus creating the need to establish new, voluntary associations; and the transition from absolutism to constitutionalism made it possible for the Galician artisans to form the required associations.

Democrats, Demonstrations and the
Politicization of Lviv's Artisans

Forced to reorganize the empire following defeat in the Italian war,

Franz Joseph had to choose between federalism, which relied on the support of the provincial nobility, and centralism, which relied on the liberal German bureaucracy. He vacillated between these alternatives, first issuing the federalist October Diploma of 1860, then replacing it with the centralist February Patent of 1861, then again inclining towards federalism until finally, in 1867, he settled upon the Compromise that divided the empire, as far as internal policy was concerned, into two separate states: Austria, dominated at first by the liberal German centralists, and Hungary, ruled by the Magyar nobility.

The Poles of Galicia, of course, had favored federalism and the widest possible autonomy for their crownland. The Democrats in particular championed autonomy and they reacted to fluctuations in imperial policy with demonstrations and torch-light processions. Already in late December 1860, when it became clear that the emperor was about to retreat from the federalist solution, Democrats organized demonstrations in Cracow and Lviv. Another patriotic demonstration took place in Lviv in 1865 when Florian Ziemiałkowski was released from prison (he had been imprisoned for his part in the East Galician Insurgent Committee in 1863), another in 1866 when Agenor Gołuchowski was appointed governor of Galicia, yet another in 1867 in support of Leszek Borkowski, a deputy to the Galician Diet who opposed sending delegates to the central Parliament.[20]

The years that were richest in demonstrations, however, were 1868 and 1869. The Compromise of 1867 had left the Poles dissatisfied with Galicia's undistinguished position in a centralized Austrian state. In reaction to the Compromise, the Galician Diet passed a Democrat-sponsored resolution in 1868 demanding the extension of the Diet's competence at the expense of the central Parliament; the resolution also demanded the establishment of a "crownland administration" on the order of a cabinet responsible to the Diet. In August 1868, when Franciszek Smolka submitted the resolution to the Diet,

> the population of Lviv improvised a torch-light procession in which everyone was represented: intelligentsia, merchants, *craftsmen, journeymen.* . . . The demonstration showed that the public opinion of our city agrees with the convictions of the Lviv deputy [Smolka].[21]

Two weeks later another demonstration marked the resignation of Gołuchowski as governor. Not all patriotic demonstrations had an overt political aim: earlier in the same year, the papal nuncio Cardinal

Falcinelli had visited Lviv and a large crowd greeted him with fireworks, banners and shouts of "Long live the pope!" In 1869 there were
several occasions for patriotic demonstrations: the discovery of the
relics of Polish King Kazimierz the Great, the three-hundredth anniversary of the Union of Lublin, a plan to return Mickiewicz's body to
Poland and the visit of Polish statesman Karol Libelt to Galicia.[22]

The pretexts for demonstrating were almost irrelevant. The main
purpose of the Democrats was to use the streets to keep pressure on
the Galician Diet and Imperial government. A contemporary satire on
Democratic strategy, published by the group of nobles known as the
Stańczyks, recognizes this. In the satire, Sicinius, the fictional captain
of the Galician social revolution, defends street demonstrations to a
lieutenant and expounds on why it makes no difference that in the
span of only a few months there are demonstrations for figures as
diverse as Cardinal Falcinelli, the Democrat Smolka and Count Gołuchowski:

> But you must know that our immediate and most proximate aim and
> task can be nothing else but winning over the masses. There is only one
> way to win them over: by continuously electrifying them, by keeping
> them in constant expectation of something, in uninterrupted motion.
> Call the movement artificial, call it galvanization, call it anything you
> please, but you cannot deny that only this one method leads to the goal.
> There is no other way.[23]

The conservative and aristocratic Stańczyks, who were to dominate
Galician politics for nearly the next half century, initially made their
career by satirizing and opposing the demonstrations of 1868–69 — an
indication of how important these demonstrations were in the political
development of Galicia. The Stańczyks even took their name from
the series of satirical letters in which they ridiculed the Democrats and
their demonstrations; the series was known as *Teka Stańczyka*
(Stańczyk's File), after Stańczyk, court jester to the sixteenth-
century Polish King Zygmunt. The Stańczyks were themselves inclined to favor autonomy, but they objected to the "demonstratio-
mania" the Democrats employed to win it. A leading Stańczyk, the
historian Józef Szujski, wrote in the group's organ *Przegląd Polski*
(Polish Review) in July 1869:

> This abuse [of demonstrations] . . . is breaking down the nerves of
> society; it is inducing in society a state of hashish-insanity and mad-

ness. . . . In demonstrations the masses learn to scorn both school and church; they learn the desire to dazzle and to dominate the natural social order.[24]

Behind the "hashish-insanity" of demonstrations, however, lay sober political calculation. In their struggle against centralism, the Polish Democrats were using a tactic widespread in nineteenth-century Europe: the mobilization of the urban crowd. As elsewhere in Europe, so too in Galicia, artisans formed a major component of the urban crowd. Therefore, although the vast majority of artisans did not have enough property to qualify for the franchise, they nonetheless became politically important in the late 1860s because they could exert pressure through demonstrations. It is in this context that the artisans' voluntary associations also became significant politically.

The voluntary artisan associations emerged during the same period that demonstrations were being organized. The largest and most active artisan association, the journeymen's society Gwiazda, was founded in Lviv after the demonstration for Leszek Borkowski in 1867 and just before the great series of demonstrations of 1868–69. It was founded, specifically, in 1868 on the Polish national holiday, the Third of May.[25] And following the ceremonial inaugural meeting of Gwiazda on that day, the assembled artisans (and Democrats) marched to the home of the popular Democratic deputy to the Diet, Borkowski.[26]

The Democrats provided the artisan associations with leadership. There has already been reference to Democratic propaganda on behalf of the artisan associations, notably the brochures of two of Galicia's foremost Democrats, Szczepański and Romanowicz. In March 1868, Romanowicz and such other leading Democrats as Kornel Ujejski and Karol Widmann participated in the public meeting to discuss the plans to found Gwiazda. This meeting, too, was a demonstration of sorts, since seven hundred people, not counting those in the galleries, crowded into Lviv's town hall to attend it.[27] Afterwards, Romanowicz drew up the statutes for several of Lviv's artisan associations.[28] The Democrats also offered lectures to the artisans in Gwiazda and wrote for Gwiazda's newspaper Rękodzielnik (Handicraftsman).

Moreover, the Democrats financially supported the artisan associations, Gwiazda in particular. The Democrat Mieczysław Darowski convinced Princess Karolina Lubomirska to buy premises for Gwiazda at the cost of 800 gulden. The artisan association newspaper Rękodzielnik was subsidized by the Democrat Alfred Młocki. The Democrats, too, during meetings of the Galician Diet's budget commission, argued heatedly with the Stańczyks (who suspected Gwiazda was a socialist hot-bed) to wrest a several hundred gulden subsidy for the association.[29] The importance of non-artisan support for the artisan associations cannot be underestimated. Gwiazda received hundreds of books and a valuable coin collection in donations. It also had much more money in its treasury than could ever have been accumulated by the pittances artisans paid in dues.[30] Non-artisan donors, then, made the associations a reality, because it was with their capital that the associations could buy or rent premises, make loans, purchase newspapers and books and even buy games for the artisans' amusement (e.g., bowling pins). Non-artisan donors were rewarded for their generosity by being enrolled as honorary members of the associations. And, according to the statutes (drawn up by the Democrats), honorary members were eligible to hold office in the associations. Indeed, the first and long-time president of Lviv's Gwiazda was just such a non-artisan — the Democrat Mieczysław Weryha Darowski, a veteran of the 1831 insurrection, with a long history of working with artisans.

Darowski had founded an early extra-guild artisan association, the ancestor of Gwiazda, during the revolution of 1848. This was the short-lived Union of Artisan Journeymen in Lviv, of which Darowski was president. The Union's goals were both economic and political. It intended to regulate questions of production, to aid in settling conflicts between masters and journeymen and to operate an employment bureau for members; but it also sought to develop the journeymen's national consciousness and to prepare them for the national liberation struggle. Probably in connection with the latter, the association assumed a military form of organization with centuries led by centurions and decades led by decurions. Each centurion participated in the presidium, but the president, Darowski, held power independently of that body. The association grew so quickly that by the end of the summer of 1848 it had a thousand members.[31] It ceased to exist after the Austrian minister of the interior, on 6 December 1848, issued a decree dissolving "all democratic and workers' clubs."[32]

Fifteen years later, during the insurrection of 1863, Darowski again became involved with journeyman artisans. He invited journeymen to his home, where a number of other Democrats were gathered, including Romanowicz[33] and Mieczysław Romanowski, a poet who died in battle in 1863. The Democrats told the journeymen about the uprising in

Warsaw and asked them if they considered themselves Poles. The Democrats then initiated a series of lectures for Lviv's journeymen. Later, when many of the male Democrats had gone off to war or jail or were otherwise occupied with affairs of state, women Democrats, led by Felicja Wasilewska (in marriage: Boberska) assumed the task of working with the journeymen. The women taught the artisans reading, writing and Polish history; they also read the artisans news of battles in the Congress Kingdom and the decrees of the National Government. The journeymen in turn taught the women how to manufacture bullets and weapons and how to prepare packages for soldiers in the camps.[34] Some journeymen volunteered as combatants; indeed, quite a few of the artisans who later emerged as leaders of the workers' and socialist movement in Galicia had fought for Polish independence in 1863.[35]

There were elements of continuity between the agitation among the artisans in 1863 and the founding of voluntary artisan associations in the late 1860s and early 1870s. Wasilewska-Boberska went on to found the Society of Women's Labor in Lviv (1874) and Darowski and Romanowicz, of course, went on to found and direct Gwiazda. Even the choice of the name "Gwiazda" betrayed a direct connection with the agitation and insurrection of 1863: the association took its name, which means "the star," from a verse of the artisan-enlightener and fallen insurgent Romanowski.[36]

The Democrats, then, and Darowski in particular, had a tradition of combining work among artisans with the political tasks of Polish Democracy. In 1848, the year of the all-European revolution, Darowski founded a journeymen's organization that was ready, by all indications, to take up arms for the Polish cause. In 1863, the year of the Polish insurrection, Darowski agitated among the journeymen to put their skills and their lives at the service of Poland. In 1868, the year of the demonstrations for Galician autonomy, Darowski founded the journeymen's association Gwiazda, which functioned as the popular arm of the Democratic party and a primary nucleus for the demonstrations.

Gwiazda's role in the demonstrations can be illustrated by the demonstration for Karol Libelt, one of the most successful that the Democrats organized and the one for which we have the fullest account. Libelt arrived in Lviv by the evening train on 11 April 1869. A few minutes after his arrival, a torch-light procession marched from the station to the square in front of his hotel:

The whole procession was divided into eighteen detachments. After each detachment carrying Chinese lanterns came a detachment with torches. Participants in the procession marched in ranks of six. . . . Two military musicians accompanied the procession. . . . The national songs played alternately by the two musicians contributed in no small measure to the elevation of the mood.

The view for onlookers was splendid: the whole of the huge expanse of St. Mary's Square appeared as a single sea of fire. The effect on the eye was all the greater since the Chinese lanterns were of different colors in each detachment: white, rose, lilac and so on. In this way the most diverse colors, carefully selected, presented a simply enchanting spectacle.[37]

One can readily appreciate how useful associations would prove in the elaborate preparation and organization required to produce such a spectacle.

The participants in the demonstration, according to a witness, were: university and technical students, secondary school students, "burghers," "uncounted throngs of the public" and "various corporations and societies," including, specifically, Gwiazda.[38] The demonstration, a friendly newspaper of the time reported, numbered three thousand.[39] No doubt the "uncounted throngs of the public" made up the largest contingent, and these probably held candles and torches instead of the intricately placed Chinese lanterns. If Gwiazda had shown up in full force, it would have contributed over four hundred marchers at the least.[40] The figures here are by no means exact, but they do indicate the contribution Gwiazda could make to the demonstrations of this period.

A final point must be raised about the connection between the artisan associations and the demonstrations: the artisan associations were unusually dynamic precisely in the city where the demonstrations took place.

Lviv was the locus of the demonstrations. This is reflected in a Stańczyk satire in which Lviv figures under the name of Tigertown (Tygrysów), since Lviv etymologically signifies "city of Leo" or "of the lion." The satire has Brutusik, a Democratic leader, urge the Democratic National Society in Lviv to pass the following resolution:

In consideration of the fact that the Diet of the Kingdom of Galilee has betrayed the confidence of the nation, the First Privileged Democratic Society of Tigertown has resolved and determined:
Article I: The Diet shall be deprived of all legislative power.

Article II: Legislative power shall be transferred to popular assemblies which the administration of the Democratic Society of Tigertown shall convene *in Tigertown* whenever the fancy should strike it.[41]

As the satire suggests, Lviv was the natural setting for demonstrations because it was the seat of the Diet which the demonstrations competed with and strove to influence. Of the eight major demonstrations held in 1867–69, seven were held in Lviv.

The one exception, the demonstration occasioned by the solemn reburial of King Kazimierz, occurred in Cracow, since the king's relics were entombed there in the cathedral of Wawel castle. Otherwise Cracow was devoid of demonstrations. But in addition to the demonstration in memory of King Kazimierz, there was also the anti-Jesuit outburst in that city in 1869 when a certain Barbara Ubryk, suffering from insanity, was discovered literally walled up in a convent.[42] This, however, was a spontaneous and destructive mob action, not the sort of organized spectacle produced by the Lviv Democrats to rouse patriotic fervor during the autonomy campaign. The nature of the Ubryk outburst only underscores that Lviv, and not Cracow, was the focal point for the organized demonstrations.

If we compare the artisan associations, both named Gwiazda, in Galicia's two largest cities, we find a disproportionate concentration of organized artisans in Lviv; this implies that the Democrats were much less interested in recruiting artisans to the association in Cracow rather than to that in the politically crucial capital city. We could in any case have expected Lviv's Gwiazda to have been twice as large as Cracow's, since Lviv's population was nearly double that of Cracow and the number of artisans in Lviv was a little more than double the number in Cracow.[43] Yet the Lviv association surpassed its counterpart in Cracow by a measure far exceeding that which could have been expected from a comparison of the demographic data. Lviv's Gwiazda had been founded in 1868, but Cracow's was only given permission to form by a rescript of the viceroyalty dated 2 March 1872, several years after the demonstrations had taken place. Cracow's Gwiazda had existed unofficially as early as 1869,[44] but was evidently too anemic to constitute itself formally. In contrast to the wealthy Lviv association, generously endowed by the local Democrats, Cracow's Gwiazda had financial difficulties. Moreover, Cracow's Gwiazda always had a small membership; there were only sixty members left in 1876 and by 1877 the police could report that the association "only exists *de nomine*," exhibiting no signs of life.[45]

By contrast, Lviv's Gwiazda had 661 members when founded in 1868 and 1,350 in 1875.[46] Lviv's Gwiazda also boasted its own newspaper, which was out of the question for Cracow. The difference in the two associations is testimony that Lviv's, but not Cracow's, artisans served the Democratic party as the base for its urban crowd.

The Austrian reforms of the 1860s therefore had a complex effect on the Polish artisans in Galicia. With one stroke they deprived the artisans of their old guild structure, and with another they permitted the artisans to form an alternative, the voluntary artisan association. The reforms also accelerated the recruitment of artisans into Polish political life.

Looking ahead, the heritage of these reforms were to influence the development of the Polish workers' and socialist movement in the decades that followed. The voluntary artisan associations would provide an institutional framework on which to build. The political experience of the 1860s would evolve in a more class-oriented direction. And the "political geography" established at this juncture — the contrast between the politicized and organized artisan class of Lviv and its rather inchoate counterpart in Cracow — would mean that the socialist movement in Galicia's two large cities would follow divergent paths.

Democrats and Craftsmen

Throughout the 1860s and early 1870s the Democratic intelligentsia displayed much interest and initiative in working with craftsmen. Partly, this concern with artisans reflected the Democrats' disenchantment with the peasantry, "the people" (*lud*) so long celebrated and appealed to in early Polish Democratic literature. In 1846 the peasants had seized the occasion of a Democratic-inspired insurrection to slaughter their landlords. In 1848 the peasants' struggle for land conflicted with the Democrats' struggle for Poland. In many cases, too, peasants had actively opposed the insurrection of 1863. The artisans, on the other hand, had demonstrated by their actions in 1846, 1848 and 1863 that they constituted a body far more politically mature and patriotic than the peasantry; the Democrats therefore looked to the artisans to form the popular basis of their national movement. As we have seen, the Democrats made use of the craftsmen's support in the struggle for autonomy. Furthermore, the Democrats espoused the program of "organic work," which encompassed the goal of developing independent Polish economic institutions such as the artisan associations. And no doubt many Democrats were sincerely moved by the poverty of the craftsmen, who were more immediately visible to the urban intelligentsia than were the peasants.[47]

In their activity on behalf of the artisans, the Democrats were by no means endeavoring to inaugurate a radical workers' movement. Quite the contrary. The Democrats tried to instill a strictly bourgeois ideology in the craftsmen's organizations. They sought to avoid dissension within the nation, to build an organic, harmonious Polish nation in which craftsmen willingly participated.[48] The distrusted what they termed "the spirit of foreign workingmen" and "the ideas holding sway among the Western working class."[49] The Democrats urged instead that the same harmony which Copernicus discovered in the solar system be maintained in society.[50]

Thus a certain "S," who contributed an article on "contemporary socialist tendencies" to the Democratic organ *Gazeta Narodowa* (National Gazette) in 1870, distinguished militant socialism, which he condemned root and branch, from "voluntary or cooperative societies tending to raise the worker to the level of the capitalist, i.e., to join the hands of the two factors of production: capital and labor. This movement does not threaten the social order with any danger." But, he warned, "class struggle in the workshops is as ruinous as the struggle on a battlefield; striving to remove the economic solidarity between the worker and the capitalist leads to destruction, not salvation."[51] Similarly, in 1871, *Gazeta Narodowa* lamented that the West European workers' movement was "poisoned with the venom of hatred." In Galicia, the paper said, the workers' movement is concerned with the workers' enlightenment and moral elevation, not with a war against capital and the destruction of society.[52]

To some extent, the Democrats were also interested in founding artisan associations to co-opt the Galician artisan movement and prevent it from developing into a working class movement of the West European type. As Alfred Szczepański had written in 1867: "Let us take measures to rescue our declining craftsman class and maybe we can succeed in avoiding the workers' question, the question of the proletariat." Tadeusz Romanowicz had implied the same in his brochure of the same year. The viceroy of Galicia, Agenor Gołuchowski, though no Democrat himself, also, for a time, felt the need to foster craftsmen's organizations in order to steal the thunder from a radical workers' movement. In March 1872, Gołuchowski issued a circular to the police in which he recommended that the local authorities and employers encourage workers' clubs, libraries and aid funds "in order that the workers' question be steered on to different tracks and not become in our country what it has developed into elsewhere." Gołuchowski also urged that craftsmen's societies be defended in the press.[53] (Towards the end of 1872, however, the viceroy changed his mind and took measures to repress the craftsmen's movement.)

Some Galician Democrats, influenced by the ideas of two Poles from the Prussian partition, Karol Libelt and Kazimierz Szulc,[54] prescribed profit-sharing as a panacea for social injustice and concomitant social unrest. One such Galician Democrat was Karol Groman, who fought in the Hungarian insurrection in 1848, was imprisoned by the Austrian government for his role in the 1863 Polish insurrection and later became cofounder, curator and honorary member of Lviv's Gwiazda.[55] In 1872, after the typesetters at *Gazeta Narodowa* asked for a raise, Groman, as "an adherent of democratic-social principles," promised the workers shares in the print shop's profits. The typesetters, at first delighted by Groman's offer, became, on reflection, indifferent and even hostile to the profit-sharing plan. Cash benefits of the shares were not at the workers' direct disposal and the shares were offered for only 5 percent of the profits. Especially irking in Groman's proposal was a clause that forbade any employee who had shares in any other printery from participating in the program. Since the printers at that time were setting up a cooperative print shop, Groman's proposal seemed to be aimed against the printers' collective enterprise.[56]

In addition to profit-sharing, a very popular antidote to workers' unrest was the ideology of Herman Schulze-Delitsch whose popularity with the Democratic intelligentsia was understandable, since Schulze-Delitsch was a believer in a harmonious society in which craftsmen helped themselves through producers' cooperatives and other forms of self-help. Schulze-Delitsch's world-view was criticized as utopian by Galician conservatives. Stefan Pawlicki, a Resurrection father writing in the Stańczyk theoretical journal in 1874, affirmed that Schulze-Delitsch was too accustomed to the humble conditions of the small town and that the modern mass workers' movement was alien to his understanding. Pawlicki felt that Schulze-Delitsch was only the tool of liberal factory-owners; he was morally and materially supported by the bourgeoisie to diminish the influence of Ferdinand Lassalle among the workers.[57] But the Galician Democrats were very fond of Schulze-Delitsch. They hoped the master craftsmen would organize a self-help society of the Schulze-Delitsch type.[58] Both Szczepański and Romanowicz had expressed a high regard for Schulze-Delitsch in their brochures of 1867. Indeed, the whole emphasis on artisan associations and self-help as the cure-all for the craftsmen's plight bears the distinct mark of the ideology of Schulze-Delitsch. Although very little of what Schulze-Delitsch had written appeared in Polish translation,[59] his ideas reached the craftsmen through the Democrats' propaganda. As the historian Walentyna Najdus has commented, "the environment of the journeyman craftsmen, who were not separated by so impenetrable a wall from the entrepreneurs as were workers in large-scale industries, constituted fertile ground for the solidaristic views of Schulze-Delitsch."[60]

The limits of Galician Democracy's social program is well illustrated by its attitude to the International Workingmen's Association and the Paris Commune. The Democratic papers *Kraj* (Cracow) and *Gazeta Narodowa* (Lviv) were not unfriendly in their reporting on the Paris Commune. But here patriotic motives, that is, the attitude of the French Republicans and the International to the Polish question, decided the papers' sympathetic posture. Polish patriots had been profoundly disappointed by their enemy's triumph over their ally, the Prussians over the French. "And that is why," Bolesław Limanowski later recalled, "the news of the March revolution in Paris and the establishment of the Commune called forth almost universal joy and awakened the hope that accounts with the Prussians had not yet been settled once and for all."[61] The International had sent emissaries to Galicia, and the head of the organization, Karl Marx, thought the International had strong support there, but what connections it did have in Galicia were concerned with the Polish question, not the workers' question.[62]

Sympathy with the International and Paris Commune ended when it came to the workers' question. Kazimierz Szulc, for example, bitterly condemned both the Commune, which he knew at first hand, and the International.[63] Maksymylian Machalski, in his 1872 lecture on the International, painted a frightening picture of the godless organization and the Commune it inspired:

> The organization I am discussing is spreading out its arms like a gigantic octopus over the whole of Europe. . . . It is already near our borders — and perhaps it has even crossed them and is making itself at home in our midst.[64]

Rękodzielnik, the Galician artisan newspaper, was the most sympathetic to the International and Commune. It even printed an abridged version of the International's statutes[65] and frequently reported on the association. *Rękodzielnik*'s support of the International, however, was qualified in a manner that reflected the influence of the paper's Democratic patrons. In Western Europe, *Rękodzielnik* explained,

> the organization can bring great benefits; in our country, however, the workers' population is still altogether modest in size, we have almost no factories in which several dozen or several hundred workers are employed, and, also, in the present circumstances loan societies and consumers' cooperatives absolutely suffice for our workers. Therefore these organizations must be founded first of all and their benefits continually alluded to.[66]

In reporting on an 1869 gathering of thirty thousand Czech workers in Prague, *Rękodzielnik* praised the action and encouraged Gwiazda's administration to take example and convoke a meeting of journeymen craftsmen. In Galicia, however, the paper stipulated, "we have no such factories where workers work fourteen or eighteen hours a day[67] and so it is not against this that we must speak out." The meeting *Rękodzielnik* envisioned would be devoted to popularizing the benefits of education and loan societies.[68]

The stamp of the Democrats was, indeed, all over *Rękodzielnik.* Its publication was paid for, as mentioned earlier, by "the noble [in both senses] Alfred Młocki."[69] The liberal economist Tadeusz Skałkowski contributed to it a series of articles on political economy that was not so much a defense of capitalism as a plea for it to descend upon Galicia. Skałkowski's articles in *Rękodzielnik* in 1869[70] touched upon such topics as the division of labor, market price and competition, but mainly dealt with a problem of particular concern to the Democrats — Galicia's retarded industrial development. He regretted that West European nations were growing rich off Galicia's backwardness. Galician hand manufacture could not compete with machine-powered factories and large capital was destroying the small workshop. Skałkowski proposed the standard remedy for this state of affairs: Galicia needed more stock companies, associations and societies.

Rękodzielnik's fiction also reflected the Democrats' influence. In the short story "Together," for instance, Polish craftsmen in a Prussian town have fallen on hard times while the German craftsmen are prospering. Enter the son of one of the Polish artisans; he is returning home from Paris, having finished his term as a journeyman cobbler. He, of course, seeks to convince the Polish artisans to form a cooperative association to purchase their raw materials wholesale. It is a difficult task to persuade the reluctant Polish masters to band together in an association and the opposition of a villainous German bureaucrat almost spoils everything, but in the end the association is effective: now it is the German craftsmen who have fallen on hard times while the Polish craftsmen are prospering. Characteristically, a powerful and wealthy Polish nobleman acts as a benign *deux ex machina* to save the hero from false imprisonment.[71]

But *Rękodzielnik* underwent an ideological evolution in 1870. After the first fifteen months of publication, the paper abandoned its Schulze-Delitsch-style motto of "Work and Thrift."[72] Thereafter it consistently reported on the militant workers' movement in the West, especially on the 1870 trial of Viennese workers' leaders. Most importantly, *Rękodzielnik* reported on and actively supported the wave of strikes in Galicia in 1870–73. Perhaps as a result of the paper's radicalization, the more moderate Marian Minkusiewicz replaced Piotr Zbrożek as editor in 1873.[73]

Radicalization

Although printers were not, in the strictest sense, craftsmen, they played an active role in the artisan movement in Galicia. As elsewhere in Europe, and especially Eastern Europe, printers constituted the advance guard in the workers' and socialist movements. In Galicia, they were the first workers to establish any sort of non-guild organization, a mutual benefit fund in Lviv in 1817;[74] they were the most highly organized, 75 percent in Lviv in 1878;[75] they were the first, in Lviv in 1870, to go on strike.

Several factors account for the printers' position in the foreground of the workers' movement. The typesetter Józef Daniluk explained it as a direct result of the nature of his work:

The very act of setting type and the need to read carefully the book to be set introduce the typesetter, whether he likes it or not, to diverse scientific and political problems, awaken his intellect, form this or that conviction. . . . Here not simple mechanical power is required, but some sort of (at least elementary) education. . . . This is why in all of Europe for the past hundred years, it is the typesetters who most quickly awaken to reflect upon and recognize their state. That is why typesetters generally lead other workers forward in various workers' movements.[76]

Tadeusz Romanowicz understood the printers' leadership to be a result of the relatively high wages they received.[77] Then, too, the printers enjoyed the same anomalous position in advance of the rest of the workers that the printing industry itself enjoyed in relation to the rest of Galician industry. In otherwise backward Galicia, the development of the press proceeded along much the same lines as in the West; the dissemination of information was conducted in a much more modern fashion than the manufacture of cloth, shoes, pots, wheels or carts. The printing concern was a modern capitalist enterprise, not an artisan's workshop. Typesetters and printery workers were deprived of the paternalism of a master towards the journeymen and apprentices who often boarded with him. So the printers, earlier than the traditional craftsmen, were forced to rely more on their own devices and to set up mutual benefit funds. Traditional artisans, masters as well as journeymen, had established loan and mutual aid societies to help withstand foreign competition, but print-shop workers had felt it necessary to do so even without the pressure of foreign factory competition.[78]

In addition to mutual aid societies, the printers also established their own educational associations which functioned simultaneously as trade unions. The initiative to found the latter type of organization came from outside Galicia, from Vienna's Progressive Society of Printers.[79] In May 1869 this society sent an appeal to the Printers' Mutual Aid Society in Lviv, summoning the Galicians to found a branch of the Progressive Society. The Viennese association sought to build a network of Progressive Societies throughout Austria and invited the Lviv printers to send a delegate to an all-Austrian printers' congress to be held in June. The Lviv printers decided not to send a delegate, but to found an independent Progressive Society. The printers of Lviv assigned Jan Hoszowski[80] and Józef Wiśniewski to draw up the statutes for the new society.[81]

The printers submitted the statutes to the viceroyalty in mid-September 1869. When two weeks had passed without the statutes being confirmed, some members of the organized but as yet unauthorized Progressive Society became impatient. Hoszowski, Józef Seniuk, Szczęsny Bednarski (all veterans of 1863), the latter's brother Karol, Wiśniewski and Edmund Lewicki formed a secret society, the Left-Wing Circle, to push matters forward. They were eager for the Progressive Society to begin its activities, especially to carry on the first wage negotiations in Galicia, something Progressive Societies had done successfully in Vienna, Prague, Budapest, Brno and Trieste. The Left-Wing Circle, which took its name (Koło Lewicy) from a similar organization in Graz (Club der Linken), at first kept formal records of its confidential meetings and continued a progressively less formal existence some time after the statutes of the Progressive Society were confirmed on 8 October 1869. The members of the Left-Wing Circle sought, and with a large measure of success, to push the Lviv printers' movement in a class-oriented direction.[82]

The Lviv Progressive Society undertook wage negotiations, in which the Left-Wing Circle and Antoni Mańkowski were very active, at the end of 1869. When the negotiations with the employers failed to produce the desired results, about a hundred typesetters went on strike on 24 January 1870. If we exclude a printers' strike confined to a single Lviv printery in 1848,[83] the 1870 printers' strike was the first strike in Galicia. The Progressive Society, especially the Circle and Mańkowski, led the strike. The strike lasted one week and ended in a victory for the workers, whose wages were raised and working day shortened.[84]

The printers' example sparked a wave of strikes in Galicia, primarily in Lviv, from 1870 to 1873. Although strikes were expressly forbidden by article 77 of the 1859 industrial law, this provision, like the provisions on corporations, was largely ignored.[85] In the beginning of June 1870 bakery workers held meetings to demand higher pay and a shorter working day and then went on strike. Locksmiths also went on strike in 1870, and even the coachmen began to threaten respectable and indignant citizens with a strike.[86]

On 26 April 1871 three hundred needleworkers went on strike, led by Jędrzej Augustyn, who had previously taken part in the workers' movement in Graz. The strike ended victoriously on 4 May 1871.[87] The printers of Lviv contributed to the needleworkers' victory by their support. On 27 April the administration of the Progressive Society issued to its members the following appeal, signed by Szczęsny Bednarski and Jan Niedopad:

> We are once again witnesses to a very saddening drama, for it is the struggle of labor with capital. A very considerable number of members of the tailor's profession, forced to the extreme, have decided to go on strike to win themselves a bettering of their lot in these days when material conditions are so difficult, especially for the working class. Let us hurry to them with aid.

The printers collected 28 gulden for the striking needleworkers.[88]

At the same time, workers from four Jewish print shops walked off their jobs for two weeks until their demands were met.[89] The cartwrights and wheelwrights went on strike at the end of May 1871. They demanded better treatment from the master craftsmen, reduction of the working day to twelve hours, an end to obligatory room and board at the master's house and a raise in wages to a gulden and a half daily. The strike met defeat in June.[90] During the cartwrights' strike, the Democratic *Dziennik Polski* (Polish Daily) admonished the masters and journeymen: "When two quarrel, a third party benefits; that third party is foreign industry."[91]

The strike movement spread to non-artisan workers as well. In mid-1872 mill workers on scattered provincial estates went on strike, and in September 1872 representatives of the tobacco industry in Lviv warned the viceroyalty that agents of the International were trying to organize their factory hands and encourage them to strike.[92] Characteristically, the strike wave did not encompass Cracow. There, in the summer of 1872, the printers also undertook wage negotiations, but achieved their goals without recourse to a strike (except in a single print shop).[93]

Virtually the last strike of the 1870s was once again the work of the Lviv printers, who started the series of strikes in the first place. At the all-Austrian printers' congress, held in Brno on 29 and 30 June 1872, the assembled delegates urged the establishment of a fixed price-list for typesetters in each crownland.[94] Szczęsny Bednarski actively propagated the congress's decisions among his colleagues,[95] so that at the end of 1872 the Lviv Progressive Society was determining anew the price of a typesetter's labor. "The employers themselves," said the printers' newspaper *Czcionka* (Character), "have acknowledged our aims in this matter to be correct and just; they await from us the presentation of the proposal [for new wages], that, after coming to a mutual understanding, it might be acknowledged as binding for both parties." "If," the paper concluded optimistically, "we shall take care of this matter through legal means and place our total confidence in our delegates, this affair will achieve a successful result."[96]

On 21 December 1872 the printers chose delegates, including Seniuk, Bednarski and Hoszowski, to represent their demands.[97] The Lviv police, however, broke up the meeting that chose the delegation,[98] a signal that the Galician authorities had begun to suppress the artisan movement, especially the printers' movement. Acting on a cue from Vienna, where the authorities had dissolved the Progressive Society on 28 November, the police not only dispersed the Lviv printers' meeting, but also, on Viceroy Gołuchowski's orders, dissolved the Lviv Progressive Society on 31 December. Gołuchowski justified his order on the grounds that the Lviv Progressive Society had exceeded the legal limitations of its statutes by establishing a wage commission.[99] Thus, the printers' hopes of successful negotiations and their optimistic intention to employ only legal means of persuasion proved to have been radically out of place; the employers refused to meet their demands and the viceroyalty, whose patience with the wave of strikes was exhausted, had turned the force of law against them.

Czcionka responded in an article that half pleaded with and half threatened the authorities. It noted that the workers' movement frightened the government and it warned that "whoever dares to oppose the awakening vitality of either progress or society is beginning a hazardous game." Is it the working class, the paper asked, or is it "capital, that greatest egotist," which constitutes a real threat to the authorities? "The experiment of dissolving the associations and confiscating their property may easily bring about an explosion that even the most skilled fireman could hardly stifle and extinguish."[100]

The printers went on strike for two weeks beginning 11 January 1873. During the course of the strike, Mańkowski, Bednarski, Seniuk and Hoszowski called a meeting of the printers on 24 January; the Lviv police dispersed the meeting as illegal. The strike ended in a compromise, bitterly opposed by Bednarski and Mańkowski: a 15 percent raise instead of the 20 percent originally asked.[101]

The printers' movement exhibited remarkable resiliency after the repression of 1872–73. The Cracow police expressed surprise that the printers of that city succeeded in organizing their own version of the

Progressive Society, Ognisko (Hearth), early in 1873. The police were certain that "the misfortune that befell the similar association in Lviv" would discourage the Cracow printers from setting up Ognisko. After months of procrastination, however, the viceroyalty confirmed the association's statutes on 1 August 1873. It was a short-lived organization all the same, disbanding on 1 January 1875 when the local printers' mutual aid society could no longer house Ognisko on its premises for only a nominal rental fee.[102]

The Lviv printers in the mid-1870s divided into left and right. When, in 1869, Lewicki and Seniuk had approached Franciszek Piątkowski, president of the Printers' Mutual Aid Society, to explain to him the plans and aims of the Left-Wing Circle, Piątkowski had asked: "Why call it the Left-Wing Circle? We have neither right wing nor center." "That will come," they replied.[103]

Their prediction was fulfilled. One of the first points of contention between left and right was the organizational structure of the cooperative print shop. Alfred Szczepański had first urged the printers to establish a cooperative printery in 1867.[104] In 1870, after the printers had proven their ability to act in solidarity during the first printers' strike, Tadeusz Skałkowski also encouraged them to set up a cooperative enterprise.[105] So, in 1870, the Lviv printers inaugurated a Savings Society to finance a cooperative print shop. Two programs, dubbed "aristocratic" and "democratic," divided the printers on how to arrange the cooperative. The "aristocrats" favored a cooperative for better-off printers and urged that prospective members pay at least 500 g. for a share. The "democrats," probably the Left-Wing Circle and its sympathizers, agitated for an arrangement in which members could purchase shares on long-term credit for 50 g. The two factions eventually settled on a compromise of 100 g. per share. The First Union Print Shop was founded in Lviv in December 1872.[106]

After the 1873 printers' strike, the printers' organ Czcionka ceased to issue radical statements. Thereafter Czcionka insisted that the printers had never harbored and did not then harbor any hostility toward the print-shop owners, since only through agreement and mutual good will could both sides achieve their goals. The paper, adopting as its motto "Through Education to Prosperity," began to stress the moral and cultural elevation of the working people; it now censured class hostility and radical measures.[107] True, an occasional anti-capitalist article still appeared in Czcionka,[108] but the general tone set by editor Leon

Zubalewicz became increasingly *déclassé*. Zubalewicz, employed as a print-shop manager since early 1873,[109] complained, in a probable reference to the Left-Wing Circle, about behind-the-scenes intrigues during the recent wage negotiations.[110] He disapproved of the division within the printers' movement between "the so-called democratic element (those who possess little) and the aristocratic element (the capitalists)."[111] In May of 1873 Zubalewicz graced the paper with an article stating that the struggle between capital and labor exists only outside Galicia and therefore Galician workers should not join the all-Austrian movement or be deluded by internationalism.[112] Thus, as the Lviv delegate to the sixth all-Austrian printers' congress in Graz in 1873, Zubalewicz firmly opposed a printers' union for the empire; he said he feared that Austrian printers would "outnumber and terrorize" Polish printers.[113]

Zubalewicz urged the printers to show solidarity with their employers by participating in the celebration to commemorate the hundredth anniversary of the Piller publishing house in Lviv. Antoni Mańkowski, surprisingly, headed the workers' jubilee committee. The banquet, held on 20 September 1873, took place beneath a banner inscribed, "Hand in hand — labor with capital." Accounts differ as to the course of the banquet, but it is clear that some speakers, perhaps Mańkowski and Bolesław Limanowski, made objection to the celebration of capital-labor solidarity, only to be rebutted by Zubalewicz.[114]

A half year later, owing to conflicts with other printers who did not share his pro-management views, Zubalewicz resigned as editor of *Czcionka*. The paper soon folded up, a victim of the division within the printers' movement. *Czcionka* was revived briefly in 1875; it was succeeded by *Naprzód* (Forward; only one issue of which appeared, on 20 January 1877) and then by *Praca* (Labor; the first issue of which appeared on 1 July 1878).[115]

There were, to be sure, other tendencies within the printers' movement that differed from Zubalewicz's. Szczęsny Bednarski, in December 1873, published in his own translation and at his own cost Ferdinand Schönhofer's *Was wollen, was sollen die Arbeiter*. Schönhofer called for universal suffrage, a fixed working day, limitations on women's labor, abolition of child labor, separation of church and state, abolition of indirect taxes, introduction of a progressive income tax and state financial support for workers' production cooperatives. In short, Schönhofer was a Lassallean. Bednarski emphasized several times that he wholeheartedly shared Schönhofer's views. He added only three specifically Galician demands to Schönhofer's list: autonomy for Galicia, reduction of the number of holidays and the exclusive use of the Gregorian calendar.[116]

An important section of Schönhofer's brochure dealt with the need for workers' organization, especially in times of repression. Schönhofer urged the workers to form trade unions to regulate wages and the length of the working day. He urged, too, that workers very carefully organize strikes. Repression, he noted, causes many workers to stand aside from the movement, but this is demoralized behavior; only through solidarity can workers overcome obstacles.

The publication of such sentiments in Lviv was timely. The police had dissolved the Progressive Society and the Lviv printers were attempting to revive it under the name "Postęp" (Progress). The statutes of Postęp, which a meeting of eighty printers approved on 26 May 1873, provided for a permanent wage commission attached to the administration. The printers submitted the statutes to the viceroyalty for confirmation on 31 May, but the statutes were returned unconfirmed on 9 June. The printers appealed then to the Austrian ministry of the interior to reverse the viceroyalty's ruling, but without success. In January 1874 the printers again submitted a revised version of the statutes to the viceroyalty and again confirmation was refused. Finally, on 6 May 1875, the viceroyalty approved the statutes of a new printers' society, Ognisko. The association, which started out in 1875 with a hundred members, lasted until 1935; it included among its chief activists Antoni Mańkowski, Józef Daniluk, the brothers Bednarski, Jan Hoszowski and Józef Seniuk. Ognisko, as the Progressive Society had done before it, annually celebrated the anniversary of the first printers' strike.[117]

Not long after the establishment of Ognisko, on 23 July 1875, the Ukrainian socialist Mykhailo Drahomanov, who was then visiting Galicia, attended a meeting of the association's administration, extended his best wishes and offered the association a small donation.[118] Continued contact of Ognisko's president Mańkowski, with Drahomanov led the police to keep a watchful eye on the printers' movement. On 9 May 1877 the police conducted a search of the premises of the Lviv Printers' Mutual Aid Society. They were looking for evidence to mount the first major prosecution of socialists in Galicia.[119]

Outside the printers' movement, too, left-wing views were making their appearance. In June 1871 a Lviv tailor, Franciszek Głodziński,[120] proposed a utopian venture in communal living to his colleagues in Gwiazda. His ideas were set forth in a brochure published at his own cost and distributed on the occasion of the consecration of Gwiazda's banner. Głodziński proposed that the Lviv craftsmen set up communal housekeeping in an association to be called "The Great Family." This would make life easier for wives, who could then share cooking, child care and other chores. The Great Family, each "family" of which required a hundred members, would benefit craftsmen by fostering domestic happiness and lowering the cost of living. Głodziński suggested that the craftsmen could raise the initial capital for the cooperative by saving a gulden a month for five years. Concerts, donations and contributions of honorary members could also help.[121] Although nothing came of Głodziński's proposal, it did attract the attention of the professed socialist Bolesław Limanowski. Limanowski placed a summary of the brochure in *Dziennik Polski* and elaborated there, with great enthusiasm, upon experiments in communal living in Europe and America. He ended his article by noting: "For us, too, this is a thing which must be done."[122]

Limanowski, originally from the Russian empire where he had been involved in Polish patriotic agitation in the early 1860s, had been converted to socialism while serving a term of exile in the Russian Far North. He came to Lviv late in 1870 and had some connection with the local artisan movement.[123] In particular, he held two lectures in Gwiazda, on 19 March and 2 April 1871, which dealt with the decline of feudalism and the rise and democratic character of the workers' movement in Western Europe. He stressed the importance of mutual aid, a principle he traced back to the Divine Teacher. Now socialists, such as Owen and Lassalle, championed the same principle. In order to do battle with capitalism, he maintained, workers in the West have no other choice but to join together in cooperative associations and trade unions. He spoke with approval of the International Workingmen's Association. Reflecting on the persecution of the workers' movement in Western Europe, Limanowski assured his listeners that "persecution is the bloody cross through which everything that has a mighty future must pass."[124]

The lectures created little stir. The only person who displayed any interest in them was Piotr Zbrożek, editor of *Rękodzielnik*. Nonetheless, mainly because he needed money, Limanowski tried to publish the lectures. *Gazeta Narodowa* considered his presentation of the worker's question inopportune and declined to print it. Limanowski decided then to publish the lectures as a brochure. He hoped to make a profit, but only half the printing costs were returned to him. He gave away a large portion of the 500 copies he had had printed.[125] It is indicative of the brochure's ideological blandness that even such a rabid anti-socialist as Kazimierz Szulc could recommend his readers to consult it on West European profit-sharing.[126]

Limanowski's reputation as a socialist spread to the Russian empire, where Polish students were taking a serious interest in socialism in the mid-1870s. To make contact with Limanowski, the students sent emissaries, Kazimierz Hildt from Warsaw and Jan Hłasko from Kiev, to Lviv in September 1875. Limanowski introduced his guests to members of the artisan associations and to his fellow journalist Bolesław Czerwieński. Hildt, Limanowski, Czerwieński, Jan Welichowski and the printer August Skerl discussed the possibility of founding an organization and a socialist periodical, but nothing went beyond discussion.[127]

In 1876 Edmund Brzeziński and Erazm Kobylański paid a visit to Limanowski. Brzeziński, a delegate of Polish socialist students in St. Petersburg, brought Limanowski a translation of Lassalle's workers' program and money — about 500 rubles — for publication. Limanowski had to rework the translation completely, but it was published in 1878, along with other works of Lassalle in Polish translation, by the First Union Print Shop.[128]

On 31 May 1877 Erazm Kobylański revisited the Galician capital. He had been sent by Polish socialists in Warsaw and St. Petersburg to establish contact with Russian, Ukrainian and Polish socialists outside the Russian empire. Kobylański arrived in Lviv from Switzerland loaded down with revolutionary brochures and letters to various people in Galicia. In Lviv he met with Limanowski and Skerl. With the latter Kobylański visited the headquarters of Ognisko, where, as the Lviv police noted, Kobylański "spent a rather long time, during which many people from the working class entered and left the premises."[129] Kobylański was soon arrested and on 10 June 1877, Limanowski, too, was searched by the police and imprisoned.[130]

In the 1860s, in connection with the Austrian reforms, the Polish

Democrats had organized the Polish artisans in Lviv and inducted them into the political process. In doing so, and contrary to their intentions, they also set the stage for the emergence of a radicalized artisan movement. In the early 1870s the artisans and especially the printers of Lviv went on strike to win higher wages and better working conditions. By the mid-1870s Lassallean and collectivist ideas appeared in the printers' and artisans' ranks. At the same time, Bolesław Limanowski, a socialist refugee from the Russian empire, publicly advocated an idealistic form of socialism and collaborated with Polish socialists from Russia. The Polish socialist movement had not yet begun in Galicia, but the preconditions for it were there. All that was required was a catalyst. This was to be provided by the Lviv police and the Ruthenian socialist youth.

Chapter Two

Ukrainian Politics, 1860–1878

While Polish socialism had its origins in a radicalized artisan movement, Ruthenian socialism started as a radical political current among the young intelligentsia. The young men who became Galicia's first Ruthenian socialists were originally members of student clubs imbued with the ideologies of Ruthenia's two rival national movements, Russophilism and Ukrainophilism (or national populism). Their conversion to socialism involved a conscious rejection of both Russophilism and national populism and an adhesion to the principles of a radical Russian Ukrainophile, Mykhailo Drahomanov.

Russophilism and Ukrainophilism (National Populism)

Russophilism, the national movement of those Galician Ruthenians who identified themselves as part of the Russian nation, can be traced back to the 1830s and 1840s when the Ruthenian intelligentsia, clerical and secular, came into contact with Slavophile propagandists from Russia. It developed as a wider trend only after 1848 and continued to be closely connected with Slavophile circles in Russia. The Slavophiles, and the Russian government itself, materially supported Galician Russophilism. The Moscow Slavonic Committee sent Russian Orthodox ecclesiastical paraphernalia to pro-Russian Greek Catholic priests and granted stipends to Russophile students in Austria. The Slavophiles also directly subsidized prominent Russophiles; in 1868, for example, they sent 200 rubles to Ksenofon Klymkovych. At least in the case of Klymkovych, who had been a founder of the rival Ukrainophile movement, the ruble was probably the decisive factor in his switch to Russophilism.[1]

It would be incorrect, however, to attribute the rise of Russophilism only to Slavophile propaganda and foreign funding without taking into account the inner logic of Russophilism as an authentic national movement of the Galician Ruthenians. A primary cause of political Russophilism, i.e., the orientation on the Russian empire as a political power, was the sense of betrayal felt by many Ruthenians after Austria turned Galicia into a virtual fiefdom of the Polish nobility in the late 1860s. Their disappointment was all the more bitter on account of their record as a *kaisertreu* people, "the Tyrolians of the East." Also, the Ruthenian clergy and intelligentsia in Galicia suffered from an ethnic inferiority complex in relation to the Poles. The Ruthenians' was a peasant culture, the Poles' aristocratic, and to compensate for this, some Ruthenians developed the "aristocratism" that led them to scorn "the language of peasants and shepherds" (the Ukrainian vernacular). By identifying with the Russian nation, the Ruthenians in Galicia could bypass their native plebeian culture, their peasant vernacular, their lack of a state tradition, and claim as their own a high culture, a developed literary language and a powerful state. Furthermore, the linguistic and religious features that distinguished the Ruthenians from the Poles were precisely the traits Ruthenians shared with Russians. Although the Ukrainian vernacular was lexically very close to Polish, a West Slavic language, it was, like Russian, an East Slavic language; it shared with Russian many features of structure and grammar as well as the Cyrillic alphabet. And although Ruthenians were, like the Poles, Catholics, the Ruthenians were Greek Catholics; in ritual, the Greek Catholic church was almost identical to Russian Orthodoxy, since the Greek Catholics were originally Orthodox Christians forcibly united by the Catholic Poles to the Roman church. In their efforts to purify themselves of Polonism, the more extreme Galician Russophiles were ready to adopt the Russian language and return to the Orthodox faith.

Some Ukrainian Marxists have stereotyped Russophilism as clerical and reactionary,[2] but this is an oversimplification that does not do justice to the Galician movement. Part of the reason Russophilism has been branded a clerical movement is that some investigators, following Mykhailo Drahomanov's precedent, have erroneously identified the Russophile party with the St. George or Old Ruthenian party. The latter was a truly clerical party headed by the Greek Catholic metropolitan in Lviv. Russophilism grew out of Old Ruthenianism, shared with it a scorn for the vernacular and a hostility to things Polish, and Russophilism influenced the St. George party, but a distinction must nonetheless be made. The Old Ruthenians were loyal to the Habsburg dynasty and formed something on the order of a pro-government party; but the

Russophiles felt a loyalty to the Romanovs. The Russophiles were more secular than the Old Ruthenians. Ivan Franko has plausibly suggested that Russophilism was the movement of the *secular* intelligentsia of the 1850s; that Ukrainian bureaucratic and judicial functionaries, gymnasium professors, notaries, lawyers and journalists developed with greater consistency the ideas already inherent in Old Ruthenianism and in this way created Russophilism; that the rise of Russophilism and decline of the St. George party was intimately connected with the growing significance of the periodical press and with the secular intelligentsia assuming leadership in the nation.[3]

The reactionary character of Russophilism has also been exaggerated. Like almost all early national movements in Eastern Europe, many of which wore conservative, clerical garb, Russophilism implied some cultural and social elevation of the peasantry. Judge Mykhailo Kachkovsky, the Galician Maecenas of Russophilism, was attacked in the Polish Democratic press for constantly siding with the peasants when disputes with the manor over forests and pastures were brought before his court.[4] In the 1870s, the Russophile priest Ivan Naumovych was recognized even by radicals as the most energetic educator of the peasants, the most talented popular writer and the most diligent promoter of cultural and economic institutions to benefit the peasantry intellectually and materially.[5]

Yet, though Russophilism had its progressive qualities, the fact remains that it was an orientation on tsarist Russia. Russophiles maintained contact with the most reactionary circles of Russian society and government: Katkov and the Slavophiles. Galician Russophiles to some extent provoked, and after the event applauded, the Ems ukase of 1876 banning publication in the Ukrainian language in the Russian empire. Orientation towards a foreign power, moreover, was socially the most passive of the alternatives before the Ruthenian intelligentsia in Galicia.[6]

Of the two rival national movements in Ruthenian Galicia, Ukrainophilism, or national populism (*narodovstvo*), was potentially the more democratic. It rejected reliance on a foreign power in favor of work within the nation and, in contrast to Russophilism, accepted the peasant vernacular as the basis for a literary language. National populism was the Galician counterpart of the Ukrainophile movement in the Russian empire. In Russia a Ukrainian literary movement, initiated by the publication of Ivan Kotliarevsky's *Eneida* in 1798, had reached a culmination in the middle of the nineteenth century in the poetry of a ransomed serf, Taras Shevchenko. Unlike in Galicia, where the Greek Catholic clergy played an important part in the national movement, in Russia the Ukrainian movement was completely secular. The Orthodox clergy had been Russified, and only part of the secular intelligentsia identified itself as Ukrainian.

Although Ukrainophile tendencies first appeared in Galicia in the 1830s and came to the fore during the 1848 revolution, national populism experienced a decade of discontinuity in the 1850s, the consequence of both the general reaction in Austria and the usurpation of political and ideological leadership by the St. George party and the Russophiles. We can therefore justly date the beginning of the national populist movement in Galicia to the early 1860s. "In the year 1860," recalled Volodymyr Shashkevych, "there were only two young people in Lviv who were already considering, but only considering, accepting the Ukrainian dialect as the basis of the further development of our literature and introducing the Ukrainian orthography into Galicia."[7] The Ukrainophile movement was at such an early stage of development that even a minor incident took on major significance: in the spring of 1861, the Galician merchant Mykhailo Dymet returned from Kiev with a number of copies of Shevchenko's *Kobzar*. Dymet had not brought enough copies of Shevchenko to satisfy the demand he had awakened. Shevchenko's cult grew rapidly and hand-copied editions of Shevchenko circulated in Galicia.[8] Also in the early 1860s a Ukrainian student from Odessa, Volodymyr Bernatovych, visited Galicia. He made quite an impression on the young national populists in Lviv:

> He was the first real live Ukrainian we had met. We listened to him, retaining in our memories every single word he said about Taras [Shevchenko], the Kievan Hromada and how things were over there [in Russian Ukraine]. We admired the beauty of his language — and we gained courage.[9]

Bernatovych's account of the Kievan Hromada, the informal organization of the Ukrainophile intelligentsia in Kiev, inspired the Galicians to establish their own hromadas. The first of these appeared in Lviv in 1861 and others emerged elsewhere in the following years.

The national populist movement in Galicia was chiefly inspired by the Ukrainian movement in the Russian empire, but the Polish insurrection of 1863 also contributed to its growth. Russophiles, of course, felt no

sympathy with Poles in rebellion against the Russia they glorified, but
for the national populists, who saw analogies between the conditions of
the Ukrainian and Polish nations under tsarism, the Polish uprising was
an inspiration to their national movement. Although conscious Ruthenians would not participate in the Polish insurrection, they wished it well
and contracted the infectious patriotic enthusiasm of the Poles. Polish
insurgents contributed directly to the rise of national populism. Late in
1863, the Russian army defeated a division of Polish insurgents near the
Galician border and the Poles fled *en masse* to Galicia, eventually
ending up in Lviv. This particular division had been formed of Polish
students from Kiev University and other young men of the so-called
chłopomańska (peasant-loving) party. They sympathized with the
Ukrainophile movement and contributed to its periodical *Meta* (Aim) in
Lviv. Among them was Paulin Święcicki, who published *Sioło* (Village) in Polish to influence Polish public opinion in favor of the Ukrainian movement. These insurgents also established the Circle of Friends of
Rus' (*Kółko przyjaciół Rusi*) in 1863.[10]

National populism, then, aligned with two democratic and secular
movements: Russian Ukrainophilism and Polish revolutionary democracy. In the beginning, Galician Ukrainophilism was itself a democratic[11] and secular movement. Unlike the Russophiles, for whom ritual
purity and ultimately Orthodoxy were important aspects of their program, the young Galician Ukrainophiles considered religion a matter of
secondary significance. When the nation can control its *political* fate,
they reflected, then it will be able to order its ecclesiastical affairs as it
wishes. What benefit, they asked themselves, could possibly accrue to
an enslaved nation from exchanging union with Rome for Orthodoxy?[12]
Some national populists went even further and sharply criticized the
clergy's role in national life, accusing the "caste of clerics" of "making a
monopoly of spiritual enlightenment" and "robbing" the peasantry,
whom the priests consider "cattle for the milking."

> O wretched nation! Poor Ruthenian orphans! Aside from the others who
> do you injury, how many times has a Ruthenian pastor taken from you
> your last milk cow, and hay as well, in payment for the burial of your
> father, your mother?!![13]

Such radical sentiments quickly vanished from the ideological declar-
ations of the national populists. So, too, did manifestations of a more

socially conscious concept of democracy. There was a curious paradox at work: precisely because of its democratic orientation, Ruthenian national populism was forced to abandon what radical democracy it had already absorbed from its Polish and Ukrainian models. This becomes all the more paradoxical when we consider that the retreat from democracy more or less coincided with the introduction of the Austrian constitution in 1867.

Ukrainophile democracy was democracy in respect to the peasantry, which made up over 95 percent of Galicia's Ruthenian population. National populism sought to draw the Ruthenian demos, the peasantry, into the cultural and political life of the nation. The 1867 constitution transformed this desire into a necessity, for if the Ukrainophiles expected to win seats in the Parliament or Diet, they required the political support, the votes, of the peasants. So from 1867 on, national populism was characterized by village-oriented work. It published newspapers for the peasants and fostered the development of institutions such as reading clubs and cooperatives in the countryside. All this might seem, on the surface, to strengthen the democratic ideology already inherent in Ukrainophilism, but in fact it had the opposite effect.

The key to the paradox is that the secular intelligentsia was unable, by itself, to work among the peasants. It was impossible for the Lviv-based intelligentsia to work directly among the peasantry, which was scattered in thousands of relatively inaccessible villages. In this situation, the intelligentsia sought the aid of the one Ruthenian class in the countryside with sufficient education and material independence to assume leadership of the national movement in the villages themselves: the clergy.[14]

With his role as mediator between urban intellectuals and peasant, the priest became an important influence in national populism. As long as national populism had remained merely an urban-based intellectual current, it could afford to be relatively nonreligious and even anticlerical. But when national populism began its transformation into a mass movement, it had to reckon with the attitudes of the clergy. This implied not only the renunciation of anticlericalism, but the clericalization and de-democratization of national populist thought. This became strikingly evident when Galician Ukrainophilism clashed with what had originally inspired it, Russian Ukrainophilism, in the middle of the 1870s.

Drahomanov and Galician Politics

The most prominent Ukrainophile in the Russian empire in the early
and mid-1870s was Mykhailo Petrovych Drahomanov. His articles on
Ukrainian and Slavonic affairs regularly appeared in the most presti-
gious Russian periodicals of his day, *Vestnik Evropy* and *Sankt-Peter-
burgskiia vedomosti*. He was at the center, too, of the ethnographic
work then being conducted by the Kievan branch of the Russian
Geographical Society. Together with another Kievan luminary, Volodymyr Antonovych, he had published an outstanding collection of Ukrainian folk songs on historical themes. Also together with Antonovych, he
emerged as a leader of the Kievan Hromada, the central organization of
the Ukrainophile movement in Russia.

Within Hromada at least two trends competed for influence. Antonovych represented the cultural trend, which saw Ukrainophilism primarily as an intellectual movement devoted to fostering the language,
literature, ethnography and history of the Ukrainian people. Drahomanov and a number of younger Ukrainophiles, however, felt that Ukrainophilism had to transcend the literary and interest itself in political and
social affairs. In fact, by the middle of the 1870s, under the impact of the
Russian revolutionary movement, Drahomanov had come to the conclusion that Ukrainophiles had to become socialists.

Drahomanov argued that the Ukrainian nation lacked a native exploiting class. The exploiters of the Ukrainian people all belonged, by
birth or assimilation, to other nationalities; they were Russians, Poles or
Jews. He boasted that the Ukrainian nation had "neither its own clergy,
nor landed nobility, nor merchant class, nor state, but has instead . . .
the peasantry."[15] The consistent Ukrainophile therefore had to do more
than propagate the peasant's language and engage in ethnographic
research. This was, in Drahomanov's view, a preoccupation with form
at the expense of content. The Ukrainophile intelligentsia was obliged
to take up the cause of the peasant's social interests. Because the nation
was the exploited peasantry, consistent Ukrainophilism had to be socialism.

For Drahomanov, socialism was inconceivable without change from
the bottom up. The peasantry had to become educated, able to share in
the intellectual life of European civilization — not as a result of the
socialist revolution, but as a precondition for the establishment of
socialism. The peasantry had to develop autonomous voluntary associa-

tions for cultural and economic purposes — again, not as the result, but as the precondition of socialism. The intelligentsia was to serve the peasantry as midwife in this transition.

In Russian Ukraine, work among the peasantry could not begin until a constitution took the place of absolutism. For this reason, democratic reforms had to be the first postulate of the socialist program in Russia. Austria, however, was already a constitutional state and therefore ripe for socialist work among the peasants. This consideration led Drahomanov to devote special attention to the Ukrainians under Austrian rule.

Of all the Ukrainophiles in Russia, Drahomanov took the most active interest in Galician affairs. He wrote for the Ruthenian press and freely offered his advice on how to further the Ukrainian cause in Austria. It was inevitable, however, that the two Ukrainophilisms, Russian and Austrian, would confront each other with suspicion in the mid-1870s. Each had evolved, but in the opposite direction. Russian Ukrainophilism, at least as represented by Drahomanov, had developed an even more radically democratic ideology than the Ukrainophilism of the previous decade. Galician Ukrainophilism, however, had come under increasing clerical influence and had muted the radical democracy of its origins.

Already in 1872, when Drahomanov first began to write for the national populist press in Lviv, there were symptoms that the two Ukrainophilisms were unable to work together harmoniously. But after visiting Lviv in the following year, Drahomanov became so indignant at Ruthenian political leaders that he drafted an open letter of rebuke to the national populist organ *Pravda* (Truth). The open letter of 1873 protested the politics of both the Russophiles and Ukrainophiles and, in the name of progressive Russian Ukrainophilism, forbade either Galician party to pose as representatives of any political tendency in Russia, be it Slavophilism or Ukrainophilism. Seventy-six Russian Ukrainophiles signed the open letter.[16]

The quarrel between Drahomanov and the Galicians reflected the lack of territorial integration of the Ukrainian national movement, the awkwardness of relations between Austrian and Russian Ukraine. This showed up even in the more petty aspects of the dispute. Drahomanov, for instance, accused the editors of Lviv's *Pravda* of being careless in the way they handled manuscripts of Russian Ukrainophiles: some were lost in *Pravda*'s editorial office; others were published, but with long, dissenting commentaries. More significantly, some manuscripts were deliberately suppressed so as not to offend the Greek Catholic clergy.

A substantive issue of controversy concerned Drahomanov's ideas on the role that Russian culture could play in Galicia. Drahomanov was fond of calling attention to two ironies of the Galician situation: first, even though Galicia was geographically more a part of Europe than Russia was, culturally and intellectually Russia was more European than the Austrian crownland; second, though the Russophiles were idolaters and the national populists disparagers of Russia, the Russophiles had the least understanding of Russia while the national populists had a better understanding and a greater attachment to Russia.

In Galician Russophilism, the cult of Russia had not been accompanied by the culture of Russia. The Russophiles produced a literature that betrayed no acquaintance with contemporary, socially relevant Russian literature. Galician literature exhibited the same abstraction from the vital interests of the people that could also be found in Galician politics. In this sense Russia was more European culturally than was Austrian Galicia. Drahomanov believed that Russian realism, if introduced into Galicia, would vitalize the sterile intellectual climate and awaken the intelligentsia to concern itself with the real problems of society.[17] According to Drahomanov, the national populists already understood Russia better than the Russophiles, since they absorbed progressive Russian culture through the medium of Russian Ukrainophilism. In reading Shevchenko, Kostomarov, Kulish and Vovchok, the Galician Ukrainophiles were exposed to the new Russian culture, one manifestation of which was the literature of the Ukrainian movement.

Drahomanov even developed a complex literary theory on the different roles to be played by "Russian, Great Russian, Ukrainian and Galician literature." Russian literature was to be the high literary tradition in both Russian and Austrian Ukraine, while the Ukrainian and Galician literatures (and Great Russian literature in ethnic Russia) were to be "for domestic consumption," peasant-oriented and functional.[18] The Galician Ukrainophiles would not accept these views. Even the statistician Volodymyr Navrotsky, who agreed with Drahomanov on many other issues, found Drahomanov's "Russophilism" unacceptable.

That the national populists rejected Russian culture is understandable: the home-grown promoters of Russian culture, the Russophiles, were implacably hostile to the Ukrainophile movement.[19] Galicia, moreover, lay outside the sphere of Russian cultural influence, so that Russian culture was truly something alien to Galicians. (Drahomanov would have agreed that the nature of Galician Russophilism confirmed this.) Also, since Galician Ruthenians rejected Polish culture in favor of developing their own independent culture, they could not understand Drahomanov's willingness, despite his Ukrainophilism, not only to retain his Russian culture, but to promote it actively in Galicia. Nonetheless, it is difficult to agree with Volodymyr Barvinsky, a leading national populist, who felt that the major source of conflict between his party and Drahomanov was precisely Drahomanov's excessive attachment to Russian culture.[20] To reduce the debate over the role of Russian culture to a question of Ukrainian national pride alone, as Barvinsky did, is to lose sight of some fundamental aspects of the dispute.

First of all, Drahomanov did not advocate an interest in Russian literature because it was Russian, but rather because it was socially relevant. Although the national populists interpreted the cultural debate as a debate over the national question, Drahomanov saw it as a debate over a social question. The national populists had not evolved to the point where they could share Drahomanov's view that Ukrainophilism was pre-eminently socio-political. On the contrary, their Ukrainophilism had retreated to the level of cultural nationalism.

Another aspect of the debate underscores how uneasy were the relations between Austrian and Russian Ukraine. There was something supercilious and patronizing about Drahomanov's insistence on the importance of Russian literature for Galicia, something that implied that Austrian Ruthenia was inferior. Drahomanov argued that the Ukrainophiles in Galicia were more progressive than the Russophiles because the former had caught some rays of Russian culture refracted through the prism of Russian Ukrainophilism. He argued that Galicia's road to Europeanization lay through Russia and particularly, at this stage, through Russian Ukraine. One Galician Ruthenian, reviewing a collection of Drahomanov's essays in 1874, paraphrased Drahomanov thus:

> You Galicians are still little children, too little to draw from the source. Wait. *We* will draw from the source. Then we'll pour everything into another vessel and give it to you.[21]

Drahomanov was indeed solicitous to dissociate what he considered the more progressive and more European Ukrainophilism of Russia

from the backward Ukrainophilism of Austria. The more he contrasted
the two Ukrainophilisms, the less he came to like the Austrian variant.
In his native Russian Ukraine, Ukrainophilism was a purely secular
movement; the clergy there was Russified and stood apart from the
national movement. But in Galicia the clergy exercised a great influence
on Ukrainophile politics and ideology, an influence Drahomanov considered unnatural and harmful. He was indignant, for instance, that the
Shevchenko Society did not publish a single line of Shevchenko's
poetry, yet each month published *Ruskii Sion* (Ruthenian Zion), the
organ of the Greek Catholic consistory and clergy. Even more appalling
was that the Shevchenko Society elected the priest Stepan Kachala as its
president.[22]

To Drahomanov the choice of Rev. Stepan Kachala was a monstrous
betrayal of the principles of Shevchenko and Ukrainophilism. One of
Rev. Kachala's brochures had, in fact, precipitated the open letter of
1873. The brochure in question, *Polityka rusyniv* (Politics of the Ruthenians), had been an attempt to formulate the national populist
political program. Much to Drahomanov's horror, the brochure advocated a concordat with the Vatican, confessional schools and privileges
for the Catholic church, while opposing such things as civil and intercon-
fessional marriages and trade on holy days.[23]

Moreover, Father Kachala, the president of the Shevchenko Society,
was the creator of an odious social theory, namely, that the Ruthenian
peasant was poor because he drank too much, spent too freely and
declined to work hard enough. This theory found its fullest expression in
his brochure, *What Is Destroying Us and What Can Help Us,* which the
national populists published in three editions in the late 1860s. Kachala's theory had all the ear-marks of a narrowly clerical doctrine. It
was quasi-theological, for it made vice the cause of poverty, implying
thus that poverty itself was morally reprehensible. Such a doctrine was,
of course, comforting absolution for the clergy, which derived its
income directly and indirectly from the impoverished peasantry. Kachala's views differed radically, then, from the Galician Ukrainophilism
of the early 1860s and even more from the Ukrainophilism of Drahomanov. This is why Kachala in the mid-1870s warned Galician students
against "the Muscovite nihilist" Drahomanov — because "Drahomanov
does not consider the poverty of the people to be the result of their
sloth, prodigality and drunkenness. . . ."[24]

Drahomanov, and other left-wing Russian Ukrainophiles, were distressed to discover that Kachala's theories of the peasantry had even penetrated the thinking of secular national populists. One national populist intellectual, Kornylo Sushkevych, who visited Kiev in 1875, allegedly made the following statement in front of some twenty Russian Ukrainophiles:

> Now you gentlemen are always grieving for the peasant and saying: "Give them land." But you don't know the nature of our peasant. If you give him land and leave him alone, why he'll just lie down beneath a pear tree; he'll go to sleep and won't do a thing![25]

The points of contention, then, between Russian Ukrainophilism and Galician national populism were fundamental. A less energetic and stubborn man than Drahomanov would surely have abandoned the Galicians altogether. Instead, Drahomanov tried his luck at converting Galician students to progressive Ukrainophilism. In this undertaking he enjoyed considerable success.

Three Epistles to the Galicians

In the mid-1870s Drahomanov was losing ground on two fronts: at home in Kiev and in Galicia. Following the archeological congress in Kiev in 1874, the Kievan Ukrainophiles, and Drahomanov in particular, came under a mounting attack from Russophiles in Galicia and Russian circles in Kiev. *Kievlianin* (The Kievan), the influential rival of the Ukrainophile *Kievskii telegraf* (Kievan Telegraph), began to publish denunciations of Drahomanov and the work of the Ukrainophiles; Galician Russophiles wrote or inspired some of the denunciations. A leitmotif of the anti-Ukrainophile insinuations was that a Polish conspiracy had spawned Ukrainophilism. The campaign against Drahomanov and the Kievan Hromada was escalating; in 1875–76 it resulted in Drahomanov's dismissal from the University of Kiev and in a decree, the Ems ukase, banning publication in the Ukrainian language within the Russian empire.[26] Also in the mid-1870s, Drahomanov had broken completely with the national populists in Galicia and was looking for fresh allies in Galician society to establish a new and progressive tendency in Ruthenia.

Students proved to be the element Drahomanov was searching for to form the advance guard in Galician political and intellectual life. Drahomanov's first overtures were to a Ukrainophile student club in Vienna, Sich (named after the cossack stronghold of early modern Ukraine). The problem of Austrian Ruthenian inferiority vis-à-vis Russian Ukraine emerged clearly during his dealings with the Viennese students. When a member of Sich, Meliton Buchynsky, expressed reservations about socialism, Drahomanov accused him of "the backwardness of an Austrian."[27] At least one student in Vienna, however, Ostap Terletsky, came around to a whole-hearted admission of Galician inferiority. After visiting Kiev for the archeological congress, Terletsky wrote to Buchynsky: "What an immense contrast between Lviv and Kiev! . . . I'll tell you the truth, honest and frank, that before the Hromada in Kiev and before all Ukrainians I also stood in opposition to the way national affairs are run in Lviv."[28] Immediately afterwards, Terletsky published in *Pravda* a scathing critique of the Russophiles and national populists, repeating many of Drahomanov's arguments.[29] He also became a socialist. Together with Serhii Podolynsky, a Ukrainian socialist from Russia, Terletsky published a series of four brochures that were Ukrainophile, seditious and socialist.[30] He was arrested for this in 1876 and Ruthenian radicalism in Vienna was suppressed. By that time, however, the center of Ruthenian student radicalism had shifted to Lviv.

Ruthenian students at Lviv University were organized in two clubs: Druzhnii lykhvar (The Friendly Usurer), which was Ukrainophile, and Akademicheskii kruzhok (Student Circle), which was Russophile. Since 1874 the kruzhok had been publishing a student periodical, *Druh* (Friend). In its first year of publication, *Druh* appeared in the jargon of the Russophiles, the so-called *iazychiie,* neither Russian nor Ukrainian, though an attempt at the former, with an admixture of Church Slavonic, Polish and German for good measure. It was not a particularly interesting periodical in 1874, but at least one article deserves mention. The priest Hnat Onyshkevych undertook a review of a number of Drahomanov's publications on Ukrainian and Galician affairs. While agreeing with Drahomanov on some points, Onyshkevych objected, as a good Russophile, to Drahomanov's preference for phonetic over etymological orthography. Onyshkevych also disagreed with Drahomanov's open letter to *Pravda*: adopting a progressive, federalist program, as Drahomanov had urged in the open letter, would amount to the political death of Galicia's Ruthenians.[31]

By his review of Drahomanov's position on the Ukrainian and Galician questions, Hnat Onyshkevych had entered into a dialogue with

Drahomanov, a dialogue which the latter was eager to continue. While regularly castigating Ruthenian political leaders in the pages of *Kievskii telegraf* in 1875, Drahomanov singled out Onyshkevych's article in *Druh* as a symptom that there were some healthy elements in Galician society. "The article shows," Drahomanov wrote, "that the efforts of the [Russian] Ukrainians to mitigate the bitter disagreements between the Galician parties are beginning, at least to some degree, to have an effect."[32] In truth, Onyshkevych had not been very favorable to Drahomanov or conciliatory to the Ukrainophiles, at least not to the extent Drahomanov's praise would lead one to believe; but considering the unrelieved hostility emanating from Galicia, especially from the Russophile camp, Drahomanov accepted Onyshkevych's review as balm and honey. What pleased Drahomanov most, as he wrote in a letter to *Druh*, was Onyshkevych's admission that Ukrainophilism was not just a Polish intrigue. In his desire to continue the dialogue with *Druh*, Drahomanov did not restrict himself to communication through *Kievskii telegraf*, but entered into direct correspondence with the editorial board.[33]

Drahomanov purposely wrote his letter to *Druh* in Russian to impress upon the Russophile student club that Galician Russophiles were ignorant of Russia, its culture and even its language. Drahomanov suggested that the editors of *Druh* compare the real Russian language of his letter with the language of their journal and admit that these were two separate tongues. Drahomanov was proved correct — *Druh* had to publish his letter in translation (not in Ukrainian translation, however, but in Russophile *iazychiie!*). In his letter, Drahomanov encouraged *Druh* to switch to the Ukrainian vernacular: "If you wrote more in the popular Galician and Ukrainian languages, your writing would come out more 'Russian' and even more 'Great Russian' than it is at present." He wanted to avoid a picayune debate over orthography, but he did insist on the importance of the vernacular language:

> In my opinion anyway, it is better not to quarrel, but to engage in work of a nature that is not subject to controversy: educating the people in its own language and bringing the upper classes nearer the people, among other ways, by means of a literature about the people and in the people's language.

Drahomanov urged the young Russophiles to read as much Russian literature as possible, because Russian realism would lead them to

khlopomaniia (love for peasants) "and *khlopomaniia* on Little Russian
soil is Ukrainophilism."

Drahomanov's first letter to *Druh* had reiterated in a relatively gentle
fashion his conviction that Galician literature must pass through the
school of Russian realism and Russian Ukrainophilism; the letter, like
many of Drahomanov's articles of that time and earlier, had tried to
delineate the logical progression by which Galician Ruthenians, of
either the Russophile or national populist camp, would necessarily
arrive at a radically democratic Ukrainophilism, *khlopomaniia*. His
second and third letters, however, altogether rejected the very essence
of Galician culture and politics — its "Ruthenism" (*rutenshchina, ruten-
stvo*) — be it Russophile or national populist; Drahomanov abandoned
the theory of logical progression, because he had come to believe that to
the core and marrow Austrian Ruthenism was rotten.[34]

Drahomanov's second epistle to the Galicians was touched off by
Hnat Onyshkevych's response to the first. Onyshkevych had blamed the
Russian Ukrainians for the Russophile-Ukrainophile division in Galicia.
Galicians do not interfere in Russian affairs, Onyshkevych argued,
therefore Russians should not meddle in Galician affairs. Galicians
would adopt neither the Great Russian nor Ukrainian literary language:
"Don't bother us with Ukrainianism and Great Russianism, we have our
own language!"[35]

The latter statement, reducing "Ukrainianism" to linguistic preference, struck Drahomanov as eminently characteristic of the mentality of
Ruthenism. His reply elaborated on the nature of Ukrainianism:

> . . . it's not only literature in the language of the people, i.e., the
> language of the majority: it's giving the people (in this language) the fruits
> of world civilization, . . . it's the dedication of the intelligentsia — which
> could educate itself only because the people work and sweat — to serving
> the people morally, politically and socio-economically with the goal of
> ridding the people of ignorance, tyranny and exploitation. What, on the
> other hand, is Ruthenism? It would be interesting to get a straightforward
> and thorough answer to this question.

Drahomanov had no patience to wait for an answer. He unleashed his
own scathing critique of Ruthenism.

Druh, he argued, in both language and content catered to the tastes of
a peculiar "Ruthene public":

> . . . priests in dread of the consistory, clerks clinging to their "positions,"
> men who long ago forgot their seminary and university notebooks, who

never think to keep abreast of European thought, who just barely sustain their appetite for literature by reading Polish and German newspapers and journals in coffee houses, and, of course, "belles" [*krasavitsy*], whom Galician men—after the German fashion—regard as cooks and—after the aristocratic Polish fashion — as concubines and salon chatterboxes, "belles" who have never read anything but a prayerbook and the Polish [magazine] *Rozmaitości* [Miscellanea]. And the literary notions and tastes of this public legislate for your writers!

Drahomanov had no hope left for Galicia's intelligentsia and clergy. The secular intelligentsia devoted more time to billiards, card playing and café loquacity than to intellectual pursuits. The clergy was an anachronism living out its last days as science universally triumphed over religion. But the clergy was no harmless anachronism: it cheated, deceived and insulted the peasantry.

Ruthene priests and intellectuals criticized the peasants for sloth and drunkenness. "Now don't you think it's time," Drahomanov asked, "to tell the people something else besides that they are drunkards and sluggards?" Writers, bureaucrats and priests slept longer, worked less and earned more than peasants; they had no right to call the peasants lazy. The peasants were not lying on their backs under pear trees; after all, they fed and clothed themselves as well as "all the landlords, Jews, priests, writers." The peasant was not poor because he was lazy or addicted to drink. Drinking was a symptom, not a cause, of poverty. Poverty in the countryside was caused by something else.

That something else is the general structure of economic relations in which the peasant is a landless or small-holding proletarian; it is the general structure of society, which does not allow the peasant even an elementary education. . . . Every kreuzer of the wealthy is nothing more than wages withheld from a worker. This withholding of wages, and its consequence — the people's poverty, will be with us until all the land and all the factories become the property of the workers.

Drahomanov appealed to the youth not to be content with the "Ruthene ideal," but to turn from the ways of their elders and to fashion for themselves a fresh world view based on the latest achievements of European culture and science. He encouraged them to learn European languages and to build up their clubs' libraries, to read Mill on female emancipation and Draper on the conflict between science and religion, to immerse themselves in modern realist literature — Dickens, Thackeray, Flaubert and Zola along with Turgenev, Belinsky, Gogol and

Dostoevsky. Drahomanov had long championed ethnographic studies, advising students to look at the peasantry in order to find out who they themselves were. Now he also called upon the youth to look at Europe, to see what they could become.

A Fanatic and a Poet: The Younger Generation

Drahomanov's letters most impressed two peasants' sons, Mykhailo Pavlyk and Ivan Franko, both of whom were to provide the intellectual leadership of Ruthenian radicalism through the 1890s. Pavlyk was born in the village of Monastyrske near Kosiv in 1853. His father, who spent fourteen years in the army, was a cottage weaver. The Pavlyk family had an *opryshok* (social bandit) background and as a child Mykhailo heard many tales of the *opryshky*, especially Oleksa Dovbush.[36] Perhaps these tales of Ruthenian "Robin Hoods" predisposed Pavlyk to dedicate his life to a fight against social injustice.[37]

In spite of very humble origins, Pavlyk managed to attend gymnasium, first in Kolomyia for four years, then in Lviv for another four. In 1874 he entered Lviv University, joining Akademicheskii kruzhok and writing for its periodical *Druh*. His parents were too poor to pay for his education. For three years he received a stipend of 60 gulden annually, but for the most part he supported himself by tutoring other students, an occupation he found distasteful. His years in school were a constant struggle for survival.[38]

Education carried with it a certain amount of prestige. As a university student Pavlyk gained access to "society"; in the Ruthenian context, this meant he could attend social functions with priests and their families. As the son of a cottage weaver, he might at most have glimpsed through the window a party in "society." But now, a student from the capital, he took a place on the sofa. He never forgot the other side of the window, however. The contrast between "society" and his origins, his everpresent poverty, awakened resentment. "In the midst of their dancing and laughter, I would sit in a corner and ponder over things I hadn't learned in school."

Perhaps a haughty rejection had contributed to his special animus against the female denizens of "society," the priests' daughters. Pavlyk called them wax dolls who know nothing except dressing up, powdering their faces, jumping, laughing, eating and sleeping; who see nothing in this world besides themselves. They dance, they drink and they even make fun of the company that from time to time peeks through the window to see these lords banqueting at their expense.

Pavlyk could not bear it when a priest's daughter slandered the peasants, her father's parishioners, or slapped a servant in the face. "Who can stand it," Pavlyk wrote, "if his father and mother are treated like dirt!"[39]

At the university, in Akademicheskii kruzhok, Pavlyk was also sensitive about his background; most of his compatriots were priests' sons, who occasionally spoke of peasants with contempt. Pavlyk felt the need to do something for his own people. For a while he agitated in his own parish to form a branch of the Kachkovsky Society.[40] In 1875 he hit upon a plan to educate the peasantry and restore to them a sense of dignity by publishing the Gospel in their own language. He felt that Father Ivan Naumovych, head of the Kachkovsky Society, would see the value of such a project. Pavlyk considered Naumovych an exception among priests, one who treated the peasants as people. Pavlyk therefore proposed a vernacular edition of the Gospel at the annual meeting of the Kachkovsky Society in Halych (August 1875). But the clergy there vehemently opposed his proposal and it was not even put to a vote. He tried to convince the other members of the kruzhok to help in translating the Gospel, but they responded by calling him "a stupid fanatic, who wants everything at the wrong time."[41] Immediately following the meeting of the Kachkovsky Society, Drahomanov's second letter arrived at the editorial office of *Druh*.

Pavlyk's close friend and later one of the finest Ukrainian writers, Ivan Franko, was born in 1856 in the village of Nahuievychi (Drohobych district). Ivan's father was a peasant and blacksmith; he died in 1865. Seven years later, Ivan's mother died, leaving him an orphan.[42]

Like Pavlyk, Franko went to school, eventually ending up in Lviv University. At first he attended the normal school in Drohobych. His handwriting teacher was a certain Pan Walko, formerly a steward on a noble's estate. On one occasion, when Franko wrote sloppily (he was then seven or eight years old), Walko punched the boy in the face; Franko bled and lost consciousness. Walko at once worried about possible repercussions from the incident. "Who is this boy?" he asked Franko's classmates. They answered: "The son of a peasant from

Na...." "A peasant's son! Bah! What the devil are peasants doing pushing their way in here!" Walko was relieved; there would be no repercussions for beating a peasant's son, everything would go on smoothly. "Only in that peasant boy's heart," wrote Franko later, "it did not go smoothly, but became the first seed of indignation, contempt and eternal enmity towards all constraint and tyranny."[43]

In the following year, 1864, "the most terrible, the most fatal year of [Franko's] life," Rev. Sofron Telesnytsky came to Drohobych. Father Telesnytsky took a perverse pleasure in beating his charges with a cane of alder. Franko himself escaped much of the beating that went on throughout the day, every day, but his close friend, a peasant boy named Voliansky, died from one of Telesnytsky's flagellations. Franko never mentioned the incident until 1903, when he described Telesnytsky in a short story brimming over with anger and unquenched hatred. "For a long time," he wrote, "I have hesitated to recreate in my soul the memories I have of him," i.e., of Rev. Telesnytsky.[44]

> The memory of those disgusting scenes [the beatings], which dragged on day after day for a whole year, engraved itself very deeply into my soul. . . . The impressions of that year have remained with me. They have not been erased, they hurt even now, and in more than one way, I feel, they have deformed my character, tainted my personality, brought me a great deal of spiritual torment all through my life.[45]

Spiritual torment put an edge on Franko's poetry and helped to make him the great artist that he eventually became. But it would also seem to have had an effect on his political formation. Franko's anticlericalism and ardent defense of the peasantry probably owed something to his years at the normal school.

Afterwards, Franko entered Drohobych's gymnasium, where life was considerably better. The teachers were more humane and even took the students on excursions. Franko joined a secret club in which Polish, Jewish and Ruthenian students gathered to read aloud from Shakespeare, Schiller and Goethe.[46] Like Pavlyk, Franko supported himself through school by combining stipends with tutorial work.[47] In his last year at the gymnasium, he became restless, dissatisfied with provincial Drohobych, and longed for the more stimulating intellectual life of Lviv.[48] In 1875 he entered Lviv University to study philosophy. He naturally gravitated to Akademicheskii kruzhok, since in his last year as a gymnasium student he had already published poetry in the club's periodical. When Franko arrived in Lviv, the correspondence between Drahomanov and the editors of *Druh* was already underway.

Drahomanov's letters, in timely combination with other factors, wrought a genuine intellectual revolution in Ruthenia's younger generation. Pavlyk memorized the first letter;[49] in response to the second, he wrote to Drahomanov:

> You do not know how comforted I was by reading it; I tell you that I even cried from joy that there could be found in the educated world such a sincere soul, one who wishes well to the down-trodden peasant and so flails without quarter all that peasant's burdensome enemies, those who stifle his mind and do not admit him to knowledge so as to fish in troubled waters. All your thoughts went straight to my heart, so that now I can never allow myself to waver from that on which I have reflected, from that for which I have suffered.[50]

Before he received the third letter, Pavlyk had already met Drahomanov personally in Lviv (March 1876).

In his letters, Drahomanov had given Galician youth a reading list and had charged them to build up their libraries, he himself sending them a great many books. Both voracious readers, Pavlyk and Franko followed Drahomanov's counsel and took up the study of Chernyshevsky, Pisarev, Lassalle, Mill (on female emancipation), Lange, Renan and Dobroliubov. They perhaps read too fast and too much to digest all to which they were exposed, but the intensity of the learning experience gave rise to an intensity of application. Radical brochures in Ukrainian, published in Vienna, also made a great impression on the youth in Lviv. The Bosnian revolt, which the new generation in Galicia followed with interest and sympathy, heightened the revolutionary mood.[51]

The first manifestation of a fresh intellectual current in Akademicheskii kruzhok was linguistic: *Druh* abandoned the *iazychiie* in the spring of 1876 in favor of the pure Ukrainian vernacular. Pavlyk was behind the change (he had been advocating the vernacular since he first entered Lviv University in 1874) and Franko seconded him. The majority of the kruzhok, however, preferred to hold on to their customary Ruthene jargon. But a new Ukrainophile majority emerged in the spring of 1876, when, with Pavlyk's and Franko's connivance, over thirty Ukrainophile students joined Akademicheskii kruzhok and expelled the leading Russophile, Stepan Labash.[52]

Closely connected with the adoption of the Ukrainian vernacular was an interest in ethnography. The students, following Drahomanov's advice and example, turned to folklore — songs, proverbs and fables — to enrich and enliven the language of their publication. In April 1876 *Druh* began to carry a special folklore column entitled "From the Lips of the People." Franko and Pavlyk in particular went on expeditions to the villages to transcribe songs, proverbs and turns of phrase. As a result of Pavlyk's agitation an unofficial student ethnographic society came into existence in Lviv. The students understood ethnography in a wide, social sense. They were not only interested in songs and fables, but also wanted to know about the peasants' "existence [and] way of life, their needs and ill fortune."[53] As Pavlyk saw it, ethnographic work was an important task of the educated; the intelligentsia should show published collections of folklore to the peasants and tell them: "Look what you yourselves have composed with your own unaided intelligence and sensitivity! Now tell us, then, what would you not have accomplished had you gone after an education?"[54]

Pavlyk criticized the Ruthenian intelligentsia for forgetting its peasant origins:

> Our intelligentsia does not benefit our nationality as much as we would wish, because each intellectual studies only for his own ends; once he is secure in a position, he consumes the good things which his acquired knowledge provides and he forgets that all the simple people have the same soul as he has and also desire for themselves some relief in their material and moral poverty. . . . So whoever pushes himself up above the people is as lost for the people as a proud eagle in the ether.

Pavlyk hoped that Akademicheskii kruzhok would keep awake the consciences of Ruthenian students. A student club should seek to form the future intelligentsia "so that each member of the intelligentsia would consider himself a means to the people's advancement and would not consider the people a means to achieving his own egotistical aims."[55] Patriotism, Pavlyk maintained, was "love for the hungry, ragged beggar-worker."[56]

Others in the kruzhok championed similar sentiments. Antin Dolnytsky summoned his fellow students to prepare for martyrdom in the name of liberty and equality:

> Liberty, freedom, equality for all, prosperity for all, including the simple, injured people — can there be anything better than all this? Is not this worth sacrificing one's life for, as the Christian martyrs did? . . . The martyrs of the nineteenth century, martyrs for liberty, for the freedom of the poor — are not these also holy martyrs like those of the first cen-

turies? All nations in Europe can boast such martyrs, even our brother Ukrainians can boast such — only we Galicians cannot.[57]

This social enthusiasm owed much to the influence of the radical Russian critics, particularly Chernyshevsky. His *What Is To Be Done?* played on the emotions of the Galician youth and Franko translated part of it into Ukrainian for *Druh.*[58] The influence of these same Russians was also evident in *Druh's* literary criticism, mainly from the pens of Franko and Pavlyk, and most strikingly in Franko's powerful and uncompromising stories of life in the oil town Boryslav. With these critical realist sketches, Franko established himself, at barely twenty years of age, as a master of Ukrainian prose, a pioneer of Ukrainian realism.

In addition to new linguistic, ethnographic, social and literary opinions, the students came to hold a new regard for science. Like many of their contemporaries outside Galicia, the students were imbued with "scientism," putting great store by science's potential to rectify social injustice.[59] They read and discussed Darwin and Draper, coming to prefer a materialist explanation of the world to a theological one. Pavlyk was a one-man ideological *avant garde* in these matters: he rejected religion and the clergy outright and valued instead "the general human spirit, not smoked up from incense, not stamped with that darkness of mind and heart which makes man a slave and beggar."[60] These were bold words for a student periodical to publish in a nation of priests and peasants. Pavlyk was the advance guard in other matters, too. Although all the students took an interest in female emancipation,[61] Pavlyk dared to reject marriage as an institution and to champion (quite chastely) free love.

The ideological ferment did not remain confined to the single student club Akademicheskii kruzhok. In line with Drahomanov's program for the union of both Galician political factions on a new, progressive basis, the formerly Russophile kruzhok and the intellectually moribund, but Ukrainophile, Druzhnii lykhvar effected a union in the summer of 1876. Akademicheskii kruzhok was to function as the general student cultural organization, Druzhnii lykhvar as the organization for financial aid.[62] Thus both Ruthenian student clubs in Lviv came under the same ideological roof. The radical students took over the function of a "central hromada" and so spread their program and distributed their favorite reading matter to gymnasium students throughout Eastern Galicia.[63] They also met with peasants and sold booklets to the literate among them, not only Prosvita (Enlightenment) and Kachkovsky brochures, but the radical Vienna pamphlets as well.[64]

All this came to the attention of elder Ruthenians and it was not long before a full-scale battle between the generations ensued. The first to object to the new currents in *Druh* and the kruzhok were naturally the Russophiles: Akademicheskii kruzhok had deserted its original Russophile allegiance, *Druh* had renounced *iazychiie* for the Ukrainian vernacular and *Druh* became the first Galician periodical to protest the Russophile-inspired Ems ukase of 1876.[65] The Russophile organ *Slovo* (Word) carried systematic attacks on *Druh* in the summer of 1876. Stepan Labash, formerly Russophile chieftan of the kruzhok, filled page after page of *Slovo* with derogatory remarks about *Druh* and its moving spirit, Pavlyk.[66] Another *Slovo* correspondent, offended by the harsh literary criticism in *Druh*, put *Druh*'s critics in their place with a remark reflecting the generational aspect of the ideological conflict: "Let the little boys play!"[67]

At first the national populists, even the most clerical among them, misread the tendency of *Druh* and assumed that the kruzhok had simply moved from Galician Russophilism to Galician Ukrainophilism (in Drahomanov's terms: from one variant of Ruthenism to another). The Greek Catholic organ, *Ruskii Sion,* even defended *Druh* against *Slovo* in July 1876 and wished the student publication "the very best success and development and, by the same token, the greatest possible distribution in Ruthenian educated society."[68] The editor of *Ruskii Sion* had evidently forgotten a little item he had published in his previous issue: a complaint by a priest and "missionary of holy sobriety" that *Druh* was taking a stand against the temperance campaign.[69]

In August 1876 Rev. Stepan Kachala reproved *Druh*'s editors for succumbing to the influence of Drahomanov's "nihilism" and socialism:

> Socialism decks itself out in the pretty plumage of European civilization and science, but disdains nationality and all that man holds sacred. The nihilist says: . . . There is no God, no soul. . . . Man is a mere animal like any other. Eat. Drink. After death there is nothing. . . . Our Young Ruthenia has been accused of political separatism, Polish patriotism and so on, for which there has been no proof. . . . Now they will call us socialists, communists or nihilists, and for this there will be proof: articles of this type published in *Druh*.[70]

If *Druh* considered the propagation of nihilism and socialism "enlightenment of the people, then we priests — we say this openly — we don't want any such enlightenment."[71]

For a short time, *Druh* had cordial relations with the secular national populists and with their organ *Pravda*. But *Druh*'s literary criticism, very sharp and given to dissecting content (according to realist canons) as well as artistic form, primarily aimed its shafts at national populist authors. In 1876 *Druh* published reviews, mainly by Pavlyk and Franko, of twenty-two Galician publications; twenty of these came in for harsh or scathing criticism.[72] The young reviewers were so merciless that they felt constrained to hide behind pseudonyms, Pavlyk choosing the symbolic pen name "Storm Cloud" (*Khmara*). In another symbolic manifestation — of students surpassing their masters, the young overcoming the old — Pavlyk and Franko singled out for a concerted offensive Franko's former gymnasium teacher, Ivan Verkhratsky — lepidopterist, Ukrainophile, amateur philologist and would-be poet.[73] Verkhratsky responded to *Druh*'s criticism with a hysterical pamphlet, ending with these words in bold type: "DO NOT SUBSCRIBE TO *DRUH*! DOWN WITH *DRUH*!"[74]

Druh's relations with the elder national populists transcended bitter literary quarreling to encompass the range of polemics that Drahomanov carried on with the Galician Ukrainophiles. In 1876 Drahomanov had tried once more to come to some agreement with Galicia's national populists; once again he was disappointed, but now — thanks to *Druh* — he had a Galician forum in which to carry on his campaign against *Pravda* and the national populists.[75]

In 1877 Drahomanov became the financial backer of *Druh*; otherwise the periodical would have had to fold up for lack of funds. Two causes lay behind *Druh*'s financial crisis in 1877: the vestiges of the kruzhok's Russophiles (in Pavlyk's words: "the old priestly-obscurantist party")[76] held on to the club's treasury and refused to finance the publication of a periodical so contrary to their views; and the number of *Druh*'s subscribers was cut in half to just 260.[77] *Druh*'s language, themes and tendencies had changed too radically and too rapidly for the subscribers; the old "Ruthene public," which had so enjoyed the pre-Drahomanovite *Druh,* now cancelled its subscriptions in mass.

One Ruthenian woman spoke for many others in her letter to the editors cancelling her subscription. "Our belles had greeted the appearance of *Druh* with a warm heart, because *Druh* [= Friend] was a true Friend and in the beginning it corresponded to our understanding, sense of decorum and dignity." But now, she complained (in an amusing variety of *iazychiie*), the orthography and language of *Druh* were incomprehensible. Moreover, the formerly modest *Druh* published a story, one of Franko's Boryslav tales, that would offend "every well bred and moral maiden." Such a maiden would "discard *Druh* with a fit of temper, shame and suspicion."[78]

Pavlyk and Franko, and their supporters, had cut the ties binding them to the "Ruthene public." They had become, in the sterile Galician intellectual atmosphere, something new, shocking and promising.

Arrests and Trials

The radical ferment among Ruthenian youth was quickened by Galicia's intermediary position between Western Europe and Russia. After Drahomanov settled in Geneva in autumn 1876, he maintained close contact with the Hromada in Kiev, using Lviv as the connecting link. In the mid-1870s, when mass arrests forced many revolutionaries to flee Russia, not a few of these emigrated to Switzerland via Galicia. Drahomanov and other political émigrés published revolutionary literature in the West and smuggled the publications into the Russian empire — very often via Galicia. Revolutionaries on missions, revolutionaries in flight, seditious publications, confidential correspondence — all these travelled through Galicia on the way to Russia from Switzerland or vice versa.

Of course, the road through Galicia was not the only revolutionary East-West trade route. Yet Galicia had a special importance because of its national structure. Here Polish revolutionaries from Russia could meet with and to some extent blend in with Galician conationals, primarily students. Ukrainian and even ethnic Russian revolutionaries could find a similar haven among the Ruthenians. All the more so once a group of radical Ruthenian students came into existence.

Pavlyk became the key contact man for revolutionaries travelling through Lviv. In the summer of 1876, Drahomanov gave him the money to rent a special room for receiving guests of Russian origin. Pavlyk did not live in this room; he used it as a "safe house" where Russian and Ukrainian socialists and populists could stop on their journeys and meet with him, hopefully without police observation. Pavlyk had visiting cards printed up and gave them to travellers on their way to Geneva or

Kiev. The travellers could turn the cards over to their comrades who, when they came to Galicia, had merely to show the cards to Pavlyk's landlady and the special room would be at their disposal for a few nights' lodging or for storage of incendiary literature. Pavlyk became involved in the transport of forbidden publications to Russia, including the series of revolutionary pamphlets put out in Vienna by the Ukrainian socialist Serhii Podolynsky and the Ruthenian student Ostap Terletsky.[79]

It is not clear how the Lviv police came upon the scent of Pavlyk's activities. The appearance of the Vienna pamphlets and subsequent prosecution of their publishers in mid-October 1876 must have alerted the police that something seditious was afoot among the Ruthenians. Most probably, too, some unreconstructed Russophile from the kruzhok had gone directly to the police and pointed his finger at Pavlyk. In any case, two of Pavlyk's Russian guests, Aleksandr Cherepakhin and Sergiusz Jastrzębski, were conversing in Lviv's Black Crab Café on 9 January 1877 when a police agent joined them at the table and provoked a fist fight to occasion their arrest. The police searched Pavlyk's special room, where they confiscated about a thousand brochures (mainly by Drahomanov and Podolynsky) which Cherepakhin hoped to smuggle into Russia. The police then arrested Pavlyk and a Russian Ukrainian, Antin (Kuzma) Liakhotsky. The four suspects were accused of belonging to a secret society at their trial of 16–20 March 1877. The jury sentenced Cherepakhin and Jastrzębski to a month in jail followed by deportation; Liakhotsky was acquitted, but deported nonetheless. Pavlyk was sentenced to eight days in prison.[80]

Just a few months later, in May of 1877, Drahomanov gave some letters and a large quantity of revolutionary literature, mainly in Ukrainian, to a Polish socialist from the Congress Kingdom visiting him in Geneva. The Polish socialist, Erazm Kobylański (known to the Austrian police as Michał Koturnicki, alias Stanisław Kremer) was to go to Galicia, deliver Drahomanov's correspondence and socialist literature, and contact Bolesław Limanowski. He arrived in Lviv on the last day of May. Before managing to deliver Drahomanov's letters, Kobylański, who had awakened the suspicions of a hotel employee, was arrested. On Kobylański's person the Lviv police found a revolver, a sword-cane, an iron file and vials of poison. The apprehension of such a desperado provoked a spree of arrests and searches. In Kobylański's room the police found the literature and Drahomanov's letters, the addresses of which led to the arrest of Pavlyk (then in a hospital) and Franko as well as Ostap Terletsky and Shchasnyi Selsky, members of Sich, the Ruthenian student club in Vienna. Limanowski was arrested, too, but was neither long retained in custody nor put on trial. The police searched the premises of Ognisko, Akademicheskii kruzhok, Prosvita, Narodnyi dom (National Home) and the Greek Catholic seminary in Lviv. They stumbled upon the trail of the national populist student clubs (hromadas) and took dozens of Ruthenian students into custody. They came to the conclusion for a while that the Greek Catholic seminary was a socialist hot house. The Viennese police joined the action and discovered that the Polish artisan association in Vienna, Siła (Power), had become infiltrated by students (émigrés from Russian Poland) of the socialist persuasion. The police began to see the outlines of an international socialist conspiracy which had now struck roots in Galicia.[81]

After the police had sifted the evidence and released most suspects, seven defendants faced charges of belonging to a secret society: Kobylański, Pavlyk, Franko, Ivan Mandychevsky (also on *Druh*'s editorial board), Terletsky, Selsky and Anna Pavlyk (Mykhailo's younger sister). Membership in a secret society was the charge most frequently brought against socialists in Galicia, since secret societies were illegal in Austria, but socialism itself was not. There was, of course, no socialist secret society at work in Galicia prior to 1878. The Austrian and Lviv police, however, were obsessed with the idea of an international socialist conspiracy spreading its net over Europe, trapping unwary Galicia. Koturnicki (the police never learned Kobylański's real name) was, in their eyes, an emissary of the International's Russian and Polish divisions under the direction of Drahomanov in Switzerland.

The socialist trial conducted in Lviv from 15 to 21 January 1878[82] is generally regarded as the starting point proper of the Galician socialist movement. It is rightly so regarded since, though tendencies to socialist agitation were evident before the trial, the quantum leap to an active socialist movement took place only in its wake. The trial electrified Galicia: no section of literate opinion ignored it, echoes of it reached the small towns and even villages. Lines were drawn, socialism achieved recognition, prematurely, as a threat to existing morality and political and social relations. The socialist movement gained many foes as a consequence of the publicity given the trial, but it acquired adherents as well.

Although the accused, with the exception of Mandychevsky, made no attempt to conceal their socialist sympathies, all denied belonging to a secret society. The evidence against them was weak. The letters produced by the prosecutor did show that Drahomanov had entrusted Kobylański with a mission, but the existence of a secret society was in no way confirmed. The prosecutor also introduced the testimony of some Russophile students to the effect that Pavlyk, Franko and company took control of Akademicheskii kruzhok through intrigue and force. Another witness against the accused was Karol Skamyna, a cook from Zahirie serving three years for theft. He had been Franko's cellmate and the political prisoner apparently attempted to convert his fellow lodger to socialist beliefs. As was to happen more than once in the course of Galician socialism's history, the prison cell proved to be an ill-chosen setting for socialist propaganda. Skamyna's testimony, however, was somewhat discounted since he had evidently confused whatever it was Franko had told him.

In spite of the poor evidence, the accused were found guilty and sentenced: Kobylański to three months in prison and afterwards banishment from Austria; Mykhailo Pavlyk to three months' imprisonment; Franko to six weeks' imprisonment and a 5 g. fine; and Mandychevsky, Terletsky, Selsky and Anna Pavlyk each to one month in prison.

The trial further radicalized its participants. Ivan Franko later admitted in his autobiography that before the trial "I was a socialist by sympathy, as a peasant, but I was far from understanding what scientific socialism was."[83] The trial changed that. The trial strengthened, to a certain degree even created, the socialist convictions of the accused. After the trial, Franko and Pavlyk consciously and openly declared themselves socialists and created a socialist movement. During and after the trial, both Ruthenian political parties — the national populists and the Russophiles — denounced the accused, and this encouraged Franko and Pavlyk to cooperate closely with the Polish workers' and socialist movement in Lviv. The accused Pole and Ruthenians expressed their solidarity in the course of the trial and close personal relations between Polish and Ruthenian socialists followed the Ruthenians' release from prison.

There were instances of isolated support for and sympathy with the accused. The teenage Feliks Daszyński, later one of the few socialist theoreticians from Galicia, was converted to socialism by the January 1878 trial.[84] Nataliia Kobrynska was then in her twenties; later, after becoming a radical feminist and celebrated writer, she recalled that "the

trial of our young socialists staggered me; I almost could not believe
that even among us such questions were being raised, that even among
us there were people dissatisfied with the surrounding circumstances."[85]

On the whole, however, established Galician society, shocked and
indignant, congratulated the police for uncovering the socialist conspiracy. The conservative Polish press censured the young socialists, as did
the conservative Ruthenian press. The Russophile *Nauka* (Lesson) had
this comment:

> From the innocent orthography of Kulish, from the negation of our old
> alphabet, some of our youth have gone all the way to the negation of the
> entire existing order. They have made the acquaintance of foreign
> fanatics and have come to reject belief in God, in law, in authority, in
> marriage. In short, they believe in none of the things that provide the
> foundation of human society today. Their doctrine is: to kill everyone
> who holds power, also priests and all owners of property; all cities are to
> be destroyed;[86] all the land is to be divided up equally and no one can
> have more property than anyone else.[87]

The Russophiles found particularly shocking the socialists' attitude
towards marriage. *Nauka* considered the socialists adherents of the
principle: "Your wife is as much mine as she is yours."[88] Attacking the
institution of marriage was, in truth, Pavlyk's passion, and he used the
courtroom as a forum for his views.[89]

The national populists directed most of their venom at Drahomanov,
who they felt had seduced for-the-most-part-innocent youth. They
argued that the Ruthenian-Ukrainian nation was immune to socialist
ideas and that the few socialists in Ukraine, imbued with a doctrine
more appropriate to the Muscovite soul, had fallen under an unnatural, unnational influence.[90] Without mentioning Drahomanov and
Podolynsky by name, one national populist referred to them as "false
prophets," "new hetmans," "exploiters of the nation and Ukraine,"
"who spend hundreds of rubles on a comfortable life in various
metropolises . . . and spend hundreds on publications benefitting the
nation as much as last year's snow."[91] Another national populist darkly
hinted that Drahomanov was an agent of the tsarist government.[92] The
national populists admitted that they had had some dealings with
Drahomanov as a scholar, but insisted that they had kept their distance
when he began to engage in socialist propaganda. Unfortunately,
Drahomanov managed to make some students "instruments of his

propaganda"; fortunately, however, the police had nipped this in the bud.[93]

Immediately after the trial, the national populist clerical organ, *Ruskii Sion,* carried a long article assessing the characters of the young socialists. Mandychevsky, who had renounced socialism at the trial, was not, the article assumed, entirely lost. Nor was Terletsky: he came from a priestly family, but was early left an orphan. There was hope, too, for Franko, because his Boryslav stories exhibited great talent and moral principle. *Ruskii Sion,* in fact, professed bafflement: how could such an obviously intelligent and dedicated young man become a socialist? Pavlyk was the villain:

> For him nothing is honorable, moral and sacred. He is, in a word, a red communist. When he leaves prison, he will continue to spread gangrene in society's healthy body.[94] Because of this, it's a shame that Austria lacks the means to render such people harmless, that we don't have uninhabited wastes where such people could freely devote themselves to their theories far from human settlements.[95]

Pavlyk, and Franko as well (in spite of the "hope" for him), were branded pariahs in Ruthenia. Franko's projected marriage crashed on the rocks of public disgrace. After the trial, Rev. Roshkevych of Lolyn forbade his daughter Olga to meet with or even to correspond with her fiancé, Franko; not long thereafter she married a theology graduate about to be ordained to the priesthood. Franko's plans to become a gymnasium teacher also fell through because of the trial.[96] His estrangement from Ruthenian society found expression in a series of three vivid sketches entitled "Ruthenes: Types and Portraits of Galician 'Personalities.'" In them, Franko subjected his contemporaries to a pitiless examination and revealed that "Ruthenes" were narrow-minded, greedy, parasitical philistines.[97]

Thanks to Limanowski's intercession, Franko's "Ruthenes" first appeared in 1878 in a *Polish* literary weekly.[98] This marked the beginning of Franko's rejection of his own "Ruthene" society in favor of more radical Poland.

By 1878 three political currents had crystallized in Ruthenian Galicia: Russophilism, national populism and socialism (or, as it was later known, radicalism). Ruthenian socialism emerged by a curious route. It would seem, were one to compare the national populism of the early 1860s with the radicalism of the late 1870s, that the latter quite naturally evolved from the former. But this was not the case. In its origins, national populism, fed as it was by the democratic Ukrainian movement in Russia and Polish revolutionary democracy, had itself been — in contrast to Russophilism — secular and democratic. However, when national populism began to make the transition from an urban intellectual current into a mass party in the countryside, it was forced to rely on the aid of the rural clergy. The clergy thus rose to a position of influence in the national populist movement, reflected in national populism's retreat from a democratic ideology and acceptance of a clerical world view. By the late 1860s one can discern an unspoken compromise between the national populist intelligentsia and the clergy.

Because of this, for Ruthenian socialism to emerge, a complete break with the whole "Ruthene" matrix was necessary, a rejection of both Russophilism and national populism as unsatisfactory and inferior. It took a Russian Ukrainophile like Drahomanov to draft the basic program of radicalism. And it took the younger generation to embrace it. Only the youth, after all, had not been immediate partners to the unspoken compromise with the clergy. They were therefore, and this is especially true of those of plebeian background, more ready than their elders to adhere to the radical and anticlerical ideas espoused by Drahomanov. The trial of 1878, together with the vituperations of the Russophiles and national populists, deepened the cleavage between the younger and older generations and ensured that Ruthenian socialism would remain a distinct political tendency in Galicia.

Chapter Three

Polish Socialism in Lviv and Cracow

The radicalization of the young Ruthenian intelligentsia was a boon to the emerging Polish socialist movement in Lviv, to which Franko and Pavlyk attached themselves. Together with a group of local Polish intellectuals, they sharpened the focus of the artisan movement that was already underway in Lviv. Within a few years, Lviv's socialists could boast of their own newspaper, a number of other publications (including two drafts of a party program), a series of successful mass assemblies and a genuine base of support in the artisan working class.

The movement in Cracow was entirely different. Here the artisans had not been politicized by the autonomy campaign of the 1860s and the local intelligentsia kept its distance from anything that smacked of social radicalism. Into this vacuum poured socialist refugees from the Russian partition of Poland, bringing with them the methods they had found necessary under tsarist despotism. They managed to set up networks of clandestine socialist cells and even to engage in acts of terrorism. But dependent on leadership from abroad and based on an artisan population more atomized and less conscious than Lviv's, the Cracow socialist movement was numerically weak and short-lived.

In Defense of the Journeymen

In June 1878 the first meeting of Lviv socialists was held at the home of Bolesław Limanowski. In attendance, besides the host, were the Ruthenians Ivan Franko and Mykhailo Pavlyk, the pharmacist Adolf Inlaender, the typesetter Józef Daniluk and the poet Bolesław Czerwieński. The gathering constituted itself as an agitation committee to direct socialist activity in the city and to prepare socialist literature.[1] With the exception of Limanowski, who was to emigrate to Switzerland in the fall, the members of the committee also functioned as the editorial board of the newspaper *Praca* (Labor), whose publisher and managing editor was Daniluk. Because throughout the 1870s and 1880s no formal socialist party was founded, the activists who put out *Praca* were the leaders of the Polish socialist movement in Lviv.

Praca began to appear in July 1878; Daniluk and Antoni Mańkowski established it to replace the printers' papers *Czcionka* and *Naprzód* which had ceased publication in 1876 and 1877. In April 1878 the printers' society Ognisko had discussed the need to revive a printers' paper, and in July it gave *Praca* 30 gulden to print its reports and minutes. Throughout 1878, *Praca* carried the subtitle "A Fortnightly Devoted to Printers' Affairs" and only changed to "A Fortnightly Devoted to the Affairs of the Working Classes" on 1 January 1879.[2]

The transformation of *Praca* from a narrow trade paper to a socialist workers' paper seems to have been primarily the achievement of Franko and Pavlyk.[3] Pavlyk began contributing to *Praca* in its third issue and first hinted at its impending transformation: "*Praca* intends to defend the workers' interests, temporarily only the printshop workers'."[4] This temporary limitation came to an end with the first issue for 1879, when the paper's subtitle changed and Franko took over as editor.[5] Franko stated in a front-page editorial that the paper was intended for "the whole of the working class."

Almost every theoretical and programmatic article to appear in *Praca* in 1878–81 came from Franko's pen,[6] and he can rightly be regarded as the newspaper's guiding spirit in its formative years. Others on the editorial board included Daniluk and Mańkowski, Czerwieński and another journalist, Bolesław Spausta, and the brothers Inlaender, Ludwik and Adolf, assimilated Jews, the first a railroad clerk, the second a pharmacist who had edited a druggists' paper for several years. Pavlyk was not involved with the paper during this period. Since 1879 he had been living abroad, where he worked closely with Mykhailo Drahomanov and Serhii Podolynsky. Along with Drahomanov, he felt that *Praca* was too Polish in orientation and aimed exclusively at the highest level of the Lviv working class (artisans), neglecting thus the peasantry and proletariat.[7]

It is difficult to gauge how popular *Praca* was among the Galician working classes. The conservative Cracow daily *Czas* (Time) surely exaggerated its influence in 1881 when it wrote that the young journeymen "greedily seize upon its tempting words" and complained that "no honest paper for the common people" has been able to survive, but "this poisonous plant prospers now for the fourth year."[8] Franko himself, however, occasionally had doubts about the popularity of the paper among Lviv workers.[9]

One difficulty the editors faced was that their readership was artisan rather than proletarian. Franko wrote that it was "saddening" that *Praca* devoted so much attention to "printers, tailors and in general workers of crafts or manufactures" and that these artisans instead of factory workers were in the foreground of the Galician socialist workers' movement.[10] It was difficult to spread socialist ideology among crafts-men. Artisans still thought in ossified concepts going back to the guilds. Printers pompously styled themselves "the Gutenberg brotherhood"; the turner despised the carpenter, the carpenter the tailor and everyone the cobbler. Journeymen considered the label "worker" insulting and applied it only to the day laborer. All of this, the socialists felt, was supported and encouraged by the existing artisan association and their Democratic curators.[11]

Dissatisfied with Gwiazda and other artisan associations, the Lviv socialists decided in 1879 to found an independent workers' mutual aid society. Franko envisioned an association that would financially support workers during periods of unemployment (whether the consequence of economic crisis or a strike) and that would control employee-employer relationships, especially making sure employers did not arbitrarily fire workers, lower their pay or lengthen the working day. In other words, Franko hoped that the Lviv journeymen would found a type of trade union.[12] To encourage thought along these lines, Franko wrote a long article about English trade unions for *Praca*.[13]

A socialist-inspired artisan association, however, did not appear until 1881, when Daniluk, Mańkowski and the cobbler Mykhailo Drabyk founded the Lviv Workers' Society of Mutual Credit and Fraternal Aid. The Society modelled itself less on English trade unions than on Gali-cia's pre-socialist artisan associations. One interesting innovation of the socialist society was that, unlike Gwiazda and similar associations, it permitted women to join.[14]

The Society was a failure. At its general meeting in January 1882, only thirty members attended, sixteen of whom were elected to office in the association. Gwiazda, by comparison, had started out in 1868 with 661 members and topped 1,000 in the next few years. There was at work, it seems, a simple rule: no money, no members. The Workers' Society of Mutual Credit and Fraternal Aid had at its disposal in January 1882 the grand total of 17 gulden 90 kreuzers. Gwiazda's

mutual aid society had tens of thousands of guldens. A sober journeyman might well have preferred investing his dues in Gwiazda's larded
coffers rather than in those of the socialists' pure but frugal association.

The disparity in funds between Gwiazda and the Society reflected, of
course, the attitude of the moneyed and propertied to the different
ideological postures of the two associations. Gwiazda, the Democrats'
spawn, received a subsidy from the Galician Diet in addition to regular,
generous donations from the likes of Princess Lubomirska and the noble
Alfred Młocki. The socialists also wanted a subsidy from the Diet, but
the Democratic deputy Teofil Merunowicz refused even to present their
request. The Crownland Administration also rejected the Society's
application for financial support. Then, too, no princesses and nobles
came forward to aid the socialist journeymen. Left to their own devices,
the journeymen could not scrape up twenty gulden, barely enough to
support one typesetter and his family for a single week.[15]

The socialists had much greater success in mobilizing the journeymen
to protest the masters' political intrigue, their attempt to strengthen
their own position at the journeymen's expense. Particularly in 1879 and
1882, master craftsmen throughout Austria — in Vienna and Prague as
well as in Lviv and Stanyslaviv — agitated for the revision of the 1859
industrial law. Galician masters held numerous assemblies in Lviv and
sent memoranda and lobbies off to parliament to demand protection of
crafts through the establishment of compulsory artisan corporations and
corporate regulation of the certification of new masters.

Although the 1859 industrial law had dissolved the guilds, it had also
urged the establishment of compulsory artisan corporations. The provisions on corporations went largely unobserved, but the masters in
1879–82 called for their enforcement and the revision of the industrial
law to put teeth into the articles on corporations. The corporations, as
envisioned by the masters, would be run by the masters. The corporation's highest authority would be the general assembly, three-quarters
composed of masters and one-quarter composed of adult journeymen
who had been working for more than a year in one workshop. The
corporation — three parts master, one part qualified journeyman —
would regulate, in accordance with the 1859 industrial law, relations
between masters and their journeymen and apprentices. The masters
also wanted the corporations to have control over the certification of
new masters.

With the abolition of the guilds in 1859, every journeyman had become free (once he had obtained an industrial patent from the local government) to set up his own workshop. To set up an independent shop required capital, of course, and here lay a major factor behind the popularity of mutual aid and loan societies among the journeyman artisans. The masters now, in 1879–82, proposed to restore to the corporations the old guild privilege of certifying new masters. Journeymen, in the masters' plan, would still be allowed to set up their own independent shops without the corporations sanctioning them as masters; they would merely be forbidden to hire any help — they were free, in other words, to compete against the masters, but only with a mortal handicap. The masters wanted masterpieces (*Meisterstücke*) from the journeymen and the right to determine their own competition; they wanted, in plain language, the return of the guilds.[16]

The masters obtained what they agitated for; the new industrial law of 1883 catered to their desires even to the point of prohibiting strikes.[17]

The masters' agitation, according to *Praca*, was a panicky and misguided response to the natural process of factory production overcoming the artisan workshop. "On all sides they send out delegations, almost day and night they convoke assemblies" to restore corporations and limit competition:

> Not only that, but our masters, seeing that capital is mainly in the hands of the Jews, passionately speak out against these latter, even creating separate associations, societies of Christian entrepreneurs. . . . Others, again, . . . would like to close the Galician border to foreign, non-Galician products.

Praca argued that the masters were swimming against the current and wanted to return to the Middle Ages. Factory production was far superior to artisanal production: it saved physical labor and produced more quickly, more abundantly and more cheaply. The editors of *Praca* believed that factory production had everything going for it, everything, that is, except that a handful of the privileged controlled it and exploited the workers. The restriction of factory production was no solution to the poverty of the Galician craftsman; the only solution was socialization of the means of production. "Forget your petty, personal interests," *Praca* addressed the masters, "and join us, gentlemen, beneath the *standard of radical* social *reform.*"[18]

Inspired by workers in Prague, who had called a mass meeting to protest the masters' assemblies,[19] the socialists of *Praca* organized a mass assembly of journeymen in Lviv on 28 December 1879. Five hundred Lviv workers attended the assembly, listened to the socialists' militant speeches and passed a series of resolutions encompassing both economic and political demands.[20] The editors of *Praca* had prepared a version of the resolutions in advance of the assembly and printed them as a supplement to the paper.[21]

The resolutions were acutely topical, specifically addressed to the journeymen's defense in the face of the masters' offensive. The first two resolutions emphatically rejected all restrictions on earning a living through craft industry (presentation of a masterpiece, certification by corporations, etc.) as well as the introduction of compulsory corporations. The resolutions favored, instead, the formation of voluntary artisan associations. Other resolutions called for the establishment of courts of conciliation to arbitrate employer-employee quarrels and Handicraft Chambers to regulate minimum wages for each craft; both the courts of conciliation and the Handicraft Chambers were to be elected directly by workers and employers on the principle of one man, one vote. Since journeymen outnumbered masters, the resolutions were, in fact, calling for journeyman control of these institutions, just as the masters had called for control of corporations. The nature of the work contract was another issue that the masters, in their proposed revision of the industrial law, hoped to settle to their advantage, and the journeymen, in the resolutions, to their own. The resolutions further demanded better working conditions, a ten-hour working day, benefit funds, industrial schools, industrial inspection and rigorous sanctions against the sale of adulterated food.

In addition to the economic demands, the resolutions put forward four moderate political demands: electoral reform in the direction of universal suffrage, educational reform to make schooling more practical, a shortened period of obligatory military service, and abolition of restrictive press laws and press taxes.[22]

After the Lviv workers' assembly had passed the resolutions, the assembled journeymen appointed a petition committee to collect signatures in support of the resolutions. In less than two months the committee collected over two thousand signatures and presented the resolutions-petition to Democratic deputy Otto Hausner to place before parliament.[23]

The economic resolutions were renewed at subsequent mass assemblies on 30 January 1881 (300 workers in attendance), 26 June 1881 (700 in attendance), 1 July 1883 (after the passage of the new industrial law) and 12 August 1883.[24] These resolutions were reprinted and endorsed in the May 1881 Program of the Galician Workers' Party[25] and in the Ukrainian socialist press in Geneva;[26] even the more populist wing of the Ruthenian national populists approved of the resolutions.[27]

A group of Polish socialists in Geneva, however, dissented; they thought the demands of the 1879 Lviv assembly smacked of reformism.[28]

The police, for their own reasons, also had reservations about the socialist-sponsored journeyman assemblies in Lviv. In 1881, the Lviv socialists had issued two extensive political programs and had begun serious preparations for founding a socialist workers' party. They called a mass assembly for 30 October 1881 in Lviv. This particular mass assembly differed from the previous ones in that it was to be an all-Galician assembly; delegates from workers' groups outside of Lviv were to attend in order, among other things, to discuss founding a political party.[29] But when the delegate of the Cracow printers arrived, he discovered that the police had forbidden the assembly.[30] Now that the socialists were about to found a political party, the police decided that the assembly — "for safety's sake and the sake of the public good" — must not take place. The assembly, after all, would seek "to spread dissatisfaction with the existing order . . . and incite workers to hatred against the wealthier classes."[31]

On 4 December 1881 the Lviv socialists tried again to hold an assembly, not as ambitious as the one that had been planned for October. The police dissolved it after several craftsmen-socialists had spoken.[32] The police forbade an assembly planned for 23, then 30, April 1882.[33] They dissolved another assembly on 29 June 1882.[34]

Harassment by the authorities in 1881–82 interrupted the socialists' campaign in defense of the journeymen, prevented them from founding a party as they had hoped and brought other consequences that we will look at at the end of this chapter.

Grappling with Theory

Theoretical work by Galician socialists in Polish was almost exclusively confined to Lviv and to the period 1878–81. The socialist movement in Cracow, until the very end of the 1880s, relied on socialists from the

Russian partition to furnish it with an ideological framework.[35] Lviv's own theoretical development was hampered after 1881 by the police harassment mentioned above and by strained relations between Polish and Ruthenian socialists, which led *Praca*'s chief and most original theoretician, Franko, to end his close collaboration with the Polish socialist movement.[36]

Franko had felt close enough to the Polish movement in 1878, in the aftermath of his trial and conviction, to refer to "us Poles" in the first theoretical document of Galician socialism.[37] This was the "socialist catechism" that Franko wrote at the suggestion of the socialists who had assembled at Limanowski's home in June. It was based in form on Louis Blanc's *Faith of the Socialists,* which had appeared in a Polish edition in Lviv a decade earlier,[38] but its contents reflected Marxist and Lassallean theory.

A second major theoretical statement of 1878 was Limanowski's *Socialism as an Inevitable Phenomenon of Historical Development.*[39] It was an original and interesting work, for all the imprecision of its formulations and almost random eclecticism of its sources. It defined socialism as "the theoretical-practical tendency that, flowing from a deep feeling of justice, demands equality for all, condemns exploitation of every sort, recognizes the leading position of labor and leads the people (the fourth estate) to complete liberation."[40] Limanowski had not read Marx, and the ideas that inspired his brochure were those of pre-nineteenth-century utopians, early-nineteenth-century radical Polish democrats, Lassalle and Schäffle.

Franko's articles in *Praca* in 1879–81 were overtly, if somewhat superficially, Marxist, with a Lassallean undertone. The same was true for the two programs published by the Galician socialists, in January and May of 1881: "The Program of the Galician Socialists" (the January program)[41] and "The Program of the Galician Workers' Party" (the May program).[42] Ludwik Inlaender, Czerwieński and Franko collaborated on the first program; Czerwieński and Inlaender drew up the second by themselves.[43] Both programs were party-oriented. The January program twice mentioned that its authors were "aiming" at the founding of a political party.[44] The May document was already intended to be the program of the projected-but-never-founded Galician Workers' Party. (The police, of course, had prevented the establishment of a party and the authorities banned both programs.)[45]

A distinctive characteristic of all this literature, in contrast to the theory (and practice) of Polish socialism in the Russian empire, and its émigré and Cracovian satellites, was its emphasis on a peaceful and legal transition to socialism. This was consonant with Lviv socialism's role as the left-wing successor to the legally organized artisan movement. Limanowski expressed the general sentiment of Lviv's socialists when he wrote that revolution was indispensable only in despotic states, such as Russia; in constitutional states, progress towards socialism could be made peacefully.[46]

Franko's catechism of 1878 spoke unequivocally of a "socialist reform," which workers' representatives in parliament "could gradually introduce." The reform would prevent "the terrible, bloody explosion, which [otherwise] . . . would have been inevitable and very damaging to all human enlightenment and progress."[47] The January 1881 program was more careful to distinguish its aim from that of "reformists," who advocate "partial improvement" and "palliatives." It foresaw a *revolutionary* transformation, which would be accomplished, however, by "gradually preparing a re-organization of society."[48] The May program also hoped that socialism would come into being "freely, gradually, without violent acts and bloody measures."[49]

The Galician socialists argued that work for gradual change was necessary in order to lay the foundation for the new social order before the collapse of capitalism.[50] That such gradual change was possible was demonstrated by the development of capitalism itself, particularly the concentration and nationalization of capital, which already prefigured social ownership of the means of production.[51] But in the end, the peacefulness of the transition would also depend on the posture of the ruling classes. According to the January program, if the bourgeoisie would come to an early understanding of the situation, it could anticipate the wishes of the proletariat: "then the transformation from the present order to the new order will be gentle and the ultimate conflict less violent."[52] The May program, too, foresaw the possibility of a peaceful revolution, if both the possessing classes and the state would "allow our movement to develop freely."[53]

A Lassallean attitude towards the state was also characteristic of the Polish socialist literature in Galicia. While recognizing the modern state as a bourgeois institution, the Lviv socialists nonetheless felt that the state should be used, whenever possible, for the benefit of the working class.[54] Thus, the May program raised the typically Lassallean demand that the state subsidize cooperative economic ventures,[55] and almost

every programmatic statement called for universal suffrage.[56] Coexisting
with this Lassalleanism was a streak of anarchism, apparently introduced by Franko under Drahomanov's influence. This was manifest in
the Galician socialists' ultimate political goal: a decentralized, free
federation of free associations.[57]

A fundamental and difficult task was proving that Galicia's social
structure and economy had already developed to a point sufficient to
sustain a socialist movement. The Galician Democrats argued that this
point had not been reached. Western socialism, they said, was based on
a critique of conditions in industrialized countries and therefore had no
basis in Galicia, where factory production was undeveloped.[58] With
similar reasoning, the Galician authorities, in an indictment of Lviv
socialists, argued that socialism had no natural basis in Galicia, "where
there are no masses of the working class," and the majority of the
population was "the village people, religious, attached to their land and
to the customs sanctified by centuries, hostile to such [socialist] innova-
tions."[59]

Limanowski admitted that the lack of factories was retarding the
development of the Galician socialist movement[60] and the January
program implied as much when it stated that the conflict between labor
and capital "is waged most actively where developed factory industry
brings out most clearly the consequences of capitalist production."[61]
Still, the January program argued that socialism had a *raison d'être* in
Galicia:

> To those who stubbornly maintain that socialism in Galicia does not have
> the proper conditions for existence and who can adduce as proof only the
> tremendous development of factory industry in Western countries and the
> lack of the same in Galicia, to them we reply along with Marx: "*De te
> fabula narratur.*"
>
> "Intrinsically, it is not a question of the higher or lower degree of
> development of the social antagonisms that result from the natural laws of
> capitalist production. It is a question of these laws themselves, of these
> tendencies working with iron necessity towards inevitable results. The
> country that is more developed industrially only shows, to the less
> developed, the image of its own future."[62]

The socialists argued not only that capitalism *will* come to Galicia, but
that it had *already* come. In contrast to Russia, for example, where
communal production remained yet in agriculture, Galicia could boast
agricultural production that was "already completely capitalist, as in the

West," with bourgeois property relations in land, an extensive credit economy, production for the general market, grain speculation, concentration of land by large capital, greater application of agricultural machinery and wide-scale exploitation of agricultural workers. Then, too, the growth of the mining town of Boryslav and the expansion of banks and railways attested to capitalist development in Galicia. They also maintained that capitalism — albeit *foreign* capitalism — was destroying small industry in Galicia and thus making a proletariat of the artisan population.[63]

Although the Galician socialists could easily pronounce their economy capitalist, it was more difficult to delimit the local equivalents of capitalism's two principal classes, the bourgeoisie and proletariat. When they wrote about the "bourgeoisie," the Galician socialists seem to have had in mind, in the first place, factory-owners, whom they knew, however, only from socialist literature, not from Galician reality. Although they never took the care to make an unequivocal statement about it, they seem also to have included a small segment of the master craftsmen among the bourgeoisie. According to the May program, which contains the most explicit statement on the subject, the term "bourgeoisie" referred primarily to "*urban* capitalists." To this (in Galicia virtually non-existent) group, "one must also add the so-called *szlachta,* the owners of great estates, unnecessary dignitaries of every sort, etc."[64] Usurers, too, were capitalists.[65] Thus, abstracting from the imaginary Galician factory-owners, the bourgeoisie in capitalist Galicia comprised the landed nobility, their inseparable companions — the usurers, and a handful of the wealthiest master craftsmen! Such was the progress Galicia had made since the era of serfdom.

As to the proletariat, the May program specified that this included "petty industrialists," i.e., the great bulk of Galicia's 27,000 master craftsmen.[66] Also, "the day laborer, the journeyman, the factory workers, the engineer, the litterateur as well as the non-capitalist master —all these are *workers.*"[67] For all the May program tells us, the four fifths of the population who were peasants were to stand idly by while the class struggle raged between Galicia's bourgeoisie and proletariat. Franko, who had no hand in drafting the May program,[68] felt differently. In his view, the Galician peasantry also constituted the proletariat.[69] The same was implied in Limanowski's brochure and the January program, which identified the peasantry as potentially the leading class in the Galician socialist revolution.[70]

The analysis of their own society proved to be a stumbling block for the

Galician socialists. They had in their minds an image of class struggle as it had been explained to them in the works of Marx and Lassalle. Where in the Western composition the bourgeoisie stood, the Galicians placed the landed nobility; where the proletariat — the artisans and peasantry.[71] That things seemed to fit in place for them is not to be wondered at, because the class antagonisms of Galician reality were just as sharp and pervasive as anything they had read in books. Only their understanding of the real nature of these antagonisms was obscured by their preoccupation with the developed capitalism of their theory. The great conflicts in Galicia were those between peasant and landlord, and peasant and usurer, i.e., the last and bitter battles from a pre-capitalist heritage. That these were the dominant contradictions in society only made the agony of the Galician artisan class more ominous. Barely emerging from the feudal womb, Galicia was already locked in fierce competition with the developed capitalist world into which it was daily more intimately integrated. The destruction of Galicia's pre-capitalist society was clearly underway, but the signs of a future development of productivity were nowhere to be seen. The Galician Democrats had correctly understood the situation, but had proposed the ineffective solution of voluntary associations. The socialists instinctively advocated a radical transformation of society, but their theoretical justification for it and vision of its course were confused. It was not until the 1890s that two Ruthenian socialists moved towards a more appropriate theoretical framework, or at least towards one that has subsequently become widespread. They analyzed their society in terms of a conflict between developed Western Austria and undeveloped Galicia, and the resolution they proposed was an independent Ruthenian-Ukrainian state with a nationalized economy.[72]

For the socialists of ethnically-mixed Galicia, where national antagonism was rife and national movements strong, the national question was of great importance. They saw no contradiction between strong national sentiments and socialism. In fact, they felt the two went hand in hand. Limanowski, as Cottam remarks, "believed that every true patriot was a potential socialist, due to his love of the people as an end in itself. Conversely, every true socialist, in Limanowski's opinion, was a potential patriot, because patriotism in Poland was also a means of establishing a regime of social justice."[73]

The Galician socialists opposed all national oppression,[74] which they felt had its origins in social injustice.[75] Socialism would eliminate national oppression by removing its basis in both the social structure and politics (with federative associations replacing the modern state).[76] They believed, furthermore, that national distinctions, and especially the national cultures of small, oppressed nations, had to be cultivated.[77] A Ruthenian perspective is evident in these formulations, especially the latter.

The January program, which objected to the oppression of Poles and Ruthenians by "governments of occupation," expressed "the wish that the Polish and Ruthenian peoples might regain independent national existence."[78] But, consistent with its anarcho-federalist principles, it stopped short of calling for the establishment of independent national *states*. As Franko had written in his "catechism," "political independence means nothing to people as long as internally there is social oppression. . . . What good will it do us to have our own king, if the usurers and capitalists continue to exploit us as before?"[79] Only Limanowski believed in the necessity of an independent Polish (but not Ukrainian) state; this view, however, had little support among the Galician socialists.[80]

The activists in Lviv intended to establish a federation in Galicia of three socialist groups: Polish, Ukrainian and Jewish. Though joined in a single, federative party, the three groups would enjoy full autonomy, including the right to enter federative unions with Polish, Ukrainian and Jewish socialist organizations outside Galicia.[81] These same principles, as several later writers have pointed out, were adopted by the Austrian Social Democratic Party at the Brno congress of 1899.[82]

In line with this, the January program stated that the socialists of one nation could not pose as the representatives of all of ethnically-mixed Galicia.[83] This principle was reflected in the original title of the program — "The Program of the Polish and Ruthenian Socialists of Eastern Galicia" — which emphasized that the program was the work of a coalition of socialists of separate nationalities, though of the same territorial unit. What happened to that title is instructive, and symptomatic of the place of national feeling in the Lviv socialist movement.

The authors sent the manuscript to Limanowski, then in Switzerland, for publication, but for some reason Limanowski omitted the words "and Ruthenian" from the title. The title thus read: "The Program of the Polish Socialists of Eastern Galicia." The blunder seemed to confirm suspicions voiced earlier by Drahomanov that in his heart Limanowski considered Polish such ethnically Ukrainian territories as Eastern Galicia. Under protest from the Lviv socialists, Limanowski printed up new titles and pasted them over the offending version. But instead of restoring the original title, Limanowski this time omitted all potentially controversial phrases ("Polish and Ruthenian" and "Eastern Galicia") and simplified the title to: "The Program of the Galician Socialists." It is interesting to contrast Limanowski's and Franko's views of this incident:

Limanowski, in his memoirs:

> All at once I received a letter from Inlaender full of bitterness and reproaches. It seems that the title of the manuscript was "Program of the Socialists of Eastern Galicia," but that it was printed as "Program of the Polish Socialists of Eastern Galicia." This made the Ruthenians indignant; they raised frightful cries, accusing us of having done this out of chauvinistic Polish patriotism. Whereas this was an unintentional blunder. Trussov, who set the type for the program by himself, did it. I, making corrections, paid no heed to it. It ended up that we had to reprint the title and scrupulously paste new titles over the old titles so as to completely cover up the adjective "Polish," which arouses such aversion and anxiety among the Ruthenians.[84]

Franko, in a letter to Drahomanov (October 1881):

> With the "Program" there's a comedy. Limanowski was sent a manuscript with the title "The Program of the Polish and Ruthenian Socialists of Eastern Galicia." By mistake he printed only "Polish." This we protested, then he corrected it, but — once again "by mistake" — he omitted both "Polish" and "Ruthenian" and left only "of Eastern Galicia." Just so he wouldn't have to print that despised word "Ruthenian."[85]

The January program had announced a place in its proposed federation for a Jewish socialist group, although Jewish socialism had not yet appeared in Galicia. The program recognized the Jews as a distinct nation, expressed solidarity with the Jewish proletariat and announced plans to publish socialist literature in Yiddish. This aspect of the program probably reflected Pavlyk's influence. In 1880 he had sent a letter to *Praca* stressing the need for Yiddish socialist literature. Among Galicia's Jews, he wrote, "are many poor and hard-working laborers (tailors, cobblers, masons, typesetters, etc.), who, although they also suffer from their own rich (bourgeoisie), nonetheless stick very close to them in their kahals (communities) and can suffer completely without cause if they do not dissociate themselves [from the rich] and join up with the peasants and workers of other nationalities. . . ."[86] Pavlyk returned to this theme in May 1881 when he prepared an appeal to "the

Christian and Jewish people in Ukraine."[87] He hoped to publish the appeal in Ukrainian and Yiddish and have it distributed in Russian Ukraine, where the first large wave of pogroms had just begun. Pavlyk's views on the Jewish question were formed under Drahomanov's influence.[88]

The Socialist Conspiracy in Cracow

The socialist movement in Lviv, as we have seen, owed a great deal to the preceding, Democrat-sponsored artisan movement. It inherited some of the institutional forms of the pre-socialist artisan movement (*Praca* and the mutual aid society), coopted some of the pre-socialist artisan leadership (Mańkowski, Daniluk) and focussed its activities on the defense of the journeymen's immediate interests. The working class was well prepared for mass action by the experience of the decade preceding 1878 and by large-scale participation in voluntary artisan associations; socialist activity was open and took a legal form.

Such was not the case in Cracow, where the pre-socialist artisan movement had been very weak in comparison in Lviv's. A Cracovian journeyman complained to *Praca* about the "stagnancy reigning in our city":

> I would like to report something about the movement in workers' circles here. But what can I write you about it, when there is almost no movement at all. You in Lviv have associations and so forth, but where we are everything is dead and turned to fossil.[89]

The organizational and leadership vacuum in Cracow permitted the sudden emergence late in 1878 of a conspiratorial socialist organization with revolutionary Marxist leaders freshly imported from Russia.

The story of the origins of Polish socialism in Russia is the story of a generation that in childhood watched its parents take up arms against the tsar in the insurrection of 1863. It was a generation born, for the most part, in comfortable circumstances, but very often impoverished by the time it reached adolescence as the estates and property of the insurgent families were sequestered. It was a generation, further, that attended gymnasia officially and openly hostile to its nationality. In the face of anti-Polish repression, these young people founded secret patriotic societies in the gymnasia and carried these secret societies with them to Russian universities in Petersburg, Kiev, Moscow and Warsaw. They entered the universities at the same time that Russian university youth were immersing themselves in radical social theories. The philosophical materialism of Warsaw positivism appealed to them, but not positivism's political program. They had no sympathy with the older generation's "organic work" and enrichment at the price of acquiescence — the elders' understandable reaction to the failure of the insurrection. The youth became infatuated, instead, with the anti-tsarist spirit of their Russian classmates and influenced by the illegal radical literature then filtering into Russia. Their secret clubs now read and discussed not Mickiewicz and Mochnacki alone, but Bakunin, Lavrov, and, in Russian translation, Marx. Some founded clandestine Marxist discussion clubs at the universities as well as underground workers' circles and strike funds outside the universities. In the summer of 1878, the tsarist authorities arrested this generation in mass; those who could fled to the West, many to Galicia.[90]

The outstanding leader of the Polish socialists in Russia was Ludwik Waryński, a young man combining a courageous, passionate temperament with a logical mind and magnetic personality. He was tall and blond, strong but very near-sighted, with a brisk gait, and given, in the course of argument, to forceful gesticulation, making a fist of his right hand and pounding it in time to his speech as though he was striking an anvil with a hammer.[91] This pounding was no idle gesture. When Waryński moved to Warsaw in 1878, he was the moving spirit behind the students' agitation among Polish workers. He convinced other students to work as apprentices in order to make contacts within the working class; thus Stanisław Mendelson, son of a wealthy banker, took up the cobbler's trade, while Waryński went to work in a smithy, whence his characteristic gesture.

Their organizational efforts were very successful, especially considering the need, in tsarist Russia, to carry on such work in the utmost secrecy. In a matter of months, Waryński and those who shared his aspirations organized between two and four hundred workers in workers' circles and strike-fund societies or "defense treasuries" (*kasy oporu*). The arrests in the summer of 1878 interrupted this flourishing organization and Waryński, together with Mendelson and others, escaped to Galicia.

Some of the refugees soon moved on to Switzerland, but Waryński decided to stay for a while in Galicia. In Lviv he came into conflict with the local socialists. He disapproved of the law-abiding direction the Lviv movement was taking, while the Lviv socialists accused him of ignorance of local conditions.[92] Pavlyk in particular opposed the influence of the Russian *"Wandersozialisten"* and charged them with trying to engineer a split in Lviv's socialist movement between the Poles and Ruthenians. Pavlyk especially objected to Waryński's plans to set up in constitutional Austria a centralized, conspiratorial socialist organization such as Waryński had established in Russian Poland.[93] Waryński, for his part, found Lviv unsuited to his temperament; he was soon to complain that in Russia, even with the repression, life at least existed, but in Austria everything was in a state of hibernation.[94] The police, who accidently stumbled upon Waryński's presence in Lviv,[95] only seem to have helped him decide to switch his field of operations to Cracow in October 1878.

In Cracow, in the organizational and leadership vacuum noted earlier, Waryński and his plans flourished. He drew a dozen or so of his Russian comrades to Cracow and the work of recruiting journeymen began in earnest. Several of the émigrés from Russia infiltrated the otherwise vegetating branch of Gwiazda in Cracow. The secretary of the artisan association welcomed them, because "from the first conversation with them, he recognized that they were educated people" and "craftsmen should always stick with people more educated than themselves."[96] As to the émigré students, they were as though in love with the artisans. Witold Piekarski, who had engaged in the socialist movement in Kiev gubernia, wrote home to his friends and relatives from Cracow:

> I know the nicest, healthiest, most promising contingents of local society — I live with the workers, the craftsmen, the sons of peasants and, in general, with the children of poverty. . . ."[97]
> . . . It's amazing how developed our artisans are [i.e., in class consciousness], and how nice they are.[98]

With such enthusiasm, it is little wonder that the network of the socialists' contacts among the artisans spread quickly.

The socialists also agitated among Cracow's student population. They had no success among the students of the Jagellonian University; apparently these privileged individuals were too much under the wing of the prevailing Stańczyk ideology. Pierkarski, who so lauded the artisanal youth, described Cracow's youth as *"garbage."*[99] Recruiting was much better in the teachers' seminary in Cracow, where the authorities soon felt obliged to expel several students for socialist agitation.[100] Perhaps the teachers' seminary was a more conducive nest for socialism than the university because the teachers' seminary attracted the offspring of the less privileged classes. Social origin had made a difference to Ludwik Wąsowicz, a student at Cracow's school of fine arts. On trial in 1880, he admitted to socialist convictions and announced that the social question had particular relevance to him, "because I am the son of a worker."[101] At St. Anne's Gymnasium secret student clubs, patriotic, with heroic fantasies of armed insurrection, paved the way for socialist ideas.[102]

Thus in late 1878 and early 1879, Waryński and his comrades had converted a sizable body of artisan and student youth to socialist sympathies. Waryński organized the converts along much the same lines he had organized workers in Warsaw, in the Russian empire: into clandestine, conspiratorial socialist cells. A copy of Waryński's "Program of Organization," confiscated by the police in February 1879, reveals the basic structure of the secret organization, the Social-Revolutionary Association of Poles (*Socjalnorewolucyjne Stowarzyszenie Polaków*).[103]

The Association was composed of a number of individual cells (*kółka,* literally: "circles"). For conspiracy's sake, the individual cells never held common, intra-Association meetings; thus members of one cell were not supposed to know the members of other cells. The discovery of one cell by the police was therefore not supposed to lead to the discovery of the remaining cells and so to the eventual eradication of the entire Association. According to the standard practice of such revolutionary conspiracies, members who betrayed the organization were to be executed. The individual cells were connected with one another only through their officers.

But since 1878–79 was a period of initial mass recruitment, the Cracow socialists modified the organizational structure to accommodate the influx of newcomers. For one thing, meetings were held more frequently than the statutory twice a month. The "preparatory cells," in fact, were meeting every evening. These "preparatory cells" supplemented the regular "revolutionary cells" and functioned something like a socialist novitiate. In the preparatory cells, members listened to lectures on socialist theory and discussed various brochures and periodicals on the same theme. Only after a member of a preparatory cell displayed a proper understanding of the basic doctrine was he invited to attend a revolutionary cell meeting. In the revolutionary cells, as the name indicates, candidates were initiated into the inner mystery of socialism: that the working class must seize power by a violent revolution. According to one who passed from preparatory to revolutionary cell, there were five revolutionary cells functioning in Cracow in 1879.[104]

In addition to meeting and discussing revolution, some Cracow socialists began to collect arms.[105] They had plans, too, to smuggle revolutionary literature into Russia[106] and to publish a socialist newspaper in Cracow.[107] They also contracted a local printer, Antoni Koziański, to publish three thousand copies of a Polish translation of a brochure by Wilhelm Liebknecht. The printer informed the police about this unusual assignment.

On the evening of 8 February 1879, messengers arrived at Koziański's printshop to pick up the brochures. The police shadowed the messengers, following them to Waryński's apartment, where they arrested Waryński and confiscated the brochures. While the police were searching the apartment, Hieronym Truszkowski, a former schoolmate of Waryński's walked in with a load of laundry. When questioned, Truszkowski said he was the son of a washerwoman from Smocza street. There was no Smocza street in Cracow; the police promptly took Truszkowski into custody. That same evening the police arrested Józef Uziembło, another refugee from Russia. They arrested Uziembło at a restaurant and were questioning his partner at the table when this partner ran to the bathroom, locked himself in and flushed some papers down the toilet. The police later retrieved these papers for evidence. The partner, the police afterwards discovered, was none other than Erazm Kobylański, the socialist emissary who had precipitated the 1878 trial in Lviv. In the meantime, the Cracow teachers' seminary expelled a few students on suspicion of socialist agitation. The police investigated the affair and arrested two students, Józef Ostafin and Stanisław Bogucki.[108] They bullied and intimidated Bogucki, who was young, ill and impressionable, until they had extorted an account of the activities and members of the socialist cells.[109] It was a major breakthrough in the case and arrests multiplied thereafter. The police displayed more zeal than intelligence in their activities, at one point even confiscating Lessing's *Laocoon* as socialist literature.[110]

The police saw no reason to treat the suspects gently. They beat Kobylański and ripped much of the beard off his chin. Truszkowski they thrashed with a cane. One officer struck seventeen-year-old Szczepan Mikołajski in the face. As for Waryński, the police beat him in the face, breaking the spectacles he so depended upon, and threw him — bound — into a cell.[111]

While the police were rounding up suspects, those socialists still at large fought back. On 27 February 1879, they exploded a petard at police headquarters. Then they posted an anonymous leaflet that, according to the police commissioner's description, "in the most brutal phrases hurls insults at the government, the police organs and the investigative judge in this case." The socialists threatened to assassinate Koziański, the talkative printer, and seem to have taken a shot at the police commissioner of Cracow, Jan Kostrzewski.[112]

Things quieted down after the police completed their round up. Many of the socialists spent about a year in prison before standing trial for disturbing public order. At first the authorities hoped to charge the suspects with high treason, but after the police finished sifting the evidence they had extorted from adolescents and fetched from toilets, it became clear that they would be fortunate to win a conviction on the trivial charge of disturbing the peace. With a cynical disregard for Polish national feeling, the police of autonomous Galicia worked hand in hand with the tsarist police, feeding the tsar's agents information about whom to arrest in Russian Poland (over forty individuals) and consuming information from the Russian authorities on the identity and past of the arrested refugees.[113]

The year in prison was a trying period for the arrested socialists and for their families. Witold Piekarski's father, Teodozy, became so distraught by his son's imprisonment that he lost all mental balance and hanged himself in March 1880.[114] The treatment of the prisoners, bad at first, improved as the prison authorities became cognizant of the social connections of the arrested émigrés. The émigrés came from good families and those families implored their more eminent and powerful friends, such as Włodzimierz Spasowicz, to visit the imprisoned, greatly impressing the petty tyrants of Cracow's prison.[115] The prisoners' situation also vastly improved after a three-day hunger strike in November 1879: the accused were given copies of the indictment to study in preparation for their defense, they were allowed to receive books and to visit each others' cells and prisoners from Galicia were set at liberty until the trial.[116] Morale was good. Even before the hunger strike, in April and May 1879, the prisoners had put out two issues of *Zgrzyt*, a hand-written periodical filled with political and satirical verse, anecdotes, riddles, puzzles and news.[117]

There were thirty-five defendants, twelve born in Russia, and twenty-three in Austria.[118] The trial opened in mid-February and did not end until two months later, on 16 April 1880. From the first, the defendants made a favorable impression on the public. Even the conservative, Stańczyk daily *Czas* commented on their "lively, one might even say merry, faces; and if it weren't for their responses, sometimes of a drastic content, betraying ruinous ideas, they would in no wise seem to be so-called socialists."[119] The defense attorney reminded the public that his clients were on trial for disturbing public order, not for socialism. He objected to the admission card he had been handed upon entering, since the card advertised the trial as a prosecution of "socialists." The attorney, Maksymylian Machalski, who had himself engaged in anti-socialist propaganda in the previous decade, explained to the court that the defense had spent a great deal of time and effort searching the criminal codex and other collections of laws for references to "socialism" and "socialists." The defense had found no such references, "socialism" was not a legal term[120] and Machalski protested the text of the admission card.

The defense remained on the offense during the whole trial. The defendants made easy sport of the prosecutor from the stand[121] and circulated caricatures of the prosecution and police.[122] By March, things had come to such a pass that the prosecutor begged the protection of the court and complained that "the trial has currently taken such a form as though he [the prosecutor] were the accused and not those who sit on the bench of the accused."[123]

Indeed, the accused were doing the accusing. They used the trial as a forum for the propagation of socialist ideology. Four years later, Cracow's police commissioner, Jan Kostrzewski, thus summed up the significance of the 1880 socialist trial:

> This trial . . . constitutes a most important moment in the Polish social-revolutionary movement. One might say that this trial contributed greatly to the dissemination of socialism among the population of Cracow. The courtroom was turned into a tribunal from which Ludwik Waryński, with his characteristic eloquence, preached his principles before a large public and expounded the same program that hitherto he had been careful to explain only in concealment, at clandestine gatherings.[124]

And it was not only that Waryński reached the people in the courtroom. The papers gave the trial great publicity and the influential *Czas* published a nearly stenographic transcript of all the proceedings. The trial became a vogue topic of discussion. In one instance, a third-year

law student in Cracow had been reading the trial proceedings in *Czas*
and began a debate with his roommate on the topic of socialism. The
law student defended socialism and almost landed in jail for a scatologi-
cal deprecation of the emperor.[125] (Curiously, this was not the first time
Czas had inadvertently aided the cause of socialism. In 1878, to expose
the socialist danger, *Czas* had reprinted a large quantity of socialist
literature in installments. These issues of *Czas,* as the trial brought to
light, were required reading in the socialist cells of Cracow.)[126]

At the very start of the trial, after the reading of the long indictment,
Ludwik Waryński was called to the stand and asked to explain the
doctrine of socialism "omitting the scientific aspects." Waryński took
his cue from the question's phrasing and responded:

> Socialism is a purely scientific question and is based only on science, so it
> is impossible to give an unscientific definition of it. . . . Our socialism
> proceeds from a critique of the present social structure. . . . If we con-
> sider that in society at present we find on the one hand accumulated
> capital and materials, i.e., everything known as the instruments of labor,
> and on the other hand only enslaved and exploited labor, than we must
> come to the conclusion that capital — as the instruments of labor — must
> stop being private property and must pass into the possession of the
> whole.[127]

The prosecution was especially interested in following up three questions that it felt would jeopardize the socialists' reputation with the
public: the questions of revolution, patriotism and religion.

Although revolution, violent revolution, was genuinely a part of
Waryński's program,[128] he felt it was better at the trial to project a
thoroughly legalist image. Thus, in explaining the practical aspect of the
introduction of socialism, Waryński maintained: "Our struggle is a
parliamentary struggle, that is, winning a majority in parliament, that is,
a struggle by way of the ballot."[129] He took care to distinguish himself
from the revolutionary socialists of Russia,[130] but he did ambiguously
warn that though his program "does not call for a revolution," it "does
foresee one."[131]

The prosecution felt it would be able to show that the socialists, if not
a revolutionary menace, were at least unpatriotic and indifferent to the
fate of Poland. But the majority of the socialists on trial were fervent
patriots, especially Piekarski, who privately held that socialists were
continuing the great Polish insurrectionary tradition.[132] Waryński and
Mendelson, however (and this the police and prosecution surmised),

were opposed to continuing the struggle for Polish independence. It was not that they were indifferent to national oppression, but rather that they felt the national struggle would detract from the class struggle, while an inevitable consequence of social liberation would be national liberation (if not necessarily state independence).[133] The prosecutor seized an occasion to insinuate that Mendelson lacked patriotic sentiment, but Mendelson turned the tables on him and declared that he stood nearer to the Polish idea than any Austrian prosecutor.[134] Mendelson's reply was just and it hit home, because the public well knew and heartily disapproved of the recent cooperation between the Galician and tsarist organs of justice.

The prosecution gratuitously included in the indictment information on the religious convictions of the accused, assuming that the socialists' impiety would work against them in Catholic Cracow, where the Jesuits had declared March a month to pray "that the Lord God might save the people from socialists."[135] Thus the indictment mentioned Edmund Brzeziński's affirmation that, though baptized in the Roman Catholic faith, the Catholic idea of God was entirely alien to him.[136] More shocking was Edmund Mikiewicz's confession of faith: he rejected an ideal God, Creator and Supreme Being, and professed instead a religion of love. (At this point the indictment provided some sordid details about Mikiewicz and his "concubine," categorically denied by Mikiewicz later in the trial.)[137] Waryński, first to testify, was called upon to explain the attitude of socialism to religion. He answered very simply that religion was a matter of conscience and that it had nothing in common with science.[138] One young Cracovian socialist, Ludwik Wąsowicz, had quite positive feelings about Christianity, at least in its purer forms. To cheer his parents, Wąsowicz wrote them a letter from prison comparing socialism to Christianity:

> If I should be found guilty, then I won't grumble about suffering, because Christ suffered even more, for the same doctrines that the socialists possess. Just as the Jews, so cruelly persecuting the Christians, were unable to eradicate the Catholic faith, just so [it will be impossible to eradicate] the faith that it is wrong for some to have more and exploit others possessing nothing. . . .[139]

Wąsowicz's letter was read aloud at the trial.

The trial drew to a close and the prosecutor gave a long and windy summation, the tedium of which was only broken up occasionally by flashes of hysteria. He wearied the jury with the history of socialism, touching upon Lassalle, the International, the Jew Marx and his agitation, Bakunin and the anarchist faction in the International. He then proceeded to a history of nihilism, which derived from Bakunin, and explained the organizational structure of the contemporary nihilist movement, headed by Petr Lavrov with his thirteen secretaries. The nihilist party, the prosecutor continued, was divided into two main groups: the Great Russian group, headed by Valerian Smirnov in London, and the Little Russian group, headed by Mykhailo Drahomanov in Geneva. Waryński and company had set up in Cracow "a social-revolutionary association of anarchists belonging to the Little Russian group of nihilism."[140] Following this far-fetched taxonomy, the prosecutor talked on and on (filling half a dozen pages of newspaper) until he concluded that since the socialists' ideas were not only contrary to law, but contrary to human nature and the Polish national character, the jury should sentence the accused severely. "Remember," he admonished the jury, "that if you spare the guilty, you hang a sword over the head of the innocent; and mercy is really merciless if it leads to ruinous consequences for the country."[141] The defense was more laconic, yet more eloquent. In fact, the speech of attorney Józef Rosenblatt was so brilliant that it was included forty years later in a Viennese anthology, *Famous Defense Speeches, 1860–1918.*[142]

The jury sentenced some of the Russian-born accused to short terms in prison for registering under false names, but they acquitted all the defendants on the touch-stone charge of disturbing public peace and order.[143] It was a great, unequivocal victory for the socialists. The police, understandably, were upset. So, too, were the Stańczyks, who argued, not altogether consistently in light of their own political record, that the acquittal of the socialists was a great blow to the Polish national cause.[144] Paweł Popiel, the veteran ideologue of Cracow conservatism, was also dismayed by the verdict. In fact, he had just finished writing, on the very day the verdict was handed down, a major anti-socialist brochure entitled, *The Illness of the Century.* The brochure held that "Jewish doctrine and Jewish goals" as well as freemasonry lay at the root of socialism.[145]

Following the trial of 1880, Ludwik Waryński and the other Russian émigrés left Cracow, mainly for Geneva, where they joined the editorial board of the Polish socialist journal *Równość* (Equality). In Cracow they had established a pattern of Russian-led conspiratorial socialism, which continued to exist in that city until 1884. The years 1880–81 were relatively quiet in Cracow, although the police did arrest an occasional socialist[146] and now and then an émigré socialist from Russia appeared in the city, usually ending up deported.[147] A quickening of Cracow's socialist movement came in 1882 when Aleksander Zawadzki was a medical student at Cracow's university.

Zawadzki, originally from the gubernia of Vilnius, came to Cracow in August 1881 from Siberia, where he had served three years for socialist agitation. Once in Cracow, he met with the local socialists, revivified socialist cells and also began experimenting with a legal, open socialist movement such as existed in Lviv. The police frustrated these flirtations with legality by deporting Russian-born socialists, including Zawadzki, and by arresting as many Austrian-born socialists as possible. The year 1883 was filled with socialist trials.[148]

In May 1883 those socialists still at liberty in Cracow issued a leaflet in response to the wave of arrests and deportations decimating the Cracovian socialist movement. The leaflet left it to the authorities to decide whether Galician socialists would take the legal or "convulsive" road. The Cracow socialists complained of their persecution: how their newspapers were confiscated and how they were imprisoned for long periods of time prior to being brought to trial. The leaflet noted that one faction within the Cracow socialist movement wanted to take revenge upon the police, but that cooler heads prevailed. Although the Cracow socialists would much prefer a legal socialist movement, the Galician police had driven them to conspiracy. If their legal rights were not respected, they promised to declare war on the authorities. "The bayonet will not be able to reach the 'red spectre'; this will not be a battle with barricades, but an underground battle, threatening because of its secret might." The Cracow socialists claimed to be so desperate, that no fear of reprisal would restrain them.

The leaflet then appealed to the ideals of democratic Polish revolutionaries of the past, but warned that without radical social reforms the ideals of freedom and equality, of patriotism and independence, would remain only empty phrases. The leaflet urged the progressive youth and workers to join together for peaceful, systematic work. It also called for the formation of independent workers' organizations. "If they push us off this road, then we shall descend beneath the earth, we shall dig ourselves down like gravediggers, we shall plant a mine that will rip off the legs of the monster, the monster that laps up blood from our open wounds and nourishes itself upon our sweat."[149]

Yet the summer of 1883 was, as the police recorded with satisfaction, a quiet summer, undisturbed by socialist activity.[150] The police did not give rein to a legal socialist movement; the socialists did not, yet, resort to terror.

In 1882 Waryński had returned to the Congress Kingdom and created an underground socialist party, Proletariat. A short-lived branch of the party was founded in Cracow in 1883. A secret agent of the Russian police uncovered the Proletariat organization in Cracow and its members were arrested, including its leading activists from Russia — Maria Zofia Onufrowicz, Józef Gostyński, and Marian Piechowski. The trial against Onufrowicz and companions was conducted in secret to avoid sensation and propaganda on 29–30 March 1884. The court sentenced Onufrowicz to four months' imprisonment, Gostyński and Piechowski to six.[151] All three were to be banished from Austria upon their release, but not necessarily deported to Russia. However, Cracow's police commissioner, Jan Kostrzewski, took an interest in the affair and urged the viceroy of Galicia to extradite the three Russian citizens to Russia. The viceroy approved Kostrzewski's recommendation and agreed to turn the prisoners over to the Russian authorities. "It is understood, of course," cautioned the viceroy, "that the above order be executed in a most discreet manner, not attracting any attention."[152] Once returned to the Russian empire, Onufrowicz was sentenced to four years in Siberia, which she survived; Gostyński and Piechowski were sentenced to five years in Siberia, which killed them both.[153]

The arrest and imprisonment of Onufrowicz and company did not eradicate the underground socialist organization in Cracow. A socialist Central Committee had kept in touch with Onufrowicz and her fellow prisoners. As Onufrowicz and the others stood trial at the end of March 1884, the Committee began considering terrorist reprisals. Apparently at the instigation of Roman Piechowski, Marian's brother, the Cracow socialists decided to assassinate police commissioner Kostrzewski.

Kostrzewski, whom we have just seen in action urging the Galician viceroy to deliver Onufrowicz, Gostyński and Marian Piechowski to the tsarist authorities, worked unofficially for the Russian secret police. He reported to them in detail on Cracow's socialist movement, for which he was awarded the tsar's Order of St. Stanislav on 24 May 1883.[154] Normally, Poles did not chase after medals from the tsar, but this one had developed a special animus against socialists. Kostrzewski had also been the man responsible for the brutal treatment of Waryński and companions in 1879.

The socialist Central Committee, determined that Kostrzewski must die, devised a plan in which a member of the Executive Committee would hurl a bomb at the police chief and would himself die in the explosion. Since an Executive Committee was not yet in existence, it was necessary to recruit members for it from the introductory cells. Early in 1884 the Cracow socialists had cautiously begun to recruit new members into the introductory cells; these included a seventeen-year-old journeyman brazier, Bolesław Malankiewicz, and a twenty-two-year-old journeyman stonemason, Franciszek Sułczewski.[155]

Recruitment to the Executive Committee was conducted in a suitably conspiratorial manner. A masked man appeared at meetings of the introductory cells and read aloud from the statutes of the Executive Committee the last article, which dealt with the death penalty as punishment for enemies of the socialist movement. The masked man asked those who wished to join the Executive Committee to stand where he indicated. Malankiewicz, who had been in the socialist movement at most a few weeks, stood in the place designated by the masked man and received from him a card with one-half of a letter of the alphabet, by which a member of the Executive Committee was known.

The volunteers who joined the Executive Committee drew lots to determine who would execute Kostrzewski. The lot fell to Malankiewicz. The Central Committee informed Malankiewicz that he would have to die with Kostrzewski in the explosion. Though he assented to the sacrifice of his own life, the Central Committee later altered the original plan and ordered Malankiewicz to escape after the assassination. Roman Piechowski constructed the bomb from pipe and gunpowder, disguising the explosive as a parcel destined for the post office. Sułczewski supplied Piechowski with the paper to wrap and pack the bomb.

Malankiewicz set about to assassinate Kostrzewski at 1:30 in the afternoon on 22 March 1884. The Central Committee had instructed him to throw the bomb through the window of an office where Kostrzewski was supposed to be working. Malankiewicz, being short, was obliged to climb up the wall a bit in order to hurl the bomb through the window. When Malankiewicz reached the window and peeked through it, he realized that there had been a mistake, that he had been directed not to Kostrzewski's office, but to the bureau of registration. Confounded, Malankiewicz was even more confounded when a clerk ran to the window and yelled at him. In his confusion, Malankiewicz fell and dropped the bomb, which exploded behind him and left him seriously injured.

Kostrzewski heard the explosion and hurried to investigate. He found the badly burned Malankiewicz and took him to the hospital. There the police commissioner questioned him. Malankiewicz stated that he was a journeyman brazier and, unaware of the identity of his interrogator, admitted that he had been trying to assassinate Jan Kostrzewski.

On the next day, Kostrzewski had Sułczewski arrested. This arrest demonstrated just how poorly the socialists had planned the assassination attempt. Not only did they select the wrong window, but in preparing the bomb, Piechowski had used a druggist's prescription to pack it with. The scrap of paper survived the explosion, Kostrzewski took it to the druggist and the druggist informed Kostrzewski that the prescription was Sułczewski's. An investigation of Sułczewski's activities turned up the fact that Ludwik Grudziński, a journeyman bookbinder, and Jan Pająk, a gymnasium student, frequently met at Sułczewski's apartment. They, too, were arrested. In the summer of 1884, Roman Piechowski was also arrested, in Prague.[156]

The police were having difficulty linking the other socialists to Malankiewicz's assassination attempt until a tsarist police agent, the Russian-born carpenter's apprentice Jan Czerwiński, appeared on the scene in Cracow in May 1884. Soon after his arrival, Czerwiński met the socialist artisan Tomasz Wesołowski and extracted from him information on socialist doctrines and on the structure of the secret socialist organization in Cracow. In September 1884, Czerwiński involved himself in a scuffle with another apprentice and was sentenced to two weeks in prison, where he was assigned to the same cell as Jan Pająk.

Czerwiński told Pająk that he knew Wesołowski and that he himself was sympathetic to socialism. Pająk hoped to win Czerwiński more decisively to the socialist cause. To this end, Pająk elaborated on socialist doctrine. Socialism aimed, he explained, at the expropriation of land and factories, so that these would be communally and not privately owned. Socialists would work to make the transition to socialism a voluntary, peaceful process; failing a voluntary renunciation of private ownership by the bourgeoisie, however, a revolution would surely break out and the means of production would be forcibly expropriated. Pająk further informed Czerwiński that to accomplish their aims, Cracow socialists had formed a secret organization divided into cells and a Central and Executive Committee. Pająk boasted that he himself was a member of the Central Committee. He also said that the Cracow socialists were trying to set up a secret printing press, but he did not know if it was in operation yet.

Eventually Pająk described, in detail, the plan to assassinate Kostrzewski. To make matters worse, Pająk gave Czerwiński, who was to be released on 25 September, a note to take to the student Ludwik Dąbrowski. Though the note was written in cipher, Pająk had taught Czerwiński the key. The note communicated to Dąbrowski that the Central Committee had once more sentenced Kostrzewski to death and with him another officer, Swolkien. Czerwiński gave the note to Kostrzewski on 27 September and repeated everything Pająk had told him in the cell. On the next day, Czerwiński filed a signed affidavit with the Cracow court and left for Odessa.

The police now had the evidence they needed. On 12–17 November 1884, at a closed trial, Malankiewicz, Piechowski, Sułczewski, Pająk, Grudziński, Dąbrowski and Adam Królikowski, a journeyman turner, were prosecuted. In the course of the trial, most of the accused spoke freely of their socialist beliefs and of the socialist movement in Cracow. At the end of the trial, Roman Piechowski was sentenced to nine years in prison, Malankiewicz to five, Sułczewski to three and Pająk to one. Dąbrowski, Królikowski and Grudziński were acquitted.[157]

Throughout 1884, apparently with the help of the same Russian police agent, Czerwiński, the police made a clean sweep of the socialist movement in Cracow. Almost all local socialists were imprisoned, and one of the main local leaders, Wesołowski, died as a result of his stay in prison.[158]

Using conspiratorial methods, the police broke up the socialist conspiracy in Cracow. The clumsiness of the socialist conspirators and their poor judgment were the truest allies of the police. In 1884, the socialist movement in Cracow was decimated; years passed before it recovered from the blast of Malankiewicz's bomb.

A Conspiratorial Experiment in Lviv

Although liberty was not a deeply rooted tradition in the Habsburg empire, least of all not in autonomous Galicia, the civil liberties guaranteed by the Austrian constitution of 1867 offered socialists in Galicia the theoretical prospect of developing a legal mass movement. No "exceptional law," such as Bismarck introduced in Prussia, fettered the Galician socialists,[159] who made use of their freedom to publish a newspaper, *Praca,* and to hold a series of workers' meetings in Lviv. Socialists in Lviv had confidence in constitutionality and agitated for the complete democratization of the state. In the early 1870s Lassallean craftsmen in Lviv called for complete freedom of the press and association as well as for the extension of other civil liberties and the introduction of universal suffrage. The socialist programs of 1881 repeated these demands and submitted that in a democratic state the socialist revolution could take place peacefully.

The situation differed radically in Russia, where socialists were not allowed to propagate their doctrines openly among the working classes. The socialists in the Russian empire, deprived of the option of initiating a legal socialist mass movement, developed, broadly speaking, two distinct tactics for accomplishing the social revolution. The first of these tactics, advocated by Drahomanov among others, placed an indispensable prior condition on beginning socialist agitation among the masses: the transformation of Russia from an Oriental autocracy into a Western-style democracy. The second tactic urged defying the law and undertaking conspiratorial, often terrorist, action in order to precipitate a socialist revolution. Advocates of the latter tactic were Narodnaia volia and Proletariat.

When Waryński and other Polish socialists came to Galicia from the Congress Kingdom in 1878, they had brought with them the conspiratorial form of organization they had found necessary in the Russian empire: the division into cells, the secrecy and aliases. The socialists in Lviv objected to these methods and accused the émigrés of not understanding local conditions. In 1880, in a contribution to *Równość,* the Lviv socialists pointed to the arrest and trial of Waryński and company as a justification of their contention that conspiratorial socialism, while unavoidable and effective in Russia, had no basis in Galicia. Here it culminated in "a great fiasco"; the Cracow trial deprived Galician socialism of some of its most valued cadres and intimidated others from openly participating in the socialist movement.

The Lviv socialists held that even the "pseudoconstitutional structure" of Austria, especially the relative freedom of the press, of association and of assembly, did provide some opportunity for legal socialist activity. Although within the framework of the constitution socialists could propagate neither the core of their doctrine nor their entire program, the Galician masses in any case were not yet ready to accept the whole socialist program. To even interest the masses in socialism required preparatory work, for which legal methods sufficed.[160]

Despite these protestations of the futility of underground organization and of the pre-eminence of legal activity in Galicia, conspiratorial socialist cells appeared in Lviv in the summer of 1882.

In Cracow there had occurred, as it were, a "Russianization" of the socialist movement. Socialists from Russia had simply transplanted their movement there. In the Lviv movement, too, a "Russianization" had occurred, but not because its leaders were imported from the East. If Galician socialists in the mid-1880s assumed a Russian character, they were surpassed and preceded in this by the Galician authorities. The newspaper *Praca* labored under heavy censorship: well over half of its issues were confiscated in 1881–83.[161] The police forbade workers' meetings scheduled for 30 October 1881, 23 and 30 April 1882, and dissolved workers' meetings held on 4 December 1881 and 29 June 1882. The Galician police furthermore, arrested socialists with regularity. In Cracow alone, there were two trials against socialists in 1880, three in 1881, three in 1882, six in 1883 and four in 1884, involving a total of eighty-eight defendants.[162] The police in Eastern Galicia were simultaneously hounding the Ruthenian socialists, forcing Pavlyk to flee to Geneva in 1879. It reached the point that even Drahomanov, champion of legal action and one-time enthusiast of the Austrian constitution, became convinced by 1881 that "in reality the individual's rights in constitutional Galicia are in no way superior to those in unconstitutional Russia."[163]

A certain amount of underground socialist work had always coexisted with mass legal action in Lviv. In 1879–80, Franko taught political economy in workers' circles that apparently were not legally constituted.[164] There is a tradition, too, disputed by the Soviet historian M. M. Volianiuk, that in 1880–81 Mieczysław Mańkowski organized a hundred Lviv apprentices into secret socialist cells.[165] Also, there were contacts between the master conspirator Waryński in Geneva and socialists in Lviv. Waryński possibly visited Cracow and Lviv in March 1881, and he certainly sent an emissary to Lviv in September 1881 — his common-law spouse Anna Sieroszewska.[166]

But the real birth of conspiratorial socialism in Lviv, the formation of clandestine socialist cells, can be traced to July 1882; it was a direct response to the police's action in dissolving the workers' assembly held on 29 June 1882.[167]

The police suspected that certain socialists in Lviv, such as the shoemaker Jan Kozakiewicz, were deliberately trying to provoke the police into dissolving the workers' meetings in order to furnish a pretext for conspiratorial action. Kozakiewicz, who had joined Waryński's Social-Revolutionary Association of Poles in 1878, was a known partisan of conspiratorial socialism; he had argued the inefficacy of legal activity and the superiority of clandestine activity in articles in *Praca* in November 1881 and in May 1882.[168] In addition to Kozakiewicz, another shoemaker, Mykhailo Drabyk, was a partisan of extra-legal activity.[169] Drabyk was the first to found a socialist cell, in July 1882. Kozakiewicz and Kazymyr Tykhovsky, a third-year philosophy student at Lviv University, founded cells in August or September.

Each of the Lviv cells met weekly, either in the home of a member or in a park. During the meetings, members read and discussed socialist literature. Sometimes the cells' organizers held lectures showing how the wealthy, the clergy and the government exploited workers. If the socialists were unable to eliminate this pervasive exploitation through legal, parliamentary action, then they would fix as their task the total destruction of the existing order, the revolutionary destruction of the capitalist class.[170] The Lviv cells, apparently with this end in view, stockpiled explosives.[171]

Representatives of the several cells met on 12 November 1882 to discuss whether or not to form a tightly-knit organization. Drabyk supported the notion of a united organization, but his proposal to unite was defeated as premature.[172] Nonetheless, the very fact of the meeting and the fact that the various cells collaborated to issue a leaflet[173] points to some measure of coordinated effort. The Lviv and Cracow cells were also in contact with one another. They issued leaflets on the same themes and at one point the Cracow group answered a leaflet from Lviv with another leaflet. The Lviv and Cracow socialists corresponded and visited each other.[174]

One feature distinguishing the Lviv cells from the Cracow cells was Ruthenian participation. Of the three cells uncovered by the police, two were headed by Ruthenians (Drabyk and Tykhovsky). Of the twenty-six accused in Lviv in 1883, eight were Greek Catholic, i.e., ethnically

Ruthenian. Tykhovsky headed a "Ruthenian cell" that included among its members two other Ruthenian students, Ivan Kuzmych and Ivan Stronsky, and a Ruthenian secretary, Roman Hapii. Three Poles also belonged to the cell, but two of them, Fryderyk Kahofer and Adam Krajewski were, in a way, almost Ruthenians: they worked for *Strażnica Polska* (Polish Watchtower), a paper very interested in Ruthenian affairs and strongly Ukrainophile.[175]

The cells in Lviv did not last long. Arrests began in the second half of November 1882. On the 16th of November, the police arrested the brothers Ludwik and Michał Sosnowski, journeyman lacquerer and glazier respectively. The next day, they arrested Drabyk and the brothers Ivan and Mykhailo Hebak, journeyman cobbler and photographer's assistant respectively.

Faced with the immediate prospect of their own arrest, Kozakiewicz and Tykhovsky wrote a leaflet summoning the workers to resist the repression of their movement. The leaflet, entitled "The Lviv Socialist Commune to the Workers" and dated 22 November, was discussed by the socialist cells and disseminated on the night of 24–25 November. The socialists hectographed two hundred copies of the leaflet and posted them around Lviv. Handwritten copies of the leaflet were also in evidence and Geneva's *Przedświt* (Dawn) reprinted it.[176] In December the leaflet was found posted on the corners of Cracow's renaissance structures.

The leaflet decried the arrests of socialist workers in Vienna, Cracow and Lviv and, without specifying how, called upon the workers, "without distinction whether Pole, Ruthenian or German," to take up the cause of their own liberation. The leaflet ended with a Biblical sentiment: "A tooth for a tooth! An eye for an eye!"

The police arrested Kozakiewicz soon after the leaflet was written. The rest of November and December was filled with arrests of students and journeymen, especially journeymen cobblers. Arrests and searches continued into January and February, throwing Lviv into a minor panic. At one point the Jesuit church was closed on a Sunday, because of rumors that socialists were going to make a terrorist attack against it. According to Feliks Daszyński in *Praca*, police agents — to earn their keep —were reporting the most fantastic things,

> what one could only read in sensational romances. Every second person is a fearsome nihilist who eats dynamite for breakfast, quenches his thirst

with gasoline and smokes a torch instead of a cigar; every third building holds a den of anarchists; every grocer's shop is a storehouse of explosive materials.[177]

The trial of twenty-six arrested socialists began on 2 May 1883; most of the suspects had spent five months in investigative imprisonment before being brought to trial. During the course of the trial, Daszyński, whom the police had not arrested, prepared a new leaflet, which threatened the Galician authorities with terrorist reprisals for the repression of the socialist movement.[178] Denouncing the exploitation of the workers and the arrests of the socialists, it delineated two roads open to Galician workers. The first was the road of the "paper constitution." Daszyński urged making use of legal methods, i.e., gathering publicly at workers' assemblies to demand independent workers' organizations and universal suffrage. If this road were not open, then there was another road:

> Let us look about us — the people are stirring. . . . All of Europe trembles from the blast of bombs. . . . Dynamite is enlightenment . . . and amidst these deafening thunderclaps one can hear from one end to the other the slogan — "Proletarians of all countries, unite!" The hour of vengeance has struck — to work, o children of slavery!

Daszyński left it up to "our extortioners" to pick one or the other of the two roads. The leaflet bore the red seal of the Socialist Executive Committee.

Perhaps in reaction to Daszyński's threatening rhetoric, the sentences handed down on 10 May 1883 were harsher than any previous sentences of Lviv socialists had been. Drabyk was sentenced to eight months and twenty days; Kozakiewicz to eight months and ten days; Tykhovsky and Apolinary Kozaczek to six months; the others to four months or less.[179]

This brief conspiratorial interlude was, it seems, Lviv's last experiment with a structured, on-the-offense underground. The socialist movement in Lviv was hurt by the arrests of 1882, but not mortally wounded, because for Lviv there always existed that other dimension of socialist activity connected with the heritage of the old artisan movement. *Praca* continued to appear throughout the 1880s, though less regularly, and the socialists recovered enough to hold mass assemblies for journeymen in July and August 1883.

For Cracow, on the other hand, the suppression of the clandestine cells signified the suppression of the entire socialist movement, because organized conspiracy was all that Cracow had known since Waryński first appeared there in October 1878. In Cracow, too, unlike in Lviv, the socialists relied for reinforcement and leadership on Polish socialists from the Congress Kingdom. After the nearly complete suppression of Proletariat in Russia in 1884, this reservoir of activists dried up.

Chapter Four
Ukrainian Socialism

Ruthenian socialism in the formative years of the late 1870s and 1880s was confronted with three serious problems. First, the Ruthenian socialists were too weak to develop an independent, institutionalized movement of their own. This placed them before the dilemma of collaborating either with Polish socialists or national populist Ruthenians; neither alternative satisfied them. Their second problem was determining a class base: who was to be their "proletariat"? They looked first to the artisans, then to the oil workers of Boryslav and finally, perhaps even reluctantly, to the peasants. The need to work among the peasantry brought them face to face with their third and probably most serious problem: how to introduce their ideas into the villages. It was one thing to publish periodicals in Lviv. It was another thing to put those periodicals in the hands of the peasants. The national populists had relied on the Greek Catholic clergy to do this for them and that is why the clergy could, in effect, censor the ideological content of their publications. Now that the Ruthenian youth had embraced radical ideas, ideas opposed to the clergy and aimed in particular at the peasantry, how were they to get these ideas into the countryside?

The Dilemma of Ukrainian Socialism

Following the trial of January 1878, the Ruthenian socialists Ivan Franko and Mykhailo Pavlyk not only worked in the Polish socialist movement, but also continued what they had begun in the student periodical *Druh,* i.e., they brought radical ideas to the Ruthenian public. In April 1878, they published the first issue of a Ukrainian-language socialist periodical *Hromads'kyi druh* (Friend of the Commune). The title symbolized the journal's solidarity with Drahomanov's periodical *Hromada* (Commune) coming out in Geneva as well as its continuity with the radicalized *Druh.* A second issue of *Hromads'kyi druh* appeared in May, thereafter — in a vain attempt to avoid trouble with the police and censors — the periodical appeared as anthologies with the titles *Molot* (Hammer) and *Dzvin* (Bell). *Hromads'kyi druh, Molot* and *Dzvin* were published with the financial backing of Drahomanov and other socialists from the Russian empire.[1]

Pavlyk, editor of *Hromads'kyi druh,* intended the periodical for East Galician students as well as for the Ruthenian peasants. He conceived of the publication as a necessary supplement to the Polish-language paper *Praca,* which aimed at a readership among what he termed "the truly industrial workers," i.e., artisans, in Lviv.[2] Such a division of labor was rational, since artisans *were* almost exclusively Polish or Polonized. The first issue of *Hromads'kyi druh* came out in six hundred copies.[3]

The periodical and subsequent anthologies contained novels by both Franko — *Boa Constrictor* in the Boryslav cycle — and Pavlyk — *Propashchyi cholovik* (A Ruined Man) and *Rebenshchukova Tetiana,* a novel advocating free love. All three novels, and a translation from Zola, reflected the realist spirit. Both fiction and nonfiction concentrated on Galician social problems. Outstanding were Franko's "Critical Letters on the Galician Intelligentsia" and the series of budgets that described the income and expenses of a priest, country weaver and Lviv typesetter. The publications of 1878 were even more radical than *Druh* had been in 1876–77. Like its predecessor, *Hromads'kyi druh,* together with its subsequent anthologies, caught the attention, none too favorable, of the elder Ruthenians and the police.

Volodymyr Barvinsky, at that time the leading spokesman of the national populists, wrote a long diatribe against *Molot* for *Pravda,* which he edited. Barvinsky accused *Molot* of being altogether too negative, "characterized by a dark and melancholy outlook on the people's existence, on all of modern life, on the whole world."[4] The editor called attention to *Molot's* frequent use of the adjective "bourgeois," which he claimed was out of place in Galicia, a land with no bourgeoisie whatsoever. He took issue with the socialists' economic determinism and, above all, with their insistence on realism. While admitting that Franko's *Boa Constrictor* showed "considerable talent and originality," Barvinsky dismissed Pavlyk's *Propashchyi cholovik* as a novel that "reveals all the weak and irritating aspects of this imagined realism."[5]

The slings and arrows of the national populists were relatively innocuous. Provoking Barvinsky's displeasure only resulted in a hostile review in *Pravda*. But provoking the police, who considered the Ruthenian socialist publications "pamphlets of the worst sort,"[6] resulted in confiscations and imprisonment. The police confiscated both issues of *Hromads'kyi druh* as well as the anthologies *Dzvin* and *Molot*. Franko and Pavlyk, however, were successful most of the time in distributing the bulk of the press run before the police found out what they had published.[7]

The editor of these publications, Pavlyk, who — the police believed — "holds in his hands all the threads of socialist agitation in Galicia,"[8] became the target of persecution. Pavlyk had already stood trial twice, in March 1877 and in January 1878. In the 1878 trial, the jury sentenced him to three months in prison, which he served — after several months at liberty spent publishing — in the late summer and fall of 1878. Pavlyk was still serving his three-month term when, in September, he was put on trial again, this time for writing and publishing *Rebenshchukova Tetiana*; the novel, it was charged, slandered the rights of the church and denigrated the institution of marriage, both punishable offenses. At the trial, Pavlyk would not renounce his views on marriage, in fact he expounded them boldly, but so clumsily as to provoke great mirth in the courtroom. He asserted, among other things, that the state itself recognized free love in the form of civil marriage contracts that expired after three years. He also developed an analogy with the behavior of birds that only backfired in laughter. For Pavlyk, however, the trial was not in the least amusing: the verdict came out guilty and he could look forward to six more months in prison.[9]

Early in January 1879, the court told Pavlyk to report within eight days to begin serving his six-month sentence. Pavlyk fled instead to Drahomanov in Geneva. He stayed in Western Europe, helping Drahomanov and Serhii Podolynsky publish *Hromada,* until 1882. In that year he returned to Galicia, served his six months in prison and then stood trial again for various other writings. This time, in 1882, he was acquitted, but nonetheless administratively escorted to his native Monastyrske.[10]

In 1879–80, in Pavlyk's absence, no Ruthenian socialist periodical came out in Galicia, although Ivan Franko was trying to get off the ground a fortnightly journal to be called *Nova osnova* (New Foundation). Because he knew that the national populist organ *Pravda* was to fold early in 1879, Franko thought that *Nova osnova* could step into the vacuum and find a wide readership. He approached several Russian

Ukrainophiles, among them the writer Oleksander Konysky, for financial backing, but no one would support the journal. Early in 1880, Franko planned to travel to Russia to solicit backing, but he lacked the money for this journey.[11] He did, however, manage to put out a series of brochures in 1879–80. This "little library" (*Dribna biblioteka*), as it was called, offered literature as well as literary and social criticism. The fiction consisted mainly of translations, but Franko's socio-psychological study of his prison experiences, *Na dni* (On the Bottom), was also published in the series. Pocket editions of essays by Pisarev, Dobroliubov and Drahomanov appeared; Franko translated a chapter of Marx's *Capital,* too, but this did not make it into print.[12]

Franko did succeed in putting out a Ukrainian-language journal, *S'vit* (The World), in 1881–82. Ivan Belei edited the journal, but Franko's writings — from lyric poetry to social criticism — filled most of the pages. Realism was once again the literary credo, and a special feature of the journal was a series of biographies of the great Russian and Ukrainian realist writers. Darwin's biography also appeared in the journal, and fittingly, too, since Darwinism was an integral part of the journal's materialist ideology. Both Ostap Terletsky and Ivan Franko contributed articles that described class conflict in Darwinist terms, as a "struggle for existence."[13] *S'vit* was radical and socialist, but quite tactfully edited compared with Pavlyk's publications. It rarely ran afoul of the police. The journal was aimed at the young intelligentsia and came out in 150 copies. It folded in 1882 for financial reasons — too few subscribers. As Franko put it, "if [*Hromads'kyi druh*] collapsed under the blows of official persecution, then *S'vit* flickered out in public indifference."[14]

Public indifference, lack of funds and police persecution made it impossible for the Ruthenian socialists to publish their own periodical from 1882 until 1890, when *Narod* (The People) appeared. There were several false starts in the 1880s: Pavlyk planned a regular Ukrainian-language supplement to *Praca* in 1883, but this fell through because of disagreements with the Polish socialists;[15] Franko and some younger disciples planned a journal in 1885, but Russian Ukrainophiles refused to subsidize it; Franko tried again in 1886–87, but the authorities confiscated the very announcement advertising the projected journal;[16] in 1888, Franko, Pavlyk and a group of students succeeded in publishing only a single issue of the journal *Tovarysh* (Comrade).[17]

Unable to publish their own periodical, the Ruthenian socialists were faced with the dilemma: either to work within the Polish socialist and left-wing press — at the price of neglecting their own nation — or to work within the Ukrainophile press — at the price of muting their social radicalism. They did both, usually unhappily, until 1890, the year the Ruthenian-Ukrainian Radical Party came into existence.

We have already seen Franko at work in the Polish socialist movement in Lviv as editor of *Praca* and coauthor of the January 1881 Program of the Galician Socialists. He left off contributing to *Praca* in 1881, partly because he could no longer afford to live in Lviv and so abandoned the city for the country, and partly because he was coming to doubt the value of expending so much effort on Polish artisans. Unquestionably, too, such incidents as Limanowski's misprinting of the 1881 program title discouraged him. He never worked intimately in the Polish socialist movement after 1881.

After some cooperation with the national populists in the mid-1880s, Franko returned to cooperation with a Polish social movement — populism. From 1886 until 1897, Franko earned his living as a Polish-language journalist, working for the publications of Bolesław Wysłouch, the founder of Polish populism.[18]

Wysłouch's political philosophy appealed to Franko inasmuch as it sought to elevate the peasantry materially and intellectually.[19] Franko was to grow less comfortable, however, with Wysłouch's nationalism, his concern to make Polish state independence "the cause of a dozen or so million people,"[20] i.e., the Polish peasants. As Wysłouch's populism took root, its nationalism became more and more explicit and Franko, as a Ruthenian, looked for a way out. Already in 1888, he considered emigrating to America to edit a newspaper for Ruthenian immigrants, telling Drahomanov:

> The pay is God knows what, some fifty dollars a month. This means just a little more than we get here at [Wysłouch's] *Kurjer Lwowski* [Lviv Courier]. But nevertheless it will be a chance to work not for others but for our own people.[21]

But Franko could not leave the paper — it was a matter of supporting his wife and children and feeding a voracious addiction to books. By the 1890s he was thoroughly unhappy. In October 1894 he complained to Drahomanov:

> You ask me what work I'm doing in *Kurjer Lwowski*? In your understanding of the word "work," I'm doing "nothing or very little," but nonethe-

less I'm making enough to eat and without it there's no way I could live. *Kurjer Lwowski* is still the most respectable of the Polish periodicals in Lviv, but I can't sympathize with its policy, especially with the policy that's come to the top lately — the Polish patriotic policy. Of course, I am unable to make *Kurjer Lwowski* go against this policy or even take a neutral stand. So I reward at least myself: I write about those things that lie outside the phraseology of Polish and Ruthenian patriotism, about social and parliamentary affairs, etc. For sure, I am very unhappy about sitting on the editorial board of a paper with which I can feel less and less solidarity — but what am I to do? Where can I turn?[22]

There was another reason, too, Franko hesitated to leave the Polish press: his aversion to the alternative — working with the Ruthenian national populists. By the latter 1880s, he preferred, he let it be known, to earn his bread working for the Poles rather than to accept "penal servitude" with the national populists.[23]

Pavlyk was far more sensitive to Polish nationalism than Franko. Like Drahomanov, he always suspected Polish socialists of plotting to resurrect Poland in its historical boundaries, i.e., with large territories inhabited by non-Poles: Lithuanians, Belorussians and Ruthenians/ Ukrainians.[24] While staying in Geneva, Pavlyk contributed reports on Ruthenian and Ukrainian socialism to Eduard Bernstein's *Jahrbuch für Sozialwissenschaft und Sozialpolitik*. These reports often polemized with the Poles. In one report, Pavlyk outlined the conditions under which "an anarchist federalism between [socialist] Ruthenians and Poles in Galicia" could come into being. Polish socialists had to confine their agitation to Western Galicia unless they were willing to adopt the Ruthenian nationality or unless they were working with Polish or Polonized workers in the cities. Polish socialists could entertain no hopes of restoring the Polish state with its old boundaries.[25]

After returning to Galicia, serving his six-month prison term and spending a few months in Monastyrske, Pavlyk moved to Lviv to edit *Praca*. His stint as editor of *Praca* was short, lasting from February until mid-March 1883, and he left Lviv for Kolomyia in June.[26] In Pavlyk's last days as editor of *Praca,* Karl Marx died and Pavlyk wrote in his memory a very revealing and controversial obituary, which Witold Piekarski denounced in *Przedświt* as a display of "idiocy" and "the most shameful ignorance."[27]

Pavlyk could not forgive Marx, the German centralist, his attacks upon Bakunin, the Slavic federalist. He felt that Marx and other German socialists were as hostile to the Slavic nationalities as were

"Bismarck and the German 'Kulturträger'!" Marx was a despot — he showed this by the way he ran the International — and his despotism proceeded logically from his conception of the future structure of society. Pavlyk saw Marx's ideal as a people's state (*Volksstaat*), highly centralized, ruled by the proletariat, kept in order by the police, detrimental to the freedom of individuals, communities, working-class associations and whole nations. Pavlyk believed that only an anarchist federation, the free association of free associations, could guarantee the liberation that socialism promised. Marx's centralist-socialist people's state was, in Pavlyk's words, "simply a utopia." Marx's plan could only find adherents among socialists of the state nations — Germans and Russians, but also Poles, who lacked a state but not the dream of historical Poland. Because of the centralization favored by Marx, the slogan "Proletarians of all countries, unite!" really translated as "Nations of the Russian and German empires, Russify and Germanize yourselves!" The socialists of oppressed nations could not adhere to Marx's ideology.

It was Marx's centralist spirit, Pavlyk felt, that led him to champion the cause of Polish independence. Marx chanted the slogan

> "Long live (historical) Poland!" and he didn't mind, or else he didn't know, that this slogan means nothing other than "Long live the Polish upper classes in Ukraine, Lithuania and Belorussia," exploiting the Ukrainian, Lithuanian and Belorussian peasantry, who show they have a right to their own land and who, in every respect, *want complete freedom of action.* . . .[28]

Pavlyk's rejection of Marxism, as the socialism of "state nations," was a position he shared with, and took from, Drahomanov.[29] Franko also came to hold this view by the mid-1880s. It was connected with their suspicions that the Polish socialists hoped to restore Poland in its historical boundaries and their insistence on the need to work for the liberation of the peasantry. In these circumstances, it is little wonder that Franko and Pavlyk left off working for the superficially Marxist Polish artisan movement in Lviv.

Both Franko and Pavlyk, after giving up on Polish socialism, tried their luck with the Ruthenian national populists. Franko was the first to do so, becoming a regular contributor to their papers *Dilo* (Deed) and *Zoria* (Star) in 1883. Drahomanov (and, for a while, Pavlyk) disapproved of Franko's cooperation with the national populists, viewing it as a form of apostasy, a return to Ruthenism. Drahomanov insisted that Franko and other radical Ruthenians work independently: "You must establish from among ourselves a community of progressives."[30] There could be no diluting social radicalism to please the Ruthenes, no compromise with the Ukrainophiles: "If an organism is still not able to take a quart of milk, then give it a tenth of a quart, but milk, not ink or milk mixed with ink!"[31] Drahomanov's impatience led him to extremes that seemed likely to destroy his friendship with Franko. At one point, in April 1886, he was ready to send letters to Kiev to protest the activities of Franko and his Galician associates, and he told Franko: "We are able to help each other out, but the former friendship between us can be no more."[32] Franko objected to Drahomanov's dictates from Geneva: "Let me say that I, here, on the spot, know what's best."[33]

Franko knew from experience that the Ruthenians could not maintain an independent left-wing journal. Nevertheless, in November of 1886, Franko took the step Drahomanov had been urging: he set forth a clear program for a new Ukrainian-language journal to be called *Postup* (Progress). The program was Drahomanovian to the core.[34] This patched up relations with Drahomanov, but had little political efficacy: the prospectus for the new periodical was confiscated by the police and *Postup* never saw the light of day. Franko was forced back to the choice between progressive Poles and politically incompatible conationals.

In the Ruthenian national populist press, Franko used "the language of facts and figures" to explore Galician social and political life.[35] Although he could neither advocate radical solutions to the problems of Galician society nor take the national populists and clergy to task, he could use the Ruthenian press to develop a thorough critique of the politics of the Polish *szlachta,* especially in the spheres of education, agrarian relations and Diet and parliamentary politics. He also used the Ruthenian press to reflect on the Polish question as a whole, standing up for the principles of an ethnic Poland ("Poland is the Polish peasantry and . . . where there is no such peasantry — there, too, is no Poland"),[36] opposing the idea of restoring Poland in its historical boundaries:

> Whoever takes a look at the history of the Polish insurrections in our century — in 1831, 1846, 1848 and 1863 — whoever does so will read in it a history of systematic and incurable blindness, a history written in characters of blood. Time and time again, facts without pity, facts that cry out, have told [the Poles] that in our century the idea of the old Polish

state, the idea of historical Poland, must be considered obsolete and
irrevocably lost. With a stubbornness worthy of a better cause, with an
enthusiasm provoking profound regret, with a truly tragic fatalism, one
generation after another has hurled itself into the fathomless abyss and
perished. Time and time again they have been forced to recognize that
all the peasants of the former Polish lands — without regard to nationality — repulse even the mementos of historical Poland.[37]

Work in the national populist press allowed Franko to express
himself fully on the Polish question, something he could not do even in
the left-wing Polish press. The Polish socialists in Galicia, after all,
held sacred the memory of the insurrections and the insurgent heroes.
Although the national populists tolerated, even encouraged, Franko's
views in regard to Polish affairs, they suppressed his analysis of
Ruthenian politics and society. Franko rebelled against the constraint
and in January 1885 contributed an article critical of the national
populists to the Polish paper *Kurjer Lwowski*. The day after the article
appeared, *Dilo* fired Franko. The national populists took Franko back
(not *Dilo*, but *Zoria*) in September 1885. He lasted one more stormy
year in the Ruthenian press, continuing to criticize the national
populists in the Polish press. The national populists were at a loss:
Franko was too brilliant a writer to lose, but too restless to harness as
they wished. Franko was expelled from the Ruthenian press in
September 1886.[38]

The whole experience with *Dilo* and *Zoria* had so soured Franko on
the national populists that for some time afterwards he wanted to have
nothing further to do with those who he felt had debased him. The
trouble with working for the national populists, he confided to a
friend, was that they treated a man like a dog treats a piece of bread:
before consuming the bread, the dog toys with it and knocks it to the
ground.[39] Pavlyk also had brief and unpleasant experiences working
with the national populists, particularly from the fall of 1888 to the
summer of 1889, when he edited *Bat'kivshchyna* (Patrimony) until he
was expelled for radicalism.[40]

In the early phases of Ruthenian socialist activity, in 1878–82,
Franko and Pavlyk had created a limited, but independent forum of
opinion in the journals *Hromads'kyi druh* and *S'vit*. These attempts at
independent work were, as the reaction of the public and the police
had shown, premature. What emerges clearly from a study of Franko's
and Pavlyk's peregrinations from Polish socialist to Ruthenian national
populist to Polish populist press is that Ruthenian socialists were

misfits in Galician political and intellectual life. They had to express themselves on Polish affairs in the Ruthenian press and on Ruthenian affairs in the Polish press. The ideas they had could not find total expression in the existing media.

Boryslav

The isolation of the Ruthenian socialists was complete. Unlike the Polish socialists, the Ruthenians were not compensated for their isolation from other political groupings by activity among a Ruthenian working class. In the case of the Poles, it mattered little if the Polish intelligentsia was hostile to the socialist movement, so long as the artisans were not. But in the Ruthenian case, that mass constituency was absent. As long as the Ruthenian socialists worked in Lviv within the Polish socialist movement, they worked among artisans, a mass constituency, but not a *Ruthenian* mass constituency. Where was the social basis for the Ruthenian movement to be found? In the early 1880s, Ivan Franko believed that this basis could be provided by the Ruthenian oil workers in Boryslav and Drohobych.

The land around Boryslav was rich in oil and ozocerite (earth wax), and in the 1870s some 15,000 workers, about half of whom were Ruthenians, retrieved and refined these mineral resources.[41] The oil boom in Galicia is demonstrated by the rapid growth of the population of its offspring, Boryslav. In 1857, Boryslav was a village of 646 inhabitants; in 1869, a town of 5,300; in 1890, a city of 12,000.[42]

Franko quite literally grew up with Boryslav and the oil industry. He was born in 1856 in the village Nahuievychi not far from Drohobych and Boryslav. Emil Haecker felt that this circumstance was decisive in the formation of Franko's outlook. While Pavlyk "became ossified in Drahomanovism," Franko was a more West European type of socialist, closer to Marxism. In Drohobych and Boryslav he was witness to the misery created by capitalism's first hesitant steps in Galicia, a misery that left an indelible impression on the young Franko, discernible in his literary works.[43]

Franko first heard accounts of the petroleum workers as a child in his father's smithy, where men would gather and tell tales about the calamities in the oil and ozocerite mines. Oil work was at that time very dangerous, since the workers were lowered on ropes into the depths of the wells, the shafts of which were poorly supported, the air of which was thin and mixed with poisonous and combustible gases. Explosions, cave-ins, broken ropes and asphyxiation were frequent occurrences in the oil and wax fields.

Franko learned more about the oil fields after 1865, when his blacksmith father died and his mother married a petroleum worker, Hryn Havrylyk. One of Franko's close childhood friends in the mid-1860s was Yasko Romanovsky, the son of an oil worker. They used to visit the oil and ozocerite fields together. Yasko's father was severely burned as a result of an explosion. Franko long remembered the elder Romanovsky suffering in the hospital and the fact that the permanently crippled worker never received any compensation, neither from the company he worked for nor from the state.[44]

The powerful impression this environment made on Franko inspired his "Boryslav cycle," a series of stories and novels portraying the life, customs and struggle of the oil workers. The cycle, one of the outstanding achievements of Ukrainian literature, began with the story "Oilman" published in *Druh* in 1877 and included the novel *Boryslav Laughs* (1881), based on the petroleum workers' strike of 1873. Franko also, in 1882, published a collection of oil workers' folklore in the journal *S'vit*.[45]

For some time Franko believed that the oilmen were the true Galician proletariat, the segment of the working class destined to lead the social revolution. In September 1880 Franko, then living in his native Nahuievychi, submitted a report on the Drohobych workers to *Praca*. In the preface to his report, he chided the Galician socialists for being too concerned with artisans and not at all with the real proletariat:

> The life of factory workers has until now hardly been discussed at all in *Praca*. This fact is at once curious and saddening. It shows that the intellectual movement in the direction of progress and the liberation of the working class has reached out to this mass of workers the least. And in the countries of Western Europe it is precisely the factory workers who stand at the head of this movement! But in our land it's just the opposite. Here printers, tailors and in general workers of crafts or manufacture are in the forefront of the movement while nothing at all is even heard of the factory workers.[46]

Later, in 1882, and again in 1885, Franko urged Pavlyk to move the center of Ruthenian socialist activity to Drohobych, since it was the workers of the industrial Boryslav petroleum region, in his view, who would be the leaders of the Galician movement.[47]

The oilmen, however, were not, as Franko thought, a disciplined and militant proletariat, conscious of its own interests. Their protests consisted of sporadic and elemental outbursts directed against practices that cheated them of their full day's wage (e.g., fines for insubordination or tardiness, payment in tokens instead of cash).

In 1873, at the end of the wave of strikes in Lviv, a strike also broke out in a refining factory in Boryslav. Three hundred factory operatives went on strike to protest payment practices, they were joined by other oil workers, somehow the oil works caught on fire, and police and gendarmes were sent in.[48] Later, in May 1881, three hundred workers rioted in Boryslav, again in protest of sharp payment practices. The gendarmes were once again sent in and one worker was mortally wounded while fighting them.[49] Another workers' disturbance erupted in Boryslav in July 1884 involving thousands of men, with thirty-two wounded and thirty arrested.[50]

These disturbances were not the organized actions of class-conscious workers. The July 1884 riot demonstrates how little workers' solidarity meant in Boryslav and how ignorant the oilmen were in matters of class interest. The riot of 1884 turned Boryslav into the battlefield of a vicious civil war, not a civil war between workers, on the one hand, and paymasters, storekeepers and mine owners, on the other, but a civil war between Jewish and Christian workers. Armed with staves, axes and stones, three thousand Jewish workers attacked the barracks of Christian workers. They did this in retaliation for the action of a band of Christian workers, who had previously attacked and destroyed a Jewish school. The hostilities had originally been touched off by a minor incident — a quarrel between a Christian and two Jews in suburban Volianka.[51]

The ethnic strife that broke out in July 1884 had long been brewing under the surface in Boryslav, where Ruthenian miners working for Jewish mine owners composed anti-Semitic folk songs and prophecies.[52] The Ruthenian miners in 1884, however, were not fighting Jewish mine owners, but Jews who were workers like themselves. Ethnic, intra-worker civil war had replaced the class struggle. But this does not exhaust the backwardness of the 1884 riot. The workers' civil war was fought against the background of French capital driving out Jewish capital, of the transition from numerous small oil wells owned, in the main, by local Jewish investors to foreign-dominated petroleum monopolies. In the 1884 riot, the chief battles were fought between Christian workers of a French-owned company and Jewish workers of the Jewish competition. The battle lines were determined, then, not only by ethnicity/religion, but by corporate allegiance.[53] Thus did the proletariat of Boryslav defend its interests. In fact the first major class-conscious, organized strikes of the Galician oil and wax workers did not take place until 1901 and 1904.[54]

Several factors probably accounted for the relative backwardness of the Boryslav petroleum workers. Neither Drohobych nor, least of all, Boryslav was a major cultural or political center like Lviv and Cracow. The oil workers therefore benefited less from the organizational efforts of the intelligentsia. Unlike the artisans, moreover, the oil workers were neither literate nor travelled and did not learn to organize themselves on their own initiative.

Extractive industry tends to be the most backward form of industry under capitalism (significantly, this was Galicia's most advanced form of industry). Workers in extractive industries often are in an amphibious state between agricultural and industrial workers. This was especially true of Galicia's oil and ozocerite workers. Most of the locally-recruited, i.e., unskilled, laborers in oil and ozocerite were peasants or at least intimately bound to the economy of the surrounding countryside. Franko, by 1882, already began to refer to the Boryslav miners as "peasants" (krest'iane, muzhiki) instead of "workers."[55] The peasant nature of the Boryslav worker is shown by the seasonal variance in the labor supply: the industry had the largest number of workers in the winter, the smallest during the harvest.[56] The petroleum workers were investing their earnings in land, and regarded their work in the oil pits as a supplementary source of income.[57] They did not, as Franko thought at first, constitute an industrial proletariat, but rather a special branch of the village proletariat, of the impoverished Galician peasantry forced to surrender life and limb to the shafts of Boryslav.

Franko and the Agrarian Question

In the middle of the 1880s, Ivan Franko abandoned his allegiance to the classic Marxian vision. He no longer believed that the industrial working class would be the leading class in the Galician revolution. He had looked for that class in Lviv, but found only artisans; he looked again in Boryslav, but he found only the village proletariat. He came to believe that Galician progressives — by this time he was less fond of labelling himself a socialist — should concentrate their attention on the peasantry. Drahomanov and Pavlyk had held this to be true from the beginning. What was for Franko a conclusion had been for them a premise.

Because Franko had been schooled in Marxism, in a body of thought that gave priority to the analysis of socio-economic processes, Franko — more so than Drahomanov or Pavlyk — took pains to understand the larger economic processes at work (or significantly not at work) in Galicia and to develop a political and economic program suited to Galicia's situation.

Franko argued that Galicia simply did not have capitalist industry and commerce. "And even for their creation in the future there is no hope," because "Galicia is a crownland economically dependent on Western capital, markets and products" and "all attempts to emancipate itself from these influences have so far resulted and will for a long time yet result in a dreary fiasco."[58]

Franko therefore turned his attention to the agrarian question, especially to the question of land holding in Galicia, "the main axis around which revolve all the [social and political] relations of our crownland." He felt that this focus was "perfectly natural in a land with such a frail development of industry, with small, semi-agricultural cities and towns, in a land whose representation [in parliament] is almost nine tenths composed of the owners of large landed estates, therefore farmers, and in which over 80 percent of the population is engaged in agriculture."[59] Franko's analysis of the agrarian question in Galicia was sufficiently expert to warrant presentation here; it will serve the dual purpose of revealing Franko's views and outlining the important socio-economic processes in the countryside.

The most characteristic feature of Galician agriculture in the latter nineteenth century was the consolidation of large estates and the parcellation of small holdings. Using statistics from 1819, 1859, 1876, Franko calculated that in these years, the number of large estates (manorial holdings) declined in the proportion 100:46:25, while at the same time the average size of such holdings grew in the proportion 100:173:350. The number of small (rustical) holdings increased in the proportion 100:154:275, and the size of the holdings shrank in the proportion 100:67:37.[60] Behind these statistics were millions of personal tragedies as peasant fathers left their sons and daughters ever smaller plots of land.

There were many burdens on the Galician peasantry that hastened its proletarianization. The very manner of the peasants' liberation in 1848 placed two weighty economic burdens on the shoulders of the peasant small holder: indemnization payments and claims for "servitudes." For political reasons, the central government in Vienna had promised in 1848 that the central government itself would pay the Galician land owners compensation for the abolition of serfdom. In the 1850s, however, the central government shifted the burden of compensation from the state treasury to Galicia's own treasury, i.e., to the Galician peasantry. Poorly managed terms of payment and amortization led to outlandish supplementary taxes for the peasants.[61]

Furthermore, emancipation left the peasants without the feudal rights to the manors' forests and pastures. The peasants felt entitled to these forest and pasture rights, called "servitudes," and involved themselves in bitter court cases with the manor to retrieve them. In the *szlachta* fiefdom of Galicia, the peasants rarely won suits against the manor. By 1881, there had been 32,000 court cases involving claims for servitudes. The peasants lost 30,000 of the cases and Franko estimated that they paid 15 million gulden in court costs.[62]

Another burden on the peasantry was "propination" — the manor's monopolistic concession on the production and distribution of alcoholic beverages.[63] Propination, in one form or another, lasted into the twentieth century. While such vestiges of feudalism were retained, other measures were introduced to aid in the capitalist transformation of the countryside. The Galician Diet in 1868 lifted all restrictions on usury,[64] which accelerated the proletarianization of the peasantry.

Various schemes were proposed to rescue the peasants from destruction. The Stańczyks favored changing the inheritance laws to introduce compulsory primogeniture in land to prohibit the division of holdings among heirs. Landless sons, the Stańczyks suggested, might go to work in industry or commerce. "This plan," wrote Franko, "looks very good on paper, but against it we might raise, I suppose, this objection: it ignores the past, the present and the future." It ignored the past, because under serfdom and even later the principle of the indivisibility of rustical lands existed formally on paper, but nonetheless peasants tacitly divided their plots. It ignored the present by ignoring peasant customary law, the unrestrained influence of capitalism in agricultural relations as well as the fact that small land holdings were already so divided and parcelled that to preserve the status quo would be to condemn the overwhelming mass of the population to gradual annihilation. It ignored the future, because "it expels the major part of future generations from the land and thrusts them into the dark corner called industry and commerce . . . of which we have almost none at all."[65]

Franko also rejected other schemes favored by the Stańczyks, such as the parcellation of manor estates for sale to the peasantry in patches.[66] He was sure this would only be done to cheat the peasantry (and Franko's suspicion was, indeed, proven true in practice).[67] Franko rejected the parcellation schemes, too, because he hoped that peasant communes would buy up manor estates whole, and not piecemeal, in order to farm collectively.

Inspired by Henry George, August Theodor Stamm and Michael Flürscheim,[68] Franko developed a plan to nationalize the land in Galicia for cooperative agricultural production. The land, he argued, was by nature the common property of the whole nation; private property in land *cum jure utendi et abutendi* was immoral. Peasants had a *right* to plots of land large enough to support themselves and their families. Since, however, there was not sufficient land for every peasant to own an independent homestead that could maintain his family, it was necessary to establish collective farms and, in general, to encourage collectivity in agricultural production as the only antidote to proletarianization.[69] Franko's agrarian program became the basis of the economic program of the Ruthenian-Ukrainian Radical Party in 1890.

Social Conflict in the Awakening Village[70]

If Ruthenian socialism were to concentrate on the agrarian question and seek its constituency among the peasantry, it had somehow to reach out into the village. A small group of intellectuals in Lviv could not hope to make the circuit of thousands of rural communities, then teach the largely illiterate peasants to read and then put into their hands publications with the proper ideological slant. This was not a problem that the Polish socialists had faced: artisans could read and they were concentrated in urban centers. It was, however, a problem that the Ruthenian *national* movement had begun to face some ten years before the emergence of the Ruthenian socialist movement in 1878.

The national populists in Lviv had also required a popular constituency. They succeeded in introducing their ideas into the village thanks
to the cooperation, albeit conditional, of the Greek Catholic clergy. The
pastors in the villages began, in the late 1860s and early 1870s, to bring
the national movement into the countryside. Often in connection with
the temperance movement, priests founded reading clubs (*chytal'ni*) in
their parishes. There were only a handful of these clubs in the 1870s, but
hundreds in the 1880s and thousands by the turn of the century. In the
reading club, the minority of literate peasants would read aloud to their
unlettered neighbors. They read popular newspapers and booklets filled
with information on saints, agricultural technique and, especially, politics. The peasant began to become aware of his or her national identity,
so that in a very real sense the growth of the network of reading clubs
was synonymous with the growth of the nation.

Some peasants emerged as leaders of the reading clubs. They would
send reports to the popular newspapers describing the conditions in
their villages, especially the progress there of the national movement.
They would also undertake ambitious programs to reform their villages
by founding cooperative stores and loan funds and by running for
election in the village government. The reformers frequently came into
conflict with three entrenched elites in the villages who opposed the
reading clubs: the tavern keepers who doubled as money lenders, the
wealthy peasants who ran the village government and the priests who
had often founded the reading clubs in the first place.

The tavern and the reading club were always at odds, and understandably, since the reading clubs were often, especially at first, associated
with the clerically sponsored temperance movement, and the clubs
never stopped competing with the taverns for the leisure time of the
villagers. The reading club looked upon the tavern as the temple of
ignorance, while the tavern perceived the reading club as a serious rival.
The tavern keeper generally also lent money to the peasants, and he
feared the competition of the mutual aid societies that the reading clubs
fostered. The natural antagonism between the peasant and the money
lender, and between the reading club and the tavern, was augmented by
a religious and ethnic difference: the peasants and reading clubs were
Ruthenian, but the money lenders and tavern keepers were predominantly Jewish. The antagonism between the "Jews"[71] and the Ruthenian
peasants was ancient, but the national awakening in the countryside
changed the forms the conflict assumed and, if we may so speak, the

balance of power. In the seventeenth and eighteenth centuries, the Ruthenian peasants were liable from time to time to rise in revolt and massacre the Jews in the villages. In the late nineteenth century, however, they were more likely to organize alternative, independent institutions that put more economic power into Ruthenian hands. The fierce jacqueries of the past had never liberated the peasantry; the "Jews" would always return, so indispensable was their socio-economic role. But in the late nineteenth century the emerging Ruthenian institutions began to take on the same social and economic functions as the tavern and lender and therefore began to supplant them.

The national awakening in the countryside also brought into the open another conflict in the village — between richer and poorer peasants. The wealthier peasants controlled the village government; their monopoly was a result of the village electoral system, which was heavily weighted in favor of the more prosperous. The village government (consisting of the chief or *viit,* scribe and councilmen) frequently abused its considerable powers to punish restive peasants and to grow rich at the others' expense. The reading clubs proved a thorn in the side of the village elites, because they often monitored the village government's revenue and expenditures as well as advanced candidates to replace incumbents considered unworthy. Moreover, the reading clubs and village governments often opposed one another on whom to support as a deputy to parliament and the Diet. In the countryside, elections to Diet and parliament were indirect. The villages would choose a few electors, usually the chief and a councilman or two, and these electors would then participate in the direct elections. The electors would often be bribed or threatened by the landlord to vote for the Polish candidate. As long as there was no reading club in the village, an elector could get away with this. But a reading club would make the elector very uncomfortable if he did not support the Ruthenian candidate.[72]

Another antagonism that came to the fore in the village was the conflict between priests and peasants. The priests at first supported the reading-club movement and provided it with leadership. But as peasants came to assume control of the reading clubs, the harmony between the pastor and his parishioners was strained. As long as the peasant was ignorant, the priest was regarded as the font of all wisdom. But when the peasant began to read or listen to newspapers, he also began to question the priest's authority. Latent economic conflict became overt as the reading clubs agitated for a reduction in the fees for sacramental rites or demanded that the priest share his pasture. The priest had endowed the peasants with new intellectual and organizational resources, but these resources could be turned against him.

Thus, as the national movement made progress in the villages, it awakened latent social conflicts, while simultaneously raising the cultural level and political effectiveness of the peasantry. At this point we are ready to see what happened when deliberate radical agitation exacerbated the social antagonism in the awakening village.

Radical Agitation in the Countryside

In the 1870s and 1880s, Ruthenian socialists attempted to propagate their doctrines in the villages of Galicia. These first efforts at radical agitation were ephemeral, marginal social phenomena involving only a small number of peasants. The history of the agitation is complicated, convoluted by many personal and familial rivalries and obscured by gaps and contradictions in the sources. The agitation is worth surveying, nonetheless, as it was an experiment that revealed much about the peasantry's grasp of a modern ideology and about the place of radicalism in the changing village.

Socialism in Kosiv

Anna Pavlyk was the first to conduct socialist agitation among the peasants. Her efforts were confined to the Pavlyks' native village Monastyrske, and to surrounding villages in the Kosiv region. Her brother Mykhailo did much to publicize the movement she initiated, but his account greatly inflated the significance of Kosiv socialism.[73] Ivan Franko complained to him in 1881 that the Kosiv movement was "neither as extensive nor as socialistic as you have presented it."[74]

The agitation began late in 1876 when Mykhailo Pavlyk sent home to his sister a packet of socialist brochures in the Ukrainian language. That Anna read the brochures aloud to some of her neighbors was not unusual. Their pastor, Rev. Yakiv Sinhalevych, like many another Greek Catholic priest, was active in the temperance movement; in an effort to replace the tavern as the center of activity on Sundays and holidays, he had instituted the custom of gathering on free days to listen to a public reading by one of the literate parishioners. Usually the pastor himself selected the reading. But in the case of Anna's reading, her brother (who, the neighbors knew, was a university student in the capital and an educational activist in the parish) substituted his authority for that of the priest. Anna's readings were in the tradition of Sunday readings, except that the texts were such as Father Sinhalevych would never have chosen for his parish's edification. The brochures Anna read were directed against the landlords, government and clergy and summoned the peasants to a socialist revolution. Anna, in a letter to Mykhailo, boasted that five peasants "understood something from these books."[75]

Anna was deeply impressed by the brochures. She began to complain that priests charged exorbitant fees for christenings, burials and other sacramental services, that priests told others to drink only water but themselves became drunk on wine with the landlords and that while at most a rich peasant might have five cows, a well-off priest or landlord had fifty. In her parish, a booklet of the temperance society was found with inscriptions, probably written by Anna, attacking the sobriety campaign.[76]

According to the Kosiv police, Anna would go about the neighboring villages, sometimes for weeks at a time without returning home, and gather village girls on the pretext of teaching them sewing, but really in order to carry on socialist propaganda. The Kosiv authorities grew suspicious; so, too, did the Lviv police, who had read Anna's letters to Mykhailo. By order of the Lviv court, gendarmes searched the Pavlyk home in Monastyrske in June 1877. In the next month, Anna was arrested. She stood trial in Lviv in January 1878 together with her brother and the other editors of *Druh*. The jury sentenced Anna to a month in prison.[77]

After her release, Anna did not abandon her agitation. Nor did the Kosiv authorities abandon their investigation. Anna was arrested again at the end of January 1879 after receiving a package of twelve copies of *Molot*, the radical anthology published by her brother. The police also arrested Mykola Kinailiuk, Stepan Pistuniak and Andrii Pyptiuk. All were accused of belonging to a secret socialist society.[78]

Kinailiuk, Pistuniak and Pyptiuk were craftsmen-peasants of Monastyrske. Kinailiuk was a tanner, but the others were weavers. Another suspected socialist, Vasyl Lysaniuk, was also a weaver; so, too, was Ivan Pavlyk, father of Mykhailo and Anna.[79] Austrian and Czech factory imports were destroying Galician cottage industry, especially weaving, in the mid-nineteenth century,[80] and this probably predisposed the village weaver to radicalism.

Among the more interesting points of this case were two attempts to proselytize local Jews. According to the testimony of Samuel Engler, money lender and tavern keeper, sometime in early 1879 (either while Anna was living in Kolomyia or had already been imprisoned), Pistuniak and Pyptiuk invited Engler to Pistuniak's home. They wanted Engler to read them a book and they would even pay him for this. The peasants said that the books, sent to them by the student Pavlyk, were in Ruthenian. "And if I read these books," Engler recounted, "then all Jews would join their group and the landlords would no longer be the masters . . . but they, that is, the peasants would be the masters." Engler declined on the grounds that he neither read Ruthenian nor had any desire to become anyone's master. Engler asked them why they did not take their books to the pastor to be read. Pistuniak and Pyptiuk replied that they could not do so "because these books are also directed against priests."[81]

Earlier, in the winter of 1877–78, Kinailiuk had attempted to convert another innkeeper, Szmaja Krauthamer. Krauthamer told the Kosiv police the following story in March 1879:

> Just last year Mykola Kinailiuk was in the habit of coming to my tavern and at that time he boasted more than once that he receives books from [Mykhailo] Pavlyk . . . , that these books are very instructive since [Pavlyk] has studied to become a philosopher and that he, i.e., Mykola Kinailiuk, is currently devoting himself diligently to studying these books, which promise the peasants a happy future.
>
> For these books maintain that the peasants will have it good only after they get rid of courts of law and introduce an equal division of property among all, but to do this they must first do away with all landowners and Jews. . . .
>
> He often explained by means of example the structure of the future society. For example, he said that if someone has two cows and Szmajko, i.e., myself, has no cow, then they will take one cow away from the person who has two and give that one to me. But it also worked the other way around. If I had two overcoats, then they would take one away from me and give it to someone who had no overcoat. He who has no money will be free to go to someone who has money and take it from him.
>
> For nothing can justify the people working for the lords, i.e., working so that lords get good money, go to casinos and smoke expensive tobaccos, while in the meantime the people have to do hard work. . . .
>
> Such were the doctrines he was in the habit of expounding before me

when he was sober; in those moments, however, when he got drunk, he
would no longer refrain from threatening that the time is coming when
they will butcher Jews and landlords.[82]

After this threat was repeated several times, Krauthamer expelled
Kinailiuk from the tavern and barred him from returning.

Anna Pavlyk and the three artisan-peasants were tried before a jury
in Lviv on 11–13 September 1879. The jury, headed by the left-wing
Democrat Kornel Ujejski, freed all four defendants.[83]

Early in 1880 the Kosiv police arrested Anna for the third time, this
time together with her younger sister Paraska. They were arrested in
connection with the Fokshei case. Since 1876, the Foksheis, a peasant
family from Moskalivka near Monastyrske, had been taking every
opportunity to speak out against the clergy and ridicule religion. The
Foksheis claimed that when the Polish priest sang *omnia saecula saecu-
lorum* it sounded like a cow lowing. They denied the sacramental
character of marriage and confession. Hrytsko Fokshei would interrupt
the priest's sermon, loudly offering the comment that the priest was
talking nonsense. The rumor spread that the Fokshei family held
readings in their home. When the police investigated, they found a
number of socialist brochures and periodicals in Ukrainian and Polish.[84]

The Foksheis were active in community politics, agitating for the
removal of their village chief. Late in 1879, Dmytro, Ivan, Vasyl and
Hrytsko Fokshei as well as two other Moskalivka peasants, Vasyl Lelet
and Hryts Balahurak, refused to pay community taxes. The village chief
ordered their property sequestered, but the Foksheis, Lelet and Balahurak forced their way into the village chancellery and took their
property back. Not long after this incident, on the night of 24–25 December 1879, someone fired a shotgun into the village chief's home.
Evidence indicated that Dmytro Fokshei, who had previously made a
threat on the village chief's life, was responsible for the shooting. The
following night, a vandal set fire to the village chief's hay, destroying
30 guldens' worth.[85]

The Foksheis, Lelet and Balahurak were arrested. So too were many
others, including the Pavlyk sisters and Ivan Franko. The latter was
arrested merely for being in the general area of Kolomyia when arrests
were made. The Pavlyk sisters also had no direct connection with the
case, though it is most probable that the Pavlyks inspired the Foksheis'
rebelliousness and provided them with radical literature.[86]

Dmytro Fokshei was sentenced to a year and a half in prison, his wife (for perjury) to one month, their servant girl (also for perjury) to fourteen days, Hrytsko Fokshei to three months, Vasyl Fokshei to one month and Anna Pavlyk to one month for writing a satirical song about judge Bogusiewicz. The rest were freed.[87]

Anna Pavlyk soon thereafter wrote her memoirs, "My and the People's Sins and the Landlords' and Priests' Righteousness," and her brother published them in Drahomanov's journal *Hromada.*[88] Anna and Paraska, who also contributed a short memoir to *Hromada,* were again arrested in October 1881 for the publication of their memoirs. A Lviv jury freed them both on 5 December 1881.[89]

The memoirs depicted two spirited Hutsul girls confident of the justice of their socialist beliefs, persecuted at every turn by the Galician police. The Pavlyk home was under unremitting surveillance. Anna was arrested many times. In addition to the instances already mentioned, Anna and her mother were arrested again in 1880 just two or three weeks after Anna's release from imprisonment in connection with the Fokshei case. They were imprisoned only six days, just to keep them away from Emperor Franz Joseph who was then visiting an exhibition in nearby Kolomyia.[90] In September 1885 the Kosiv police again arrested Anna and her brother for socialist agitation; she was sentenced to a month in prison on 2 January 1886.[91]

As though confinement was not punishment enough, Anna's arrests brought additional suffering. Ivan Pavlyk, Anna's father, died while Anna was in prison and the police tried to impress upon her that her father had died of grief and worry over her and Paraska.[92] Anna's suitor, Antin Melnyk, broke off their relationship as a result of her arrests.[93] The neighbors in Monastyrske turned against her, blaming her, not the Galician authorities, for the wave of arrests in the Kosiv district.[94]

Ivan Maksymiak

In a different part of Galicia, another intellectual peasant socialist, Ivan Maksymiak, carried on agitation among the Ruthenian peasantry. Maksymiak was the son of a poor peasant from Kupnovychi in the district of Rudky. When the police investigated him, in fact, the only document he could produce to identify himself was a certificate of poverty drawn up by the village scribe.[95]

Perhaps this certificate of poverty was issued to Maksymiak when he applied for a stipend, since Maksymiak, in spite of his social background, had attended Drohobych gymnasium through the sixth class. In Drohobych he became the friend of Ivan Franko.[96] Franko introduced Maksymiak to socialism and to the socialist newspaper *Praca.* Maksymiak soon tried his pen on the doctrine. In November 1882, he wrote a poem, "Do Cesarzów" (To Emperors), and submitted it to *Praca,* but editor Daniluk apparently found the poem too radical to publish.[97] In the summer of 1883, an article of Maksymiak's appeared, in German translation, in the Viennese liberal daily *Neue Freie Presse.*[98]

For one reason or another, Maksymiak's education was interrupted and he returned to his native village in the summer of 1883. Here "Monsieur Jean Maxymiaque à Koupnovitze," as he styled himself,[99] did not abandon his literary efforts. In Kupnovychi he wrote a brochure, *Our Poverty and What is Socialism,* as well as a poem of some two hundred lines.[100]

In addition to writing, Maksymiak engaged in oral agitation. Three times he assembled the community of Kupnovychi and "spoke to them the word of truth." As a result of his efforts, twenty peasants stopped paying taxes and going to church. Over half the community, the pastor complained, stopped believing in God. One of Maksymiak's followers even beat the priest with a cane in a dispute over a trespassing pig. Maksymiak's agitation, of course, earned him enemies in the village, notably the pastor, the school teacher and his own father. In October 1883, the priest denounced the Kupnovychi agitator to the starosta in Rudky; the starosta had Maksymiak expelled from the village and dispatched military forces to quell the unrest. According to Maksymiak, the military "greatly destroyed the village."[101]

Afterwards, Maksymiak kept up contact with Franko and other Galician socialists. On 27 March 1885, the tsarist border police arrested Maksymiak for attempting to smuggle socialist literature (works by Franko and Czerwieński and copies of *Praca*) into Russian Ukraine. He was imprisoned in Russia; the authorities released him and deported him back to Austria in July 1886.[102]

Anticlerical Agitation in Dobrivliany and Volia Yakubova

Radical agitation was also conducted in the countryside surrounding the oil towns of Boryslav and Drohobych. Two adjacent villages, Volia Yakubova and Dobrivliany, were the centers of this agitation. Both villages had some tradition of peasant radicalism. Dobrivliany, whose manor was the property of the Roman Catholic church in Drohobych,[103] was one of the villages, not altogether rare in Galicia, that interpreted the 1867 law of communal autonomy very literally. From 1867 to 1873, the village government of Dobrivliany acted independently of all other state authority (district, crownland and central).[104]

The other rural community, Volia Yakubova, had participated in the series of peasant disturbances that followed the Napoleonic wars; in 1819 the peasants of this village attempted a forcible seizure of the manorial pasture. In 1843 the community of Volia Yakubova refused to pay taxes and the military had to be sent in to sequester the peasants' property. In both of these actions in Volia, the Melnyk family played a prominent part.[105] A Melnyk was also the chief radical activist in Volia Yakubova in the mid-1880s.

On 21 August 1881, a reading club opened in Dobrivliany. Songs were sung to celebrate the occasion and four lectures read to the assembled peasants. Guests from neighboring Volia attended, including Panas Melnyk. Melnyk even delivered one of the lectures, on agricultural methods.[106] The reading club expanded slowly; almost a year after its founding, the Dobrivliany reading club had only fifteen members.[107]

Hryhorii Rymar, a smallholder, and Hryhorii Berehuliak, cantor, were the moving spirits behind the reading club. Both had attended elementary school in Dobrivliany. Rymar, who showed exceptional talent, was encouraged by pastor Antin Chapelsky to continue his studies. Rymar succeeded only in finishing the second class of gymnasium when, since he was older than the other gymnasium students, he was drafted into the army. Stationed in Vienna, Rymar continued studying on his own. The army trained him in pyrotechnics, a skill he later employed to enliven some reading-club events with a display of fireworks. From the army Rymar entered the gendarmerie and attained the rank of commandant. While serving as a gendarme, Rymar frequently visited his native village, where Rev. Chapelsky welcomed him as though Rymar were his own son. When he finally retired from the gendarmerie, Rymar returned to Dobrivliany and assumed the position of village scribe. He was a figure respected in the whole district. His former schoolmate, Hryhorii Berehuliak, who had neither travelled nor studied as much as Rymar, looked up to the erstwhile gendarme and the pair became inseparable companions devoted to the enlightenment of their village.[108]

After the example of Dobrivliany, Volia Yakubova also established a reading club, mainly through the efforts of Panas Melnyk. When it was founded, the reading club had about thirty members, mainly unmarried sons of farmers (*parubky*).[109] Melnyk himself was at this time only twenty-one years of age.[110] The reading club grew quickly: by early 1882 Melnyk boasted in a report to a popular newspaper that it had sixty members.[111] The reading club went carolling on Christmas to collect money to join Prosvita and the Kachkovsky Society. Prosvita donated forty books to the reading club and Melnyk subscribed to the popular *Hospodar' i promyshlennyk* (Proprietor and Industrialist [Artisan]) on its behalf. By January 1882 the reading club in Volia owned 104 volumes.[112]

From the very first, Panas Zubrytsky was the leader of the older, more established, landed peasants (*starshi gazdy*) who opposed the Volia reading club. Zubrytsky was an influential figure in the community: at various times he had been village chief, a member of the district council and an officer in the church committee.[113] Zubrytsky's enmity was a reaction to the threat that the reading club posed to the established authority in the village, since Melnyk and his supporters embarked on a concerted effort to reform Volia Yakubova by attaining dominant positions in every village institution.

The reading club planned to sabotage economic monopolies in the village by establishing a cooperative store, communal granary and loan association,[114] but these plans, it seems, were never realized. The reformers' main targets turned out to be the village government and the church.

Within weeks of the founding of a reading club in Volia, the members publicly announced their intention to campaign in village elections.[115] By early 1882 the secretary of the reading club, Andrii Nalyvaiko, was appointed village scribe.[116] In that same year the reading club approached the chief officers in the village government, the so-called communal authorities (*zverkhnist' hromads'ka*), and demanded to know what happened to the 136 g. that the commune had paid to the tax department in Drohobych. "And as a result of this," Melnyk wrote in a newspaper report, "more than one highly-placed person in the village found himself in an uncomfortable position."[117]

By 1884 the reading club had partially succeeded in electing a reform government. Of eighteen council members, ten (including Melnyk) belonged to the reading club.[118] But the top positions were still occupied by the reading club's foes.

The reading club took every occasion to agitate against the communal authorities. One such occasion was a typhus epidemic that broke out in Volia in February 1882. The reading club demanded that the communal authorities inform the starosta in Drohobych of the epidemic and request a physician for the village. Many in the village opposed the reading club on this issue; they mistrusted doctors and feared their fees, preferring to rely on folk medicines, charms and "ignorant hags." As the epidemic grew more serious, the members of the reading club, in particular the village scribe Nalyvaiko, threatened to lodge a formal complaint with the starosta if the communal authorities did not send to the starosta for a doctor. As a result of these threats, the communal authorities complied. The starosta assigned a physician to pay weekly visits to Volia Yakubova. The physician gained the villagers' confidence by speaking to them in Ukrainian and by giving money to indigent patients to buy food and medicine necessary for their recovery. The reading club prided itself on its contributions to the victory of science over superstition in Volia Yakubova, a victory surely the more sweet for discomfiting the communal authorities.[119]

In spite of their success during the epidemic, the reading club failed to gain the highest posts in village government during an election in 1885. The reading club's candidate, Melnyk, lost the election for village chief by one vote.[120] The reading club also campaigned, with more success, during the 1885 primary parliamentary elections. In May 1885, the community of Volia Yakubova chose the three top officers of the reading club, including Melnyk, to act as their electors.[121]

It is worth noting that Melnyk and the other activists of the reading club, in addition to waging a political stuggle and sending letters to the popular press, also used a more time-honored method of defeating their opponents: the village reformers occasionally administered a thrashing to recalcitrant foes.[122]

At first, in 1882, relations between Volia's reading club and church were distinguished by the spirit of cooperation and mutual support. The reading club intended to present a theatrical performance to raise money for repairing the church building;[123] it also put a stop to the custom of visiting the Jewish tavern keeper on Christmas and singing him a special carol, composed by the villagers, that made sport of the Christian faith. Panas Melnyk even became cantor in the parish. The pastor, Rev. Mykhailo Harbinsky, encouraged the reading club and subscribed to *Bat'kivshchyna* on its behalf. Since the old church brotherhood had ceased its activity, Rev. Harbinsky established a new one made up chiefly of reading-club members.[124]

By 1884, however, the reading club had abandoned its tactics of conciliation and infiltration with regard to the church; church and reading club had become antagonists. Zubrytsky, head of the church committee, complained that the reading club gave him no peace. The reading club bade the church committee, which Melnyk at some point joined, to fix the church roof, clean the cemetery, finish constructing the fence surrounding the church and give a public accounting of disbursements from the church treasury.[125]

Although personal issues contributed to, perhaps initiated, Rev. Harbinsky's estrangement from the reading club,[126] factors of more social significance became the focal points of discord: the clash of the priest's and his parishioners' economic interests and the competition between pulpit and reading club — religious and secular (even anticlerical) doctrines — for influence in the village.

Economic friction developed over the use of pastor Harbinsky's pasture and over the amount Harbinsky charged for performing various religious rites. For years Rev. Harbinsky had rented out his pasture to a certain Chaim for 90–110 g. and the community had to sublease the pasture from Chaim for an additional 100 g. The villagers asked Father Harbinsky to rent the pasture directly to them, hoping in this way to save the 100 g. The good father agreed to rent to them directly, but for 200 g., i.e., at the same rate as Chaim. The community was enraged and Melnyk reported the incident in *Bat'kivshchyna*.[127]

Melnyk also inaugurated a campaign to reduce the fees the pastor collected for sacramental rites. He urged the villagers to pay the priest only the amount stipulated by Austrian law.[128] (The anticlerical Emperor Joseph II had issued a patent in 1785 that established a price list for sacramental rites. Although still technically binding in the nineteenth century, these artificially low norms were no longer enforced and clerical fees rose.) Owing to Melnyk's agitation, disputes over these fees broke out in Volia Yakubova. In one incident, in 1886, the widow of a poor peasant could not afford Rev. Harbinsky's fee for the funeral services for her husband (9 g.). In an attempt to get the pastor to lower his fee, two of the widow's relatives interceded on her behalf. Father Harbinsky called the relatives scoundrels and socialists, beat them and threatened to have them arrested.[129]

The reading club made life unpleasant for the pastor in other ways as well. Rev. Harbinsky was president of the village school council until Melnyk accused him of neglecting his catechetical and supervisory duties. The pastor was dismissed from his position and new elections were held; Melnyk was elected the new president of the school council.[130] In 1884, Rev. Harbinsky felt constrained to lock up the choir loft; reading-club members, he complained, were taking newspapers with them up to the choir loft and reading instead of praying during the Liturgy.

Also in 1884, one member of the reading club brought a newspaper to church and there, in the churchyard, read aloud to the assembled parishioners about the Stundist sect in Russian Ukraine. (Ukrainian/ Ruthenian socialists, especially Drahomanov and Pavlyk, had long publicized the Stundists, a Protestant sect in Ukraine that dispensed with a clergy.) When Father Harbinsky discovered what the parish was listening to, he took the offending reader to court. Witnesses were summoned to testify in Drohobych, but the accused was released since the newspaper he read from had not been banned. According to Melnyk, who was himself perhaps the accused, Father Harbinsky avenged himself on the reader. The reader had been summoned for induction into the army and petitioned the authorities to exempt him from military service. The pastor, however, altered the parish register so that the reader's petition would be rejected. When the reader's father came to plead for his son, Rev. Harbinsky rebuffed him with the words: "Your son has become a thorn in my side. Let him go to the army. I'll teach him!" He added that he would do the same to every member of the reading club.[131]

The neighboring village of Dobrivliany was also the scene of animosity between priest and reading club. This was not so in the beginning, during Rev. Antin Chapelsky's pastorate. Father Chapelsky had been pastor in Dobrivliany for close to forty years before his death in January 1885. He was beloved by his parishioners for a number of reasons: for inviting the peasants to his home during holidays and weddings, for his efforts at educating his parish and encouraging talented young men (such as Hryhorii Rymar) to go on to further study, for supporting the reading club and permitting his daughters to take part in its activities and for performing sacramental rites gratis for his poorer parishioners, maintaining himself and his family exclusively from his salary, his farm and the gifts of more prosperous villagers.[132]

In 1884, Father Chapelsky became too ill to care for the parish and his son-in-law, Rev. Yosyf Yavorsky, was assigned to administer the parish temporarily. Hryhorii Rymar, the former gendarme, and Hryhorii Berehuliak, the cantor, had known Father Yavorsky from before 1884, when as a graduate theologian, Yavorsky had courted Nataliia Chapelska. At that time, and for the first few weeks of Father Yavorsky's administration, the peasants and the priest got on well and Rev. Yavorsky frequented the reading club. Soon, however, the amicable relations disintegrated. During the blessing of the fields, the new pastor went to bless the manorial field, which belonged to the Latin rite church in Drohobych. Cantor Berehuliak objected to this action, claiming that Father Yavorsky was just trying to curry favor with the manor and that the former pastor had never blessed the Polish church's field. Berehuliak refused to participate in the procession to bless the field, Father Yavorsky would not tolerate the disobedient cantor and Berehuliak quit his post.[133]

Another point of contention between the new pastor and his flock concerned fees for sacramental services. In contrast to Father Chapelsky, who had performed baptism, marriages and funerals without charge, Father Yavorsky collected fees for these services. The pastor met with opposition from the parishioners, an opposition all the stronger for being led by an "expert" in liturgical matters, former cantor Berehuliak, and by the educated and respected village scribe, Rymar.[134] Even after Rev. Yavorsky was replaced by another priest, Rev. Hrabovensky, the discord between pastor and villagers lingered on.[135]

Anticlerical agitation in Dobrivliany had escalated by the mid-1880s into radical antireligious agitation conducted by means of clandestine meetings and lithographed leaflets. Rymar and Berehuliak had, in fact, set up a secret organization whose influence extended far beyond Dobrivliany. Participants in the clandestine meetings included Fedir Derhalo, cantor from Zavadiv (Stryi district), Mykhas of Morozovychi (Sambir district), Novakivsky of Torky (Przemyśl district) and Ivan Franko of Lviv. Panas Melnyk of Volia Yakubova was also involved in the meetings, which were held either in Rymar's home or in the woods. Very elaborate precautions were taken to deflect the suspicions of the police.[136]

Hryhorii Rymar owned a lithographic plate that he used to publish radical leaflets. He printed the leaflets in twenty-five copies and disseminated them by posting them in the street and placing them in peasants' carts on market day. He also sent Hryhorii Berehuliak's young nephew,

Petro Berehuliak, to distribute the leaflets to other villages, including the village of Morozovychi near Sambir. According to the younger Berehuliak, the leaflets were written by Ivan Franko. The radicals in Dobrivliany received Franko's manuscripts indirectly, through Edmund L. Solecki, editor of *Gazeta Naddniestrzańska* (Dniester Gazette). Petro Berehuliak made special trips to Solecki in Drohobych to pick up the texts.[137] Since none of these leaflets have been discovered, it is impossible to confirm, on the basis of style analysis, whether Franko was really the author of these agitational works.[138] What is beyond dispute, however, is Franko's connection with the reading clubs of Volia Yakubova and Dobrivliany: he published several articles dealing with the history of the two villages,[139] he corresponded with Panas Melnyk and Melnyk intended to visit Franko in April 1884 in Lviv,[140] and Franko addressed at least one secret assembly organized by Rymar in the summer of 1885.[141] Other intellectuals who maintained contact with the reading clubs included editor Solecki in Drohobych and the young Polish socialist Ignacy Daszyński.[142] The intellectuals provided the reading clubs with radical literature: the Genevan publications of Serhii Podolynsky and Drahomanov, the 1878 anthologies of Pavlyk and Franko, and a radical Polish pamphlet.

Opponents of the reading club in Volia Yakubova had petitioned the viceroyalty to close down the offending institution in 1884. Father Harbinsky and Panas Zubrytsky sponsored the petition and collected signatures in church. They did not succeed in collecting many signatures and the viceroyalty did not order the closing of the reading club.[143] Later, more serious denunciations provoked the authorities to action.

By 1885, Andrii Nalyvaiko, communal scribe in Volia and formerly one of Melnyk's partisans, had turned against the reading club. To understand Nalyvaiko's change of heart, it must be kept in mind that the position of village scribe was potentially very lucrative. The scribe kept track of the community finances and very often succumbed to the temptation to embezzle. According to Melnyk and editors sympathetic to the reading club, Nalyvaiko wanted to follow the traditional route of scribal enrichment, but was prevented from doing so by Melnyk and other reformers.[144]

Nalyvaiko, the pastors of Volia and Dobrivliany, and the Greek Catholic bishop of Przemyśl denounced the "socialist agitation" to the authorities. Thus early in March 1886, the police arrested Rymar, Berehuliak and Melnyk together with other reading club members and imprisoned them in Sambir. Searches turned up radical literature in both Dobrivliany and Volia Yakubova; in the latter village, the literature was found hidden in a barrel of sauerkraut. The police also searched the editorial offices of *Gazeta Naddniestrzańska* and the living quarters of editor Solecki in Drohobych, but found nothing incriminating there.[145]

During preparations for the trial, an incident occurred that revealed something about the size of Melnyk's following in Volia Yakubova. Nalyvaiko and Harbinsky had submitted to the court a certificate of morality (testament of character) that portrayed Melnyk as malign and dangerous. But to counteract this certificate, the commune of Volia Yakubova submitted two certificates of morality commending Melnyk; the two certificates submitted by the commune bore almost a hundred signatures.[146]

The reading-club activists were tried in secret before a jury in Sambir (31 May–3 June 1886). All were acquitted of the charge of belonging to a secret socialist organization, but three of the accused, from Dobrivliany, were found guilty of blasphemy. For this crime of blasphemy, Rymar was sentenced to two years' imprisonment, Berehuliak to one and a half years, and Ivan Stupak to two months. Melnyk was found guilty of publicly reading forbidden books and sentenced to six days in jail or a fine of 30 g. The fifth defendant, a certain Prusky of Volia Yakubova, was acquitted of all charges.[147]

The Russophiles seized the occasion of the Sambir trial to denounce the Ukrainian national party. They claimed that no such scandal would have erupted if the reading clubs in Volia Yakubova and Dobrivliany had been supplied with the Russophile popular publications *Russkaia rada* (Russian Council) and *Nauka*. Members of the Ukrainophile party, the Russophiles said, were mistaken in assuming that "because they were enemies of Russia, they could with impunity overturn the social order."[148] The Stańczyks, too, made an issue of the Sambir trial. Ruthenian political leaders had been complaining that the viceroyalty was slow to approve the statutes of new reading clubs and seemed to be hindering their development. After the Sambir trial, the Stańczyks posed the question: "Is not the caution that the authorities exercise at the founding of new reading clubs justified?"[149]

These three cases of radical agitation in the Ruthenian village — Kosiv socialism inspired by Anna Pavlyk, the agitation in Kupnovychi led by

Ivan Maksymiak and the radical reading-club movement in Volia Yakubova and Dobrivliany — were the first attempts of Ruthenian socialists
to establish a socialist movement in the countryside and they represent a
transitional, or preparatory, phase of rural agitation. Later in the 1880s,
the Ruthenian socialists would apply new techniques of propaganda
among the peasantry. After the founding of the Ruthenian-Ukrainian
Radical Party in 1890, Ruthenian socialists would systematically conduct agitation in the village, with improved propaganda techniques,
until the isolated incidents examined above took on the proportions of
an institutionalized, radical social movement.

There is some direct continuity between these first attempts at radical
agitation and the more widespread social movement led by the Radical
party in the 1890s. Franko and Pavlyk would both still be the chief
intellectual forces behind radicalism. The Fokshei family would become
active in the Radical party's political society Narodna volia (People's
Freedom).[150] Kupnovychi would remain a center of radical agitation.[151]
Families affected by the anticlerical movement in Volia and Dobrivliany
would later produce some of the most effective political agitators of the
Radical and social democratic parties: the brothers Novakivsky and
Semen Vityk.[152] In Morozovychi, a village that had close connections
with the movement in Dobrivliany, a reading club affiliated with the
Radical party was to be established in the mid-1890s and a radical, Ivan
Mykhas, was to be elected village chief.[153] Perhaps this is the point to
mention a direct discontinuity. Panas Melnyk of Volia Yakubova was
not able to participate in the Radical Party in the 1890s: he died young,
of a lung disease contracted in Sambir prison.[154]

The dilemma of the Ruthenian socialists in the 1880s was that they were
forced to work either for the Polish socialist and populist press (at the
expense of submerging their national identity) or for the Ruthenian
national populist press (at the expense of submerging their social
radicalism). The only resolution to this dilemma was to establish an
independent movement.

The Ruthenian socialists, however, faced almost insurmountable
obstacles to creating a popular mass movement. Unlike the Polish
socialists, the Ruthenian socialists did not have the option of agitating
among Ruthenian artisans, of whom there were just too few. The Polish

socialists could afford to ignore the peasantry (and they did), because they had an approximation of an industrial working class in the journeyman artisans. This working class was not too large, had many overlapping networks of personal contacts, was generally literate and travelled, but incitable, and was most conveniently concentrated in the two large urban centers of Lviv and Cracow. The Ruthenian socialists, however, had no choice — the "workers" in Boryslav underscored this fact — but to concentrate their efforts on the peasantry. In contrast to the artisans (of whom there were thousands), the peasants (of whom there were millions) were uneducated and dispersed in thousands of relatively autarkic villages. How, then, was it possible to organize the peasantry?

The Ruthenian national movement had begun to face the same problem no more than a decade earlier than the Ruthenian socialist movement. The national movement, however, had been able to rely on the help of the Greek Catholic clergy. The priest in the village was the natural bridge connecting urban Ruthenian patriots with the raw ethnic material of the countryside. It was the rural clergy that introduced into the villages a network of nationally-oriented institutions.

But the Ruthenian socialists were fanatically anticlerical, and this was the crux of their dilemma; it was hard enough to organize peasants as opposed to artisans, but to attempt to do so without the clergy, in fact with the enmity of clergy, was surely, it seems, to attempt the impossible. Yet, in 1890, an agrarian socialist party — the Radical party — came into being and in succeeding decades sent representatives to parliament and won mass support from the peasantry. How, then, did this isolated handful of Ukrainian socialists, based in Lviv, unable even to support their own periodical, penetrate the village and develop a mass movement?

The answer is that the Ruthenian socialist movement in the village rode on the back of the national movement. As the national movement penetrated the village, it brought to the fore certain social conflicts: between peasants and clergy, peasants and village governments, peasants and tavern keepers-lenders. Reading clubs often developed into forums of peasant interests. The early attempts at radical agitation in the villages (Kosiv, Kupnovychi, Dobrivliany-Volia Yakubova) show the workings of this process of radicalization in the countryside.

The Ruthenian socialists, especially after the founding of the Radical party, would step into this fray in the countryside and give full support to the reading clubs and peasants, encouraging them in their struggle against the village governments, clergy and tavern keepers-lenders. The reading club, moreover, would prove easy to penetrate, since literature could be sent through the mails.[155] And for a national populist reading club to transform itself into a socialist reading club involved little more than switching subscriptions from nationally-oriented to socialist periodicals.

Chapter Five

The Formation of Political Parties

The emergence of socialist political parties in 1890 would have been difficult to predict from the vantage point of the middle 1880s, the lowest ebb in the fortunes of Galician socialism. The Ruthenian socialists were weak and isolated. The Polish socialists, too, were sapped of strength. The police had suppressed the movement in Cracow and had also reduced the effectiveness of socialist activity in Lviv. The passage of the 1883 industrial law discouraged the Lviv artisans and deprived them of an issue around which to rally. Moreover, the Lviv movement suffered from the defection of the intelligentsia. Ivan Franko left the Polish movement in 1881, disenchanted over the national question and the artisan base of the movement. By the mid-1880s Bolesław Czerwieński and the brothers Adolf and Ludwik Inalender also drifted away from active participation in the socialist movement. The movement's decline was accompanied, perhaps inevitably, by internal dissension, the exact causes of which are obscure.

The problems facing the socialist movement in the mid-1880s were serious, but under the surface two revivifying processes were at work, gaining momentum as the decade drew to a close. First, class conflict itself had not abated and the working classes could still be organized for united action. Thus, in the late 1880s, Lviv socialists engineered a series of strikes and convened artisan assemblies at an increasing tempo. The Ruthenian left also organized mass assemblies, but for peasants. Second — and most important — a radical student movement swept Galicia in the latter 1880s, providing a new and more stable intellectual leadership for both the Polish and Ruthenian movements. The combination of these two factors led to the establishment of a Polish and a Ruthenian socialist party in 1890.

Strikes and Assemblies

Following the strike wave of 1870–73, Galicia had been free of strike activity until March 1886, when sixty carpenters went on strike for ten days in Lviv. All the carpenters worked at a single enterprise, the Wczelak brothers' factory, an anomaly in the Galician industrial world: it employed eighty workers and it used machines. It was one of the very few Galician enterprises that made the transition, by expanding personnel and introducing mechanical power, from an artisan workshop to a modern factory. It was a domestic manifestation of the process that was impoverishing the artisans by making handicraft production obsolete.

The Wczelak artisans, undergoing transformation into factory hands, resented the new methods and relations of production. One of the striking carpenters' demands, for instance, concerned the new relations between employer and employee in a thoroughly capitalist enterprise, where the paternalism of the artisan workshop had no place: "Treatment of workers-journeymen should be humane and polite, not like it is now with the worker in a factory considered living inventory." Artisans valued the individualization of their handiwork, which also had no place in the factory. The striking carpenters therefore demanded extra pay if more than two workers were assigned to the same job. Classical, in its artisanal resentment of the machine and in its opposition to capitalist labor relations, was the demand to stop the machines and to work by hand if there was not enough work to go around. The owners understandably refused to accede to the latter demand.

The carpenters also demanded a ten-hour working day with an hour break, but settled for a ten-and-a-half hour day with two fifteen minute breaks. They demanded, too, a minimum wage of 9 gulden weekly (a third of the carpenters had been earning less than 5 g.), but settled for 7 g. The owners gave in to other demands completely: that wages be paid regularly every Saturday, that workers be given two weeks' notice before dismissal, that all drawings and explanations be delivered to the worker "in proper order," that fresh water be on hand and that the premises be kept clean and well ventilated.

The organizers of the carpenters' strike included two radical carpenters, Marian Udałowicz and a certain Zwiernicki, as well as two leaders of the Lviv socialist movement, Antoni Mańkowski and Feliks Daszyński. After the strike, Daszyński helped the carpenters set up a cooperative workshop. Other Lviv journeymen of all trades supported the strike by collecting 250 g. for the Wczelak strikers. Predictably, the Lviv police intervened on behalf of the brothers Wczelak by arresting several workers.[1]

The next strike in Galicia, the bakers' strike of 1888, also broke out in Lviv. Unsanitary working conditions and long hours (sixteen to twenty-one, but with breaks) contributed to the dissatisfaction of journeyman bakers. The journeymen were also upset that the masters hired far too many apprentices. Apprentices, of course, were cheaper than journeymen, so masters preferred to hire them. In one bakery a twenty-seven-year-old "apprentice" was working, though by law, no apprentice could be over twenty years of age. The journeymen claimed that in Lviv bakeries the proportion of apprentices to journeymen was six to one.

On 1 July 1888 the journeyman bakers of Lviv confronted their masters with six demands: that the working day last no more than twelve hours; that journeymen receive 1.5–2 g. for the night shift, 1–1.7 g. for the day shift; that bakeries cease operation from 5 AM Sunday to 5 AM Monday; that masters hire no more than three apprentices for each journeyman; that apprentices attend school; that the masters provide beds where the journeymen could rest during breaks. The masters had six days to respond to these demands. On 6 July 1888 the masters suggested certain compromises that the journeymen refused to accept.

On that very day, 228 journeyman bakers — Ruthenians, Poles and Jews — vacated Lviv and established a camp in Lysynychi, a wood outside the city. The spectacle of a bakers' camp — with old men deliberating on the workers' question and young men playing on their harmonicas — captured the hearts and imaginations of the citizens of Lviv. The populace made excursions to the wood, bringing sausage, beer, milk and — ironically —bread to the bakers. When it rained, the owner of a nearby brewery let the journeymen sleep in his warehouse. Contributions flowed in, from 30 to 40 g. daily. In advance of the strike, the leaders of the Lviv bakers had appealed to workers in Cracow, Chernivtsi, Prague, Brno, Budapest and Vienna for financial support.

The Galician authorities called in the military. On the day the bakers set up camp, a division of soldiers was dispatched to patrol Lysynychi, but the the division was recalled that evening, so peaceful were the bakers. The army temporarily donated 120 military bakers to man the deserted bakeries of Lviv. The military finally broke up the camp on the night of 14–15 July; 30 gendarmes and 50 deputized soldiers escorted 133 obstinate bakers (there had been desertions from the camp) to police headquarters. Interrogations and nine arrests followed. The masters refused to re-employ the journeymen most active in the strike movement and did not meet the strikers' demands.[2] (According to one source, there was another bakers' strike in February 1889. It followed the same pattern as the 1888 strike, except that this time the journeymen set up camp in a park.)[3]

Ruthenians were very much involved in the bakers' strikes. The 1888 strike was led by the journeyman Dudykevych (whose brother was a prominent Russophile), and several Ruthenians then associated with the Polish socialist movement (Viacheslav Budzynovsky, Mykhailo Drabyk, Mykola Hankevych) were active in agitating among the bakers. Hankevych and Budzynovsky also figured in the 1889 bakers' strike, as did the Ruthenians Ivan Franko, Osyp Makovei and Klymentyna Popovych. Polish socialists, too, such as the students Zygmunt Seweryn and Władysław Arciszewski, were prominent in their support of the 1888 strike, as was Udałowicz, leader of the carpenters' strike of 1886.[4]

In 1890, journeyman chimney sweeps, again in Lviv, went on strike for higher wages (12 g. weekly), priority in the dispensation of chimney sweeping concessions, limitations on the use of apprentices and a voice in approving apprentices' passage to journeymen. After two weeks, the masters agreed to the chimney sweeps' demands, but their victory was pyrrhic: the masters fired a large percentage of the striking journeymen. According to various accounts, twenty, twenty-five or thirty journeymen went on strike, ten, thirteen or fourteen of whom the masters then dismissed.[5]

In June 1890, four hundred journeyman carpenters, led by Udałowicz and Piotrowski, presented the Lviv masters with a list of demands. The demands included an eight-hour day, the abolition of piece work and a raise in wages. When the masters rejected the demands, about five hundred journeyman carpenters, including seventy Jewish carpenters, went on strike for two weeks. Although Vienna's *Arbeiter-Zeitung* forwarded contributions from all over the empire to the striking Lviv carpenters, the journeymen eventually gave up and returned to work under the previous terms.[6] Also in 1890, in August, journeyman locksmiths in Lviv presented their masters with demands for a ten-hour day, the abolition of piece work and the regulation of the number of apprentices. It is not clear whether they eventually went on strike or not.[7]

A few strikes also occurred outside Lviv during this period. In 1889, two thousand Polish coal miners went on strike in Jaworzno. They demanded that the working day be reduced from twelve to eight hours, that miners be allowed to leave the mines immediately after finishing work, that no penalty be incurred for a few minutes' tardiness and that the price of powder and dynamite (which miners supplied at their own cost) be lowered. The authorities reacted by calling out the military and closing the taverns.[8] The Jaworzno strike differed from the Lviv strikes in that it was not an artisan strike. At least one *artisan* strike did occur outside Lviv — a hundred brushmakers in Kolomyia, demanding 5 g. a week and an eleven-hour day, went on strike in 1890[9] — but Lviv was certainly pre-eminent in artisan activity.

In Cracow, no strike broke out. In fact, the only instance of workers' resistance in this period was not a strike, but a riot: several hundred Cracovian cobblers in 1888 tore apart a new shoe store that sold factory imports. The police and army attempted to defend the shoe store. Many of the rioting cobblers were wounded and thirty arrested. The artisans' anti-factory heroics were in vain: after repairs, the new shoe store re-opened.[10] The contrast between artisan activities in Lviv, where a series of strikes pitted journeymen against masters in an organized fashion, and in Cracow, where a single riot pitted artisans *as a whole* against the encroachments of capitalist industry, reveals again the divergence between Lviv, with its organizational infrastructure, and Cracow, with its organizational and leadership vacuum. It is the same divergence that showed up in the contrast between legal socialism in Lviv and conspiratorial socialism in Cracow, a divergence that goes back to the organizational activities of the Polish Democrats in the 1860s.

The strikes in Lviv from 1886 to 1890 were, for the most part, unsuccessful, at least as far as immediate gains were concerned. In the long run, however, the experience of these unsuccessful strikes paved the way for the much more successful ventures of the 1890s and 1900s. In particular, the Lviv strikes gave an impetus to the formation of trade unions.

Trade unions were in the process of formation in the late 1880s. Although the 1883 industrial law intended to strengthen the master at the expense of the journeyman, it did contain one provision that the journeymen eventually made good use of. The law had satisfied the masters by setting up compulsory corporations run by the masters, but it also, within each corporation, provided for a College of Journeymen (Zgromadzenie Towarzyszów), albeit with very vague statutes. By the late 1880s, socialists infiltrated key positions in the Colleges. Józef

Daniluk, for example, the editor of *Praca,* presided over the College of Journeyman Printers; the left-leaning Kazimierz Tabaczkowski presided over the College of Journeyman Locksmiths. In 1889, the socialists talked of forming a Union of Colleges of Journeymen. Later that same year, presidents of the Colleges of Journeymen met to discuss changing the Colleges' statutes to specify the Colleges' duty to defend journeymen in their struggle for higher wages, a shorter working day and better treatment of journeymen and apprentices.[11] Most significantly, it was the Colleges of Journeymen that presented masters with the journeymen's demands in the 1888 bakers' strike, and in the carpenters', chimney-sweeps' and locksmiths' strikes of 1890. By 1890, in fact, the Colleges of Journeymen had evolved into trade unions in all but name.

During the same period in which they were pursuing their *economic* interests by going on strike, the Lviv journeymen also pursued *political* aims. In the years 1887–90, Lviv artisans — once again, *not* the artisans of Cracow — participated in a great number of assemblies and meetings, primarily in order to win an extension of political representation for the working class. Lviv artisans had, of course, participated in assemblies in 1879–83. The earlier assemblies had all placed emphasis on opposition to the master's proposed revision of the industrial law. The assemblies of 1887–90, however, gave more emphasis to the wider problem of the political rights of the working class.

With the passage of the new industrial law of 1883, the earlier series of artisan assemblies had come to a natural end since the cause had been lost. But a new cause emerged in October 1886, when a Liberal deputy, Ernst von Plener, proposed that parliament establish Workers' Chambers with limited parliamentary representation. In Austria as a whole, working class leaders rejected Plener's proposal as unsatisfactory; workers demanded universal suffrage, not such palliatives as Workers' Chambers with limited representation. Throughout Austria, with one exception, workers' assemblies refused to endorse Plener's project. The one exception was the workers' assembly in Lviv, organized by Antoni Mańkowski and Adolf Inlaender.

The Lviv workers' assembly — the first since 1883 — convened 6 February 1887. The assembled artisans passed a resolution stating that only universal suffrage could satisfy workers, but that the Lviv assembly was ready nonetheless to support the Plener proposal as a first step towards full workers' representation. The assembly, however, made its endorsement of the Plener bill conditional on the following revisions:

that the Workers' Chambers send as many deputies to parliament as the Chambers of Commerce, that enfranchisement extend to include female workers, agricultural workers and all workers over twenty-one years of age and that Workers' Chambers enjoy representation in the Diets as well as in parliament. The assembly sent its resolution to the Liberal deputy Ferdinand Kronawetter.[12]

Support from Lviv was unable to salvage Plener's unpopular proposal in 1886, but in 1889 another democratic deputy, Pernerstorfer, revived a version of the Workers' Chambers plan that was more acceptable to Austrian workers. Pernerstorfer envisioned twenty-nine Workers' Chambers in Austria, corresponding to the twenty-nine Chambers of Commerce. The Workers' Chambers, to consist exclusively of urban workers, would send nine deputies to parliament. Duties of the Chambers would include working out proposals relating to wages, the length of the working day and hygiene in shops and factories.

On 13 January 1889 Antoni Mańkowski presided over an assembly of 150–400 Lviv journeymen who had gathered to discuss Pernerstorfer's project.[13] At this time the Lviv socialist movement was divided into two camps, Mańkowski's and Daniluk's. Mańkowski backed the Pernerstorfer proposal, as he had Plener's, while Daniluk and his partisans opposed it. Daniluk objected that the Workers' Chambers could only suggest and propose ways to better the workers' lot; its decisions would have no binding force. Enfranchisement for the Chambers excluded illiterates (a large percentage of Galicia's population), workers under twenty-four years of age, workers who had not worked two consecutive years in the district of the given Chamber and workers who had collided with the authorities. "So," Daniluk concluded, "the Chambers in no way satisfy workers, who will always strive for *universal suffrage.*"[14] Udałowicz, the carpenter activist, spoke in the same vein as Daniluk.

Notwithstanding these criticisms, the assembly decided to support the project, proposing the same revisions the assembly of 1887 had proposed. The 1889 assembly, again against the wishes of Daniluk and his associates, voted to send Mańkowski and Tabaczkowski to participate in an inquiry in Vienna, in which workers from all over Austria would discuss the Pernerstorfer proposal.[15] Although nothing ever came of Pernerstorfer's project, the agitation connected with it helped vitalize the workers' movement in Lviv. The Lviv delegates at the Vienna inquiry (23 February 1889) made a very favorable impression on the other Austrian workers' delegates.[16] Mańkowski's and Tabaczkowski's report to the Lviv workers after the inquiry provided occasions to call three further artisan assemblies in Lviv (16 March, 19 and 30 May 1889).[17]

Lviv socialists found many occasions to assemble the journeymen in the years 1888–90. Socialists attended an artisan assembly in Lviv on 18 March 1888 and criticized the masters, who had summoned this particular assembly, for attempting yet another revision of the industrial law.[18] The socialists also turned the funeral procession of Bolesław Czerwieński (d. 3 April 1888) into a workers' demonstration.[19] On 16 June 1889, Daniluk chaired a journeymen's assembly that petitioned parliament in regard to accident insurance for workers.[20] Jewish artisans, led by the socialist Herman Diamand, gathered in the Lviv synagogue on 8 March 1890 to demand that Jewish workers have Saturday off instead of Sunday.[21] Socialists and workers gathered on 30 August 1890 to commemorate the twenty-sixth anniversary of Lassalle's death.[22] About a hundred socialist journeymen attended a banquet on 29 September 1890 to celebrate the repeal of Bismarck's antisocialist law.[23] This latter gathering took place on the eve of the founding of a Polish socialist party in Lviv. In short, socialists were seizing every opportunity to bring the Lviv journeymen together under their leadership.

This agitation reached a culmination on the first of May 1890. On 30 May 1889, an assembly of Lviv workers had decided to send Józef Daniluk to attend the founding congress of the Second International (Paris, July 1889).[24] The Paris congress resolved that workers everywhere should celebrate Mayday as an international labor holiday. The Lviv socialist papers, Daniluk's *Praca* and Mańkowski's *Robotnik* (Worker; founded in 1890) took up the Mayday issue, urging Lviv workers to demonstrate their solidarity with workers outside of Galicia.[25] A committee, formed of the presidents of the Colleges of Journeymen, called a journeymen's assembly for 23 March 1980 to discuss participation in a Mayday celebration. The assembly, chaired by Daniluk and attended by six hundred journeymen, voted to hold a Mayday demonstration, especially in order to win universal suffrage and an eight-hour working day.[26] On 13 April 1890, Mańkowski addressed the members of Gwiazda at their annual banquet, urging them to demonstrate on Mayday.[27] Lviv typesetters voted, at a secret meeting on 25 April 1890, to refrain from work so as to join in the Mayday demonstration.[28]

As Mayday 1890 approached, a mood of panic swept Lviv. Viceroy

Kazimierz Badeni, on 26 April 1890, sent to all Galician police depart-
ments a circular categorically forbidding demonstrations on the first of
May. On 27 April, Badeni empowered all starostas to set up extraordi-
nary punitive courts to deal with demonstrators. On the eve of Mayday,
police in Biała, a mining and metallurgical center in Western Galicia,
opened fire on a crowd of workers demanding an improvement in
working and living conditions; the police killed three workers immediately and mortally wounded ten others.[29] Two days before Mayday, the
workshop of the Karl Ludwig railroad in Lviv burst into flames. The
military surrounded the railroad station and, according to Ignacy Daszyński, "wealthier people equipped themselves with revolvers, a
circumstance that gun dealers profited from."[30]

Although all omens augured otherwise, Mayday 1890 in Lviv was a
peaceful, if militant, affair. Without hindrance from the police, four
thousand workers gathered in the city hall square for an imposing mass
assembly over which Daniluk presided. After speeches, the workers
demanded an eight-hour day, universal suffrage, the abolition of a
standing army and the rejection of a project for confessional schools.
The workers also resolved to send a wreath to the grave of Lassalle and
to establish a new workers' association.[31]

Assemblies of Ruthenian peasants also played a role in the development of socialism in Galicia. Peasant assemblies were a traditional part
of the Ruthenian national movement. Ruthenian leaders convoked such
assemblies both to demonstrate popular support for the national cause
and to inspire patriotism in the peasantry. The Supreme Ruthenian
Council had convoked many assemblies in 1848–49. The annual meetings of the Kachkovsky Society, 1874–76, assumed the aspect of peasant
assemblies. In 1880, 1883 and 1884 the national populists and Russophiles joined forces to organize peasant assemblies in Lviv. For the
history of the socialist movement, however, the most important assemblies were those of 1886 held in Kosiv (31 August), Kolomyia (29 September) and Stanyslaviv (8 December).[32]

The organizers of the 1886 assemblies were a band of young provincial intellectuals in correspondence with Mykhailo Drahomanov. The
"Stanyslaviv group," as it was known, was to be a major source of
leadership for the Ruthenian-Ukrainian Radical Party in the 1890s. The
group included: Teofil Okunevsky, an aspiring lawyer; Severyn Danylovych, also an aspiring lawyer, an old comrade of Ivan Franko with
whom he met frequently in 1879–81 to discuss socialist literature;[33] and

Iliarii Harasymovych. Harasymovych was the son of a Russophile priest, pastor of the Hutsul village Mykulychyn. As a gymnasium student in Stanyslaviv, Harasymovych joined the Ukrainophile hromada led by Volodymyr Navrotsky and Ostap Terletsky. Like Terletsky, he went to Vienna to study, there joined the student association Sich, met Drahomanov and occasionally contributed a note to *Kievskii telegraf*. Because of his family's poverty, however, Harasymovych was unable to complete his education. After serving in the Austrian army, he returned to his native region and eked out a living on the land, subsisting on potatoes. When Danylovych and Okunevsky found him in the mid-1880s, Harasymovych differed little from his peasant neighbors.[34] This combination in one person of peasant and intellectual was very useful, first to the Stanyslaviv group and later to the Radical party.

In 1885–86, the Stanyslaviv group founded six reading clubs in villages near Stanyslaviv and regularly gave popular lectures in these clubs.[35] Their conscious purpose was to politicize the Ruthenian peasantry. Okunevsky made this explicit in a letter to Drahomanov: "We are mainly concerned that our peasant, who barely comprehends the business of the commune let alone the crownland or — what is more — of the state, might understand the connection that exists between his own well-being and what transpires in the District Council, Diet or parliament."[36]

In the fall of 1886, the Stanyslaviv group directed most of its efforts at organizing mass peasant assemblies in south-eastern Galicia. Okunevsky felt there were two evident benefits from these assemblies:

> First. The masses of the nation, who until now have not thought at all or have only thought a little about their social position, are coming — very slowly, it is true — to consciousness concerning their vital interests. Second. Younger people — since only these, in the main prepare their talks at assemblies — are beginning to examine and more profoundly penetrate into the urgent needs of our people, i.e., they are familiarizing themselves with our people's current political and economic situation.[37]

Although generally the Stanyslaviv group was critical of the older national populist intelligentsia,[38] they did appreciate the earlier efforts of the Stanyslaviv national populists Leonid Zaklynsky and Yevhen Zhelekhivsky. These two had founded reading clubs in the Stanyslaviv area and in general had "significantly set in motion the masses of the peasantry."[39] This was clear from the contrast between assemblies held in Kolomyia and Stanyslaviv. In Kolomyia, where there had been no intellectuals working among the peasants, the assembly was marred by a low level of political consciousness. In fact, about a third of the peasants attended with the idea that the intellectuals who spoke at the assembly could be engaged gratis to take up specific court cases.[40] The situation was quite different at the Stanyslaviv assembly, where "the peasants displayed more interest and understanding of affairs. . . . It was evident that the work of Zhelekhivsky, Leonid Zaklynsky, etc., did not go to naught."[41]

The speakers at the assemblies were mainly intellectuals, members of the Stanyslaviv group or well-known national populists such as Yuliian Romanchuk and Oleksander Ohonovsky. On the advice of Drahomanov, however, the Stanyslaviv group also coached peasants to speak. At the Stanyslaviv assembly, peasant speakers, such as Huryk and Hudyk, caused the greatest sensation.[42] The Stanyslaviv assembly, in fact, foreshadowed the mass peasant assemblies organized by the Radical party in the 1890s.

The work of the Stanyslaviv group spread as the members themselves moved from Stanyslaviv. In 1888 Danylovych transferred his activities to Kolomyia, where he opened a law office. Harasymovych went with him. Soon thereafter, Okunevsky opened a law office in Horodenka.[43] During the same period, 1888–89, Kyrylo Tryliovsky, another aspiring lawyer, carried on work similar to that of the Stanyslaviv group in Sniatyn.[44]

The Stanyslaviv group expanded its activities beyond working with reading clubs and organizing peasant assemblies. In 1887–88, the group planned to publish a monthly journal in Stanyslaviv.[45] In 1886 the Kolomyia assembly resolved to set up a Hutsul industrial cooperative to market the wood carvings and other craft products of this Ukrainian mountain tribe. Iliarii Harasymovych was the initiator and guiding spirit of the cooperative, which opened for business in February 1888.[46] In 1889 the Stanyslaviv group — by this time resettled in Kolomyia and environs — entered electoral politics. As a result of its agitation, it sent Okunevsky to the Galician Diet as deputy from the Kolomyia district.[47]

In sum, the Stanyslaviv group — under the influence of Drahomanov, Terletsky and Franko — conducted systematic agitation in the countryside, using the smaller Galician cities such as Kolomyia and Stanyslaviv as bases of operation. In the 1880s they worked hand in hand with the national populists, using national populist methods (read-

ing clubs, assemblies) to politicize the peasantry. At this time there was
no clear distinction between them and the national populists, except
that the Stanyslaviv group was younger, more energetic and potentially
more radical.

Student Radicalism in the 1880s

The Impact of Russia

Poles from Russia had already had a tremendous impact on the socialist
movement in Cracow from 1878 to 1884; and in the second half of the
1880s they also had a great influence on the radical Polish student
movement throughout Galicia, playing a role similar to that which
Drahomanov had played in relation to the Austrian Ruthenian students:
they contrasted their own progressiveness to the backwardness of the
Austrians and urged the Galician students to embrace more radical
social doctrines.

If there is any one figure who most approximated a Polish Drahomanov, it was Bolesław Wysłouch. Although Wysłouch and Drahomanov did not see eye to eye, they had certain essential features in
common: both advocated a doctrine of peasant radicalism (populism),
both formed their world views in Russian left-wing circles, both devoted
themselves to the social enlightenment of their Galician conationals,
especially students. Wysłouch, however, unlike Drahomanov, moved to
Lviv and obtained Austrian citizenship. He therefore could dispense
with the correspondence upon which Drahomanov had to rely almost
exclusively. The loss to the historian is great. Drahomanov's arguments
are clearly laid out in hundred of letters. So, too, are the responses of
Ruthenian students, whose almost day-by-day radicalization we can
trace in the Drahomanov correspondence. Since there is no equivalent
Wysłouch correspondence, we cannot so clearly document his role in
the process of radicalization.

Wysłouch's influence on the Galician socialist movement was limited
to the 1880s. Thereafter he and the peasant movement he sponsored
had little in common with the artisan-based Polish socialist movement.
Wysłouch's populist doctrine itself had no influence on the development
of Polish socialism in Galicia. His contribution consisted instead in a

general stimulation of Galician intellectual life through publications and a salon.

Of the several publications that Wysłouch founded or bought after coming to Lviv in 1884, the short-lived *Przegląd Społeczny* (Social Review) was the most outstanding.[48] Only eighteen monthly issues appeared in 1886–87, but they were filled with contributions by the very best Polish, Ukrainian and Jewish writers and thinkers. Contributors included the Polish socialists Bolesław Limanowski, Ludwik Krzywicki, Wilhelm Feldman, Edward Przewóski and Kazimierz Dłuski as well as the Ukrainian socialists Mykhailo Drahomanov, Ivan Franko and Mykhailo Pavlyk. From outside the socialist camp, Wysłouch himself, Zygmunt Balicki, Jan Kasprowicz, Zygmunt Miłkowski, Witold Lewicki and Alfred Nossig wrote for the journal. As Wilhelm Feldman noted a quarter-century later: "Here are the germs of all the more important ideas that would plow Polish soil for the next twenty years: populism, national democracy, Marxist socialism, zionism, assimilation, bourgeois radicalism, Ukrainophilism — all those currents, which would later vehemently battle each other, here yet stand side by side, some new-born, some already covered with wounds."[49]

Although *Przegląd Społeczny* was not a socialist organ, the Lviv police believed that "socialist propaganda is the aim of the periodical," and they noted with consternation that "the monthly is frequently to be found among the youth."[50] The Ruthenian socialist Viacheslav Budzynovsky, then a gymnasium student in Lviv, regularly mailed copies of *Przegląd Społeczny* to a secret student club in Ternopil gymnasium.[51] *Przegląd Społeczny* was also required reading in socialist student clubs in Lviv gymnasia. Władysław Arciszewski told a group of socialist gymnasium students in Lviv:

> Several local progressives, who have gotten together and asked for the collaboration of a number of Warsaw writers as well as Jeż [Zygmunt Miłkowski], Limanowski, Sosnowski and Dłuski in emigration, have founded a social review. They want to use this review especially to influence youth. It is our duty to become familiar with this fresh movement.[52]

Wysłouch's home was like a living *Przegląd Społeczny*. Here one could meet such contributors as Franko, Nossig and Krzywicki or veterans of the Lviv socialist movement such as the brothers Inlaender; Maria Wysłouch, an outstanding figure in her own right, was also present. Young socialists — Feliks and Ignacy Daszyński, Zygmunt Seweryn and probably many more — dropped into Wysłouch's salon and certainly benefited as much from the conversations there as they did from the pages of the journal itself.[53]

In addition to Wysłouch, other Russian-born Poles contributed to the radicalization of the young Polish intelligentsia in Galicia. From the mid-1880s, Russian-born Poles formed a much larger percentage of Galicia's student population. The increase in Russian enrollment derived from the Apukhtin affair. In Russian Poland in the spring of 1883, the Chief School Inspector of Warsaw, Aleksandr Apukhtin, "a man of limited intelligence who hated Poles,"[54] had a number of students arrested for reading socialist literature. Student protests ensued and one student — an ethnic Russian — struck Apukhtin in the face. As a consequence of the Apukhtin incident, over three hundred Polish students were suspended from Warsaw University and the Puławy Agricultural Institute. Many of them continued their education in Galicia. This was the first large wave of Russian Polish youth to emigrate to Galician universities and, in the face of undiminishing anti-Polish repression in Russia, the flow of Russian-born students continued. The Russian-born students tended, on the whole, to be more radical than their Austrian-born fellows and formed the majority of the so-called "Draconians," or extreme leftists, at Galician universities.[55] The Russian students influenced their contemporaries and contributed to the over-all radicalization of Galician youth.

Then, too, Galicia in the late 1880s was still a convenient half-way station for Polish socialists travelling between Russia and Western Europe as well as a potential refuge for Polish socialists escaping arrest in Russia. Ludwik Krzywicki, the first to translate *Capital* into Polish, came in 1885 to Lviv and here worked closely with Feliks Daszyński and edited the socialist newspaper *Praca*.[56] Witold Jodko-Narkiewicz, who came to Lviv to study, also worked with Krzywicki and Daszyński in *Praca*. The police arrested him and the authorities deported him in December 1885.[57] More Russian-born socialists were arrested and deported in 1888–90, among them Stanisław Padlewski,[58] Władysław Gizbert,[59] Wincenty Sikorski,[60] Florian Skarzyński,[61] Szymon Michał Szpunt[62] and Izaak Kassjusz.[63] The case of Kassjusz especially upset his Lviv comrades, because the Lviv police, by order of the Austrian Ministry of the Interior, turned Kassjusz over to the Russian gendarmes.

Anti-socialist cooperation between the Austrian and Russian authorities was very close in 1889–90. By 1890 it became official Austrian policy to deport Russian socialists directly to Russia, where they were imprisoned, rather than to Western Europe.[64] On 8 September 1889, the Russian embassy in Vienna installed a special attaché to work with the Austrian police in the fight against socialism. The Galician viceroy allowed the Russian secret police to set up a headquarters on Galician soil, in Podwołoczyski near the Russian border, in order to combat socialist agitation.[65] Such efforts testify to the importance of Russian-Galician contacts in the development of Polish socialism in the Austrian crownland.

The Student Movement in Lviv

Lviv's student movement owed much to a talented and energetic native of Galicia, Feliks Daszyński, who originally became interested in socialism after the 1878 trial. He was born in 1864 in an East Galician town on the Russian border, Zbarazh, but after the death of his father, a district official, in 1875, the family moved to Stanyslaviv. Here Feliks attended gymnasium and, at the age of sixteen, initiated his political career.

In Stanyslaviv, as elsewhere in partitioned Poland, there was the custom of gathering in the cemetery on All Souls' Day (1 November) to honor the memory of slain insurgents. For the 1880 commemoration, Feliks — motivated by Polish patriotism — composed an anti-Habsburg verse. His young brother Ignacy hectographed it and distributed it to the youth at the cemetery. Three days later the brothers were arrested. Feliks spent weeks in investigative imprisonment in Stanyslaviv before a jury unanimously acquitted him of disturbing the peace. The prosecutor had earlier dropped charges against Ignacy.[66]

The brothers in this period were the most fervent of Polish patriots. They belonged to a secret patriotic club composed of Polish students from all the secondary schools in Stanyslaviv. The club enjoyed the patronage of Władysław Dzwonkowski, a veteran conspirator and émigré from the Congress Kingdom. Dzwonkowski's son, also named Władysław, joined the club and became a close friend of Feliks Daszyński.

The club met in the home of the Dzwonkowski family or else made excursions to the countryside outside Stanyslaviv. On the excursions,

the young patriots practiced military arts to prepare for the next insurrection. This secret organization considerably altered its ideology in
1881 under the influence of a group of Ruthenian students. The new
ideology was a variant of Slavophilism. Together, the Polish and Ruthenian students worked out a program of primitive Slavic communism.
In October 1881 delegates were dispatched, Feliks Daszyński to Cracow and Władysław Dzwonkowski to Lviv, to propagate the program
among the more famous socialists of the time, including Franko. The
delegates, however, returned with a whole library of socialist literature
and the secret club of some thirty Slavophile schoolboys was transformed into a nest of socialists.[67]

On 28 February 1882 the prosecutor's office in Stanyslaviv received a
confidential denunciation, emanating from the local Russophiles, that
Stanyslaviv students had formed a secret socialist cell. The denunciation
specified that Feliks Daszyński and the young Władysław Dzwonkowski as well as two Ruthenians, Ivan Porubalsky and Mykola Yaky-
movych, led the socialist organization. The police arrested the four and,
after further investigation, also arrested three others. One of these
others, Wiktor Balicki, then an elementary school teacher in the Sambir
district, was delivered to Stanyslaviv in chains. The prosecutor first
hoped to charge the students with high treason, but for lack of evidence
instead prosecuted them for belonging to a secret society. On 4 August
1883, after appeals, the Stanyslaviv court sentenced Feliks Daszyński
to six weeks in prison.[68]

In the meantime, in the fall of 1882, Feliks Daszyński moved to Lviv
and stayed there off and on until the fall of 1886. In Lviv he engaged in a
wide spectrum of socialist activity. He joined, it seems, one of the
conspiratorial cells that emerged there in the late summer of 1882. He
was definitely the author of the inflammatory leaflet of May 1883 that
threatened the authorities if the arrested socialist conspirators were not
acquitted.[69] In the fall of 1883 he took part in engineering and carrying
out a daring jail break for one of the convicted conspirators, Zygmunt
Balicki, a Russian subject in danger of deportation.[70] He wrote for
Praca, Cracow's *Robotnik,* and *Ziarno* (Seed; a left-leaning periodical
edited by Adolf Inlaender). With Ludwik Krzywicki, he attempted a
reform of *Praca,* and he worked for a while with Wysłouch.[71] He
agitated among workers in the taverns. He helped Udałowicz compose
the statutes of a carpenters' cooperative. However, Feliks Daszyński's
most lasting contribution to Galician socialism was the kindling of the

radical student movement. He campaigned among Lviv students on behalf of Cracow's radical periodical *Przyszłość* (The Future) and recruited a great many Lviv students to the socialist cause, including Władysław Arciszewski and Stanyslav Kozlovsky.[72]

In the mid-1880s, the Daszyński brothers (Ignacy had joined Feliks in Lviv) provided the initiative to establish socialist student clubs in the Lviv gymnasia.[73] The clubs put out a manuscript periodical, *Propagator,* in February 1885, and met — sometimes in groups of forty — to listen to lectures or to read and discuss Lassalle's workers' program, *The Communist Manifesto* and related literature. The police arrested several members of these clubs in December 1886 and, quite out of character, released them without prosecution.[74]

Other leaders of the socialist gymnasium students, besides Ignacy Daszyński, were Jan Zalplachta, Władysław Arciszewski, Zygmunt Seweryn, Wilhelm Feldman and Viacheslav Budzynovsky. Of these only Feldman was not enrolled in any school. Completely self-taught, he worked full time as a secretary for the Jewish kahal (autonomous community organization) and part time as a journalist.[75] Feldman also tried his hand at belles-lettres on Jewish themes and in 1884 one of his short stories appeared in the socialist paper *Praca.*[76] He kept a diary, too, and this gives us some insight into the emotions and thought processes of the young socialists in Lviv. On 28 September 1886 he made the following entry in his diary:

> In general I am no enemy of religion, but religiousness is an obstacle to the dissemination of socialism. As long as the poor man looks to heaven for recompense for his poverty, things will be in a sorry state.

On 14 December 1886 he wrote in his diary:

> I consciously and soberly take up this work. I know the consequences of socialist agitation, I know that I am sentencing myself to material poverty. I know this, but I will work for the ideal, for the future, for the idea in which I see the realization of liberty, equality and fraternity. Long live the social revolution![77]

Zygmunt Seweryn wrote a short autobiography that also affords a glimpse into the feelings of the young socialists:

> I am a realist. I respect in myself the man, the Pole, the socialist. I am an atheist in region, a *collectivist* in sociology.[78]

Although Feldman was Jewish, he made no attempt to set up a

separate Jewish circle for gymnasium socialists. Viacheslav Budzynovsky, however, a Ruthenian, did establish a distinct Ruthenian circle. Budzynovsky became a socialist, as a fifth-year gymnasium student (1884?), after reading an antisocialist brochure by a Polish priest.[79] In February 1886 he joined a secret Ruthenian club at one of the Lviv gymnasia and there delivered a controversial talk on Darwinism. The club was not socialist, although the Russophiles denounced it as such and the club disbanded.[80] Then Budzynovsky joined the Polish socialist groups in the gymnasia. Soon thereafter he founded his own socialist circle of sixteen–eighteen members, mainly Ruthenians.[81]

The leaders of the Lviv gymnasium students — Daszyński, Zalplachta, Arciszewski, Seweryn, Feldman and Budzynovsky — graduated within the next few years to agitate among the students of the universities and higher schools.

In the mid-1880s, the center of radical intellectual life in Galicia's higher schools was Lviv Polytechnic. Here Feliks Daszyński had carried on agitation prior to his departure for Switzerland in the autumn of 1886. Here two of his loyal friends, Arciszewski and Kozlovsky, continued agitation into the late 1880s. In 1887–88 they dominated the legally registered student club Zachęta Naukowa (Scholarly Encouragement). The club worked on a translation of an essay by Karl Kautsky and entered into close cooperation with the Kółko Filozoficzne (Philosophic Circle) of Lviv University.[82]

Disturbed by the activities of these clubs and by a "Slavonic Circle" (Kółko Słowiańskie) at Lviv University, the police, probably on the viceroy's nod, issued an order to the student organizations either to revise their statutes or to disband. As it was, the police argued, the club's meetings had taken on the character of public assemblies, with non-members participating in meetings and with discussions at the meetings ranging over topics well beyond the limits of the club's statutes. The police further demanded, at least twenty-four hours in advance of every club meeting, a detailed agenda.[83]

The police probably issued their order in May or June 1888,[84] but the Lviv students did not take decisive action until the new academic year began in October. On Kozlovsky's initiative, Lviv students of both the university and polytechnic held an assembly at the university on 31 October 1888 to protest the police order. The assembly unanimously voted to appeal to the viceroy and parliament to rescind the police order. In the text of the appeal, the students referred to the police order as "an attack on academic liberties." Many professors agreed with the students and sent a declaration to the viceroy in November 1888 to argue for the repeal of the order.[85]

Following the assembly, again at Kozlovsky's initiative, Lviv students adopted another strategy to supplement the protest action: the establishment of a new association uniting students from several higher schools, but not strictly a student club, therefore unaffected by the police order. In November (or perhaps later), Kozlovsky, Budzynovsky, Kazimierz Górzycki, Teodor Kasparek and Aleksander Klimaszewski began to meet to work out the statutes of the projected association. In April 1889 they also invited three students from the Dubliany Agricultural School outside Lviv to participate in the meetings.[86]

This same group of students interrupted its deliberations on the establishment of a new association to call another student assembly, which met for two days, 9 and 10 March 1889. The aim of the assembly was to unite all Galician students into a single organization. Representatives of Lviv University, Lviv Polytechnic, the veterinary school and the Dubliany Agricultural School addressed the assembly. Although no representatives from Cracow attended, the Cracow students were inspired by the Lviv assembly to plan (but never actually to convoke) their own assembly. Kozlovsky presided over the assembly and others active in the preparations and proceedings included Budzynovsky, Kyrylo Tryliovsky and Joachim Fraenkel — future activists of the Ruthenian and Polish socialist parties. Three to five hundred students attended the first day's proceedings, eight hundred the next day's. High attendance was guaranteed by the cooperation, very short-lived, between socialist-leaning and Polish nationalist students at Lviv Polytechnic.

The assembly was most important as a stimulating experience in rebellion, rather than for any concrete accomplishments. The assembly did elect a student executive committee and also announced ambitions to publish a progressive journal in Polish and Ukrainian, but both the executive committee and the journal plans were forgotten after the assembly. The assembly passed a resolution condemning the Academic Senate of Lviv University for supporting police restrictions on student clubs; it also called for the separation of church and state and for the resignation of the unpopular Austrian minister of education, Baron Paul von Gautsch. Following one session of the assembly, some hundred students made a tour of Lviv's editorical offices, stopping to cheer Wysłouch's *Kurjer Lwowski* and to jeer the conservative *Przegląd* (Review).[87]

The assembly polarized opinion in the Lviv student population. In the aftermath of the assembly, Polish nationalists in the university's Czytelnia Akademicka (Scholastic Reading Club) issued a declaration censuring the assembly. In an open letter to the newspaper, the nationalist students declared that "cosmopolitans" had arranged the assembly and that the assembly had taken up no specifically Polish cause. Czytelnia Akademicka held a stormy general meeting on 23 March 1889 to determine the club's position on the matter. After heated discussion, the nationalists triumphed by a vote of fifty to forty-nine and the left wing of the club, unable to endorse a condemnation of the assembly, quit the club altogether. The Fraternal Aid Society of Lviv Polytechnic and the Ruthenian student club Akademichne bratstvo (Scholastic Brotherhood) broke off all relations with the nationalist Czytelnia Akademicka.[88]

Others who reacted negatively to the assembly were the university authorities and the Lviv police. Lviv University expelled Kasparek and Budzynovsky;[89] the Polytechnic expelled Kozlovsky and Adolf Schleyen.[90] In the months following the assembly, the police investigated the student movement, eventually making over a dozen arrests in July, including the arrest of Wysłouch. Wysłouch and six students (among them, Kozlovsky) spent almost three months in prison before prosecution in late September for belonging to a secret socialist society.[91]

During these same years, 1888–89, Lviv students began to cooperate more closely with the artisan movement, especially with the socialists grouped around *Praca*. In 1888 members of the university student club Czytelnia Akademicka gave lessons to the journeymen in the Catholic artisan association Skała. Joachim Fraenkel taught German and stylistics; Ernest Breiter taught Polish, Polish history, geography and arithmetic.[92] (Both Fraenkel and Breiter were later active in the Polish socialist party.) To some extent in 1888, but more so in 1889, Lviv students — especially Budzynovsky and Kozlovsky — worked closely with *Praca,* contributing articles and lending a hand in the editing.[93] The students also took part in organizing the artisan assemblies in 1889. The Lviv police even concluded that Kozlovsky was directing the whole artisan revival of that year. Kozlovsky did organize, or help to organize, several artisan assemblies, including the assemblies of 13 January 1889 (to discuss the Pernerstorfer project for Workers' Chambers) and of 16 June 1889 (dealing with workers' accident insurance). Kozlovsky also spoke at the 30 May 1889 assembly; in fact, he was the one to propose that the Lviv workers send a delegate to the Second International's founding congress in Paris.[94] The participation of Lviv's socialist students in the artisan assembly of 16 March 1889 gave *Praca* occasion for rejoicing:

> The day of March 16th must remain memorable in the history of our social-democratic party. . . . After a few speeches — sincere and bare of empty, noisy phrases — a festive mood, encompassing all participants, united the black, sinewy hands of the workers with the smooth, yet ready-for-action, hands of the socialist students in a fraternal clasp. An alliance has been concluded.[95]

Cracovians

By the turn of the century, Cracow was no longer the staid and stifling city that we have come to know, the nest of the Stańczyks and Jesuits, and the home of an artisan population distinguished by its passivity and backwardness.[96] Instead, in the 1890s the artistic phenomenon known as "Young Poland" blossomed in Cracow and the socialist party had become an important political force in the city. The seed of this metamorphosis was a small group of students who published the periodical *Ognisko* (Hearth) and who accomplished what one of them later called "an Icarian emigration beyond the boundaries of the contemporary youth's convictions."

These students were in conscious and open revolt against "the backwardness of the environment" and hoped to "move closer to Europe." They lived a Bohemian life of "eternal defects in footwear, communism in clothing and bedding, thin tea for breakfast, lunch and supper, a cold, unheated room." Hungry and sniffling from colds, they spent sleepless nights in theoretical discussions, exploding with heat and passion, about how to "provide 'bread' for the millions of mankind's pariahs." They were called "outcasts of Cracow society," but they considered themselves a "wave in the enormous sea of nameless, suffering throngs, roaring with the accusation of centuries, emerging ever more threateningly from the seabeds of the world."[97]

From the *Ognisko* group came some of the great critics and poets of "Young Poland": Kazimierz Tetmajer, Franciszek Nowicki and Artur

Górski. The group also contributed activists to the Polish socialist party in Cracow (Gabriel Górski) and Lviv (Ernest Breiter). Feldman travelled frequently from Lviv to Cracow to work with the *Ognisko* group. Although Ignacy Daszyński stayed on the periphery of the group, his long-time friend, Roman Baraniecki, entered *Ognisko*'s editorial board.[98]

Gabriel Górski and Franciszek Nowicki initiated the project of publishing a student periodical early in 1888 at a meeting of Jagellonian University's student club, Czytelnia Akademicka. Górski and Nowicki spent a full year looking for financial support for the journal. Górski appealed to the university youth in Warsaw for support, but the Warsaw students promised nothing, since they distrusted their "backward and sleepy" fellows in Cracow. Górski eventually did, however, collect 200 g. to begin publication of the journal *Ognisko*.[99]

The journal was ephemeral owing to suppression by the university and state prosecuting authorities. The first issue came out on 5 April 1889 and, for legal reasons, immediately afterwards the journal ceased publication. The first issue of a legally different journal, but with the same title, staff and tendencies, appeared in May 1889.[100] Only a few more issues appeared in 1889 and the last issue of *Ognisko* came out as a brochure in Lviv in 1890.[101]

The leftward tendencies of *Ognisko* are evident from the list of authors invited to contribute to the journal: Ludwik Krzywicki,[102] Edward Przewóski, Limanowski, Pavlyk, Drahomanov and Franko.[103] In his letter to Franko, Gabriel Górski described the tasks of the journal as "awakening sympathy for the populist ideal (*idea ludowa*) among Polish student youth and recruiting youth to influence the people."[104] In its first programmatic article, *Ognisko* declared that it primarily sought to formulate goals for Polish youth. It promised to rely exclusively on scientific methods in the formulation of these goals.[105]

The national question was a recurrent theme in *Ognisko*'s articles. *Ognisko* called for the independence of Poland, but always made sure to specify that it was referring to an ethnic, and not historical, Poland. The journal supported the Ruthenian national movement without reservation and even published an occasional article in the Ukrainian language, in the Cyrillic alphabet. The journal's pro-Ruthenian orientation, adopted under Drahomanov's influence, provoked the ire of Polish nationalist students throughout Galicia. *Ognisko*'s vision of an independent Poland differed from that of the nationalists not only on the

question of boundaries, but on the question of socio-economic structure; *Ognisko*'s Poland was a socialist state. *Ognisko* argued that
expropriation of the landholders and capitalists was patriotic, because
land and capital were rapidly passing into German and Jewish hands.
Capitalism, furthermore, was now everywhere in its last phase before
collapse. Although *Ognisko* ridiculed the concept of harmony among
contending social classes, it denied the necessity of deliberate engage-
ment in the class struggle or the forcible suppression of the privileged
classes. History, *Ognisko* believed, would do the work of revolution by
itself.[106]

In accord with this determinist doctrine, the *Ognisko* group as yet
made no attempt to enter into contact with the working class of Cracow.

Ruthenians

The radical student movement of the second half of the 1880s affected
Ruthenians as well as Poles. There has already been mention of secret
Ruthenian circles in the gymnasia and Ruthenian participation in the
student assembly of March 1889. Also, two of the most active leaders of
the Galician students were ethnic Ruthenians: Viacheslav Budzynovsky
and Stanyslav Kozlovsky.

In 1888, Kozlovsky and Budzynovsky decided to publish a periodical
in the Ukrainian language. They invited two of their Polish comrades,
Arciszewski and Seweryn, to join the editorial board. They also invited
Franko and Pavlyk to help edit the periodical.[107] Furthermore, Budzynovsky and Kozlovsky encouraged other Ruthenian students to write
for the journal: Osyp Makovei (later an outstanding satirist), Mykola
Hankevych (later active in the Radical and social democratic parties)
and Kyrylo Tryliovsky (later active in the Radical party).[108]

With this crew of editors and writers, the end product, *Tovarysh*
(Comrade), was a leftist publication. *Tovarysh* was most closely related
to Franko's old publication *S'vit*: more theoretical than agitational, an
attempt at a rounded socio-political and literary review with socialist
tendencies. It collapsed after a single issue appeared in June 1888.

Tovarysh collapsed for two reasons. First, there was the old problem
of money. The editors went into debt on the first issue.[109] Second, the
editors fell out among themselves. A split occurred along the lines of
age: the "elders" were Franko and Pavlyk, the "young" — Budzynovsky, Kozlovsky, Tryliovsky, Hankevych and Makovei. Budzynovsky

and Tryliovsky were particularly vehement in their opposition to the "elders," accusing Franko of filling the journal with the writings of old men, to the neglect of the students who had founded the journal in the first place. The young also accused Franko of leaning towards anti-Semitism and nationalism. Some objected to the publication of an article by Drahomanov.[110] This was the first instance in the Ruthenian left of the division between the elders and the young that was to plague the Radical party until a split resolved dissensions in 1899.[111] A personal animosity developed between Budzynovsky and Franko, also between Tryliovsky and Franko, which was to disturb the harmony of the Ruthenian left for the next dozen years.

The doctrinal overtones of the split concerned the opposition of Marxism to Drahomanovism, since Budzynovsky and Hankevych were both enamored of Marxism, while Franko and Pavlyk were the pillars of Drahomanovism. The division in *Tovarysh* did not correspond completely to the ideological lines, since Tryliovsky — himself an orthodox Drahomanovist — also opposed Franko. The conflict between the followers of Marx and Drahomanov was also felt in the Ruthenian student club at Lviv University, Akademichne bratstvo. Budzynovsky quit the club because the Drahomanovian Tryliovsky was elected president in the autumn of 1888. A former president of the club, Yevhen Kozakevych, was an ardent Marxist who did not recognize Drahomanov's theories as socialist.[112]

In spite of these differences, an incident occurred in 1889 that served to bind together the Ruthenian left: the Degen affair, a remarkable display of bungling and inefficiency on the part of the Austrian and Galician authorities. It all began when several students from Russian Ukraine, Sergei Degen and his two sisters as well as Bohdan Kistiakivsky and Apolinary Marszyński, decided to visit Galicia. All of them were having problems with their health and looked forward to hikes in the Carpathian mountains. They were eager to learn about Ruthenian life in Galicia, to improve their spoken Ukrainian (the Degens had little opportunity to speak Ukrainian in Kiev) and to consult Franko's excellent library. The students had political connections with Russian opponents of absolutism, but they had not come to Galicia on any political mission.[113]

Nonetheless, the Austrian vice consul in Kiev, Franz von Spóner, on the basis of an anonymous report he received, sent a letter to the Austrian foreign minister, Kálnoky, on 17 July 1889. Spóner's letter warned the minister that Degen and consorts were coming to Galicia "on the instructions of a certain Drahomanov" to incite the Ruthenians against the Polish nobility.[114] Perhaps Drahomanov was only "a certain Drahomanov" to the vice consul, but to the Galician police he was well known as the "chief of the Little Russian section of nihilists,"[115] the representative of an international conspiracy to overthrow law and order throughout Europe. In the mythology of the Galician police, Drahomanov was the evil genius behind many of the clandestine socialist organizations discovered, or fabricated, by the police in the 1870s and 1880s. The mere mention of this "certain Drahomanov" roused the Galician authorities to action: the Russian students were arrested along with over a dozen Galicians, mainly students associated with the socialist or national movement. Prominent among those arrested were Franko, Pavlyk, Volodymyr Okhrymovych, Yuliian Bachynsky, and Kyrylo Tryliovsky — all founders of the Radical party in the following year.

Having turned a summer holiday into a dangerous conspiracy, the Galician authorities were faced with the almost impossible task of defining the purpose of this conspiracy. An important clue, it seemed to them, was that the students from Russia had attended an ethnographic evening at which was sung the Ukrainian national hymn, "Shche ne vmerla Ukraina" (Ukraine Lives On). Obviously, the conspiracy was directed against the territorial integrity of the Habsburg and tsarist empires and aimed at the creation of an independent Ruthenian-Ukrainian state. Several months later all suspects had to be released from prison owing to a complete lack of evidence.

The Degen affair, then, was little more than a concoction of the police, a paranoid fantasy translated into the realities of arrest, investigative imprisonment and the threat of the gallows for high treason. It was significant, however, as an external event binding the suspects, the Ruthenian left, into a group foreshadowing the socialist political party that would emerge in the following year.

The Founding of Parties

The Ruthenian-Ukrainian Radical Party

By 1890 the left-wing Ruthenian intelligentsia was numerous enough to establish its own political party. Three separate groups formed this left wing: the veterans Franko and Pavlyk, the former Stanyslaviv group (by 1889 known as the Kolomyia group) and the radical students. Tendencies toward unified action had already appeared in the late 1880s. In 1888 the periodical *Tovarysh* united, albeit briefly, the veterans with the young students. In 1889 the Kolomyia group, particularly Severyn Danylovych, was corresponding with Franko and Pavlyk about the possibility of publishing a joint periodical and eventually creating a Ruthenian "peasants'-workers' party."[116] As a result of this correspondence, Franko and Pavlyk began to publish the journal *Narod* (The People) in Lviv on 1 January 1890. They invited students — Volodymyr Okhrymovych, Mykola Hankevych, Yevhen Levytsky and others — to contribute to the periodical. In this way *Narod* became the common organ of all three elements in the Ruthenian left. *Narod* started out with about a dozen subscribers in January 1890; by June, it had attracted 251. The secular intelligentsia made up the largest contingent of subscribers, but students, associations, peasants, emigrants to America and even a surprisingly large number of priests also subscribed to *Narod*.[117]

Although the Ruthenian left grouped around *Narod* constituted a party in the wide sense, a political party in the strict sense only emerged in October 1890. A relatively minor incident provided the occasion for the formal establishment of a Ruthenian socialist party. In the summer of 1890, Galician Poles were preparing to transfer the relics of Adam Mickiewicz from Paris to Cracow. They invited the Ruthenians to participate in the solemnities of the transferral, but the national populist leaders — Yuliian Romanchuk, Natal Vakhnianyn and Ivan Belei — refused, in the name of all Ruthenians, to participate. This refusal angered two segments of the Ruthenian public: Oleksander Barvinsky and other like-minded national populists who hoped to make a political alliance with the Polish nobility (the so-called "new era"); and the Ruthenian left, who collaborated closely with socialist and populist Poles.

One of Barvinsky's adherents, the student Pavlo Kyrchiv, summoned all the left-wing malcontents to a meeting at Franko's home in late June or early July 1890. About fifteen or twenty of these malcontents attended, mainly students. Kyrchiv hoped to organize a collective protest against Romanchuk *et al.*, but Viacheslav Budzynovsky changed the focus of the meeting by suggesting that there were now enough young, progressive Ruthenians to establish a separate political party. He even selected a name for the party, the Radical party, "because they call us radicals anyway." The assembled malcontents forgot about Mickiewicz's relics and the division among the national populists. Instead they discussed Budzynovsky's proposal and appealed to Franko and Pavlyk for their opinion. Franko settled the question when he said: "Gentlemen, comrades, I didn't think our thoughts had crystallized enough, nor that our number sufficed to found a distinct party. But if you think the time is ripe, then — in God's name — let's begin!" The assembled radicals agreed to call the party's founding congress in the fall.[118]

Less than thirty[119] Ruthenians attended the founding congress of the Ruthenian-Ukrainian Radical Party (Lviv, 4–5 October 1890). No list of founders was ever compiled, but the following were certainly present: Franko, Pavlyk, and Ostap Terletsky; the student radicals Roman Yarosevych, Yuliian Bachynsky, Budzynovsky, Yevhen Levytsky, Volodymyr Okhrymovych, Mykola Hankevych and Kyrylo Tryliovsky; the Kolomyia group — Danylovych, Harasymovych and Okunevsky.

Serious differences emerged at the congress, especially between the young Marxists and older Drahomanovists (including the Kolomyia group). The congress attempted to patch over the differences by approving a party program with maximal and minimal parts. Young Marxists — Levytsky, Hanevych and Okhrymovych — drew up the maximal part of the program; Franko, Pavlyk and Danylovych — the minimal.[120]

The very short maximal program declared that the party adhered to "scientific socialism" and aimed at "the transformation of the means of production in accordance with the achievements of scientific socialism." It called for "a collective system of labor and collective ownership of the means of production."[121] The Drahomanovist postulates of rationalism, realism and communal autonomy also figured in the maximal program.

The economic portion of the minimal program proposed a series of reforms aimed at preventing the rapid proletarianization of the rural population. The program demanded the abolition of property tax and the introduction in its place of a progressive income tax (from which a fixed minimum necessary for existence would be exempted). It opposed legislation prohibiting peasants from dividing their land among heirs, since the indivisibility of peasant holdings would only augment the number of agricultural proletarians. These points of the minimal program were derived in part from Danylovych's economic studies, but chiefly, it seems, from Franko's article, "Land Ownership in Galicia," written for Wysłouch's *Przegląd Społeczny* in 1887.

Franko's studies of the agrarian question were the point of departure for yet other reforms proposed in the minimal program, especially the "reforms aimed at creating a standing communal organization of popular production." The aim of these reforms was the acquisition of manorial estates by the rural communes and, in general, the fostering of communal ownership. The program therefore called for a complete ban on the division of communal property, for the reform of inheritance laws to benefit the communes, for the purchase of manorial estates by the communes and for legislation making such purchases easier.

The program also demanded state financial reforms, universal suffrage for both men and women, the abolition of the standing army, free elementary and secondary education and the widest possible autonomy for Galicia. With regard to the national question, the Radical party contented itself with a statement that it would strive to "elevate the sense of national consciousness and solidarity among the masses of the entire Ruthenian-Ukrainian nation by means of literature, meetings, congresses, associations, demonstrations, lectures, the press, etc."

The relationship between the "scientific socialism" of the maximal program and the reforms advocated by the minimal program was uneasy at best. According to the Soviet historian S. M. Zlupko, "the concrete demands of the minimal program deprive the maximal part of any real meaning."[122] A social democrat, writing in Vienna's *Arbeiter-Zeitung* in 1890, also believed that some points of the minimal program directly contradicted the maximal program. He argued that the reforms aimed at hindering the peasantry's proletarianization were contrary to the inherent historical development of capitalism. He also pointed out that the program represented the interests of the peasant petty bourgeois, not those of the working class proletarian.[123] Polish socialists in Galicia echoed these and similar arguments, noting that "the small-holding peasant doesn't want socialism, but land, his own land, as much as possible."[124] The left wing within the Radical party was eventually to take up these same arguments.

Even though emasculated, the Marxist phraseology of the maximal program disturbed the right wing of the new party. Okunevsky refused to sign his name to such "thunderous things as collectivization of the means of production" and so refrained from endorsing the Radical program. Like the social democrats, he also recognized the contradiction between "scientific socialism" and "the prevention of the creation of a proletariat."[125] Danylovych also at first refused to sign a party

program that openly called for socialism, but other party members
prevailed on him to endorse it.[126]

Dissension at the first party congress in October 1890 also broke out
over the national question. Budzynovsky (perhaps taking his cue from
the charge in the Degen affair) proposed the creation of an independent
Ruthenian state as a maximal postulate for the party program and the
division of Galicia into separate Polish and Ruthenian parts as a minimal postulate. Using Marxist terminology, Budzynovsky argued that
only the separation of Austrian Ruthenia from the rest of the empire
could overcome the backwardness of Ruthenia's agriculture and industry. Danylovych opposed Budzynovsky on the grounds that the Radical
party must strive for solidarity among the proletarians of all countries
and the demand for dividing Galicia would hinder that solidarity. Pavlyk
refuted Budzynovsky with Drahomanovian orthodoxy: the proper goal
is not the creation of a Ruthenian *state,* but the construction, from the
bottom up, of a federation of free communities. Franko, who carried
the most influence in the new party, argued that the Polish peasant must
join the Ruthenian peasant if the power of the nobility in Galicia were
to be broken; the division of Galicia would result in the loss of a
valuable ally. The founding congress of the Radical party almost unanimously rejected Budzynovsky's program. There were, in fact, only two
supporters of the independence platform: Budzynovsky himself and
Yuliian Bachynsky (later author of *Ukraina irredenta*).[127] The question
of independence, like the problem of Marxism, would remain a permanent feature of internal party debate late into the 1890s.

The Workers' Party

The Polish socialist movement was also ripe for founding a political
party in 1890. Strikes, assemblies and the Mayday celebration had
instilled a militant spirit in Lviv's working class. The pulse of the
socialist press quickened when Mańkowski began publishing *Robotnik*
early in 1890 to rival Daniluk's *Praca*. *Praca,* which had hitherto
appeared irregularly and at long intervals, responded to *Robotnik* by
coming out regularly every two weeks. The radical student movement of
the late 1880s also gave renewed impetus to the socialist movement. The
founding of the Second International and the Austrian Social Democratic Party, both in 1889, suggested to the Lviv socialists that it was
time to establish their own party. According to Ignacy Daszyński, it

was, finally, the emergence of the Ruthenian Radical party that encouraged the Polish socialists in Lviv to create their own political party.

A group of ten decided to establish the party: Józef Hudec (a typesetter), Władysław Dzwonkowski (the old comrade of Feliks Daszyński), Ludwik Janikowski and Franciszek Nowicki (both from the *Ognisko* group), Teodor Kasparek, Kazimierz Górzycki, Stepan Pidkovych, Herman Diamand and Joachim Fraenkel (student activists in Lviv), and Ignacy Daszyński, who had just returned from Galicia after deportation from Russia. Led by Daszyński, the group formed a conspiracy to infiltrate the two Lviv workers' papers, *Praca* and *Robotnik,* and to persuade them to unite to form a political party. Daszyński, who had good contacts in Russian Poland, used his influence there to deflect funds destined for *Robotnik* into his hands. He used this financial leverage to pressure Mańkowski into following his plan.[128]

As a result of this subterranean agitation, *Robotnik* on 15 November 1890 and *Praca* exactly one week later announced the creation of the Workers' Party (after 1892; the Galician Social Democratic Party). Both papers thereafter bore the subtitle: Organ of the Workers' Party. The leadership of the Workers' Party rested in the editorial boards of the two papers. *Praca*'s editorial board consisted of Daniluk and Hudec (typesetters), Piotr Eliasiewicz (cobbler), Jan Neubauer (carpenter), and Daszyński; *Robotnik*'s: Mańkowski and Józef Obirek (typesetters), Julian Baar and Aleksander Smokowski (artisans) and Górzycki (student activist). In the Workers' Party, unlike in the Ruthenian-Ukrainian Radical party, doctrinal issues counted for very little. In fact, the closest the Workers' Party then approached a programmatic statement was its laconic declaration that it adhered to "social democratic principles."[129]

The Parties and the Masses

With the founding of modern political parties, both Polish and Ruthenian socialism could undergo transformation into mass movements. Although this took place beyond the chronological limits of this study,[130] one aspect of it fits so closely into our thematic framework that a brief sketch of it is required: the socialist parties organized their constituencies according to models developed by the non-socialist national movements. The Polish party recruited artisans into voluntary associations, and the Ruthenian radicals used mass assemblies and reading clubs to unite their peasant adherents.

On Mayday 1890 the Lviv workers had resolved to establish a workers' association. The association, called "Siła" (Power), was formally organized in mid-February 1891 with two hundred members. By mid-1892 branches of Siła also existed in the mining town of Biała and in Cieszyn in Silesia. Professional socialist agitators, students and former students, were sent from Cracow and Lviv to establish other branches of Siła in Tarnów and Nowy Sącz. Branches of Siła also appeared in both Cracow and its suburb Podgórze. The growth of the Cracow Siła was particularly rapid: from 300–500 members in August 1891 to 1,196 members in December 1892. This organizational success among the traditionally atomized Cracow artisans reflected the emergence in that city of a socialist intelligentsia that could provide leadership for the movement.[131]

Siła, which functioned unofficially as the Workers' Party's basic organizational unit, was closely modelled on the Democratic-sponsored voluntary artisan associations like Gwiazda. According to Siła's statutes, the society aimed at "the elevation of the intellectual formation of the workers and the stimulation of social life as well as material aid." Means to attain these goals included maintaining premises with a library, organizing dances and games, establishing an employment bureau and offering financial aid to members. The association's treasury was to be built up primarily by members' contributions and voluntary gifts. Members were both honorary (non-worker) and regular.[132]

In only two significant points did the society differ from its Democratic models. First, instead of referring to itself as an *artisan* association and to its prospective members as *artisans,* the association labelled itself a *workers'* society which any *worker* residing in the city could join. This represented a change in consciousness rather than a change in constituency. The leading activists in Podgórze were still a mason, carpenter, cobbler and miller. At the end of 1892, in Cracow's Siła, a quarter of the members were masons, a sixth were carpenters and another sixth were cobblers.[133] The second way in which Siła differed from its Democratic predecessors was that only ordinary members could be elected to the executive. Non-workers could not buy their way into power and influence as the Democrats had done so successfully in Gwiazda.

The equivalent of the voluntary artisan association as an organizational unit in the Ruthenian movement was the village reading club. To provide the clubs with material for public readings, the Radical party began to publish its own popular newspaper for the peasantry, *Khliborob* (Farmer). Its circulation grew from two hundred in 1891 to a thousand in 1895.[134] In all but its rebellious and anticlerical content it was the equivalent of the Russophile *Nauka* and national populist *Bat'kivshchyna*. That is, it was written for the peasants and — partly — by the peasants, who contributed reports on the progress of radicalism and enlightenment in their villages. In 1893 the Ruthenian radicals also established their own umbrella organization for the reading clubs allied with their party. This was Narodna volia (People's Freedom), akin to the Russophiles' Kachkovsky Society and the national populists' Prosvita.

The pre-existing network of nationally oriented reading clubs opened the countryside to the party's influence. Without ever having to set foot in a particular village, the radicals could expose that village to socialist and anticlerical propaganda. All it had to do was send sample copies of its publications to a reading club affiliated with Prosvita or the Kachkovsky Society.[135] It is not surprising, then, that the subscription list of the reading club became a point of contention, especially between radicalizing peasants and the local pastor.[136]

The radicals also retained another organizational-agitational form from the national movement: the mass peasant assembly (*viche*). In fact, in the 1890s, the radicals made much more frequent and effective use of mass assemblies than had either the Russophiles or the national populists.[137] A key element in the success of radical assemblies was that the main speakers were peasants. Wilhelm Feldman once described his own sensation after attending one of the radical peasant assemblies at the turn of the century:

> Anyone who has ever been present at an assembly of Ruthenian Radicals and has seen peasants in their sheep-skin jackets with the wool turned outside on their wide collars, with their hair plastered down with grease, making notes on scraps of paper supported on their knees in order to participate in the discussion; anyone who had heard Huryk,[138] Novakivsky or Ostapchuk speak, . . . that person perforce has been filled with wonder and respect for this nation's intelligence and its capacity to develop.[139]

Conclusions

The Polish and Ruthenian nations in Galicia differed in the heritage of historicity and nonhistoricity. This meant for one thing, that the Polish nation — but not the Ruthenian nation — retained in its social structure a historical ruling class, the nobility. In the restructuring of the empire in the late 1860s, the Polish nobility was able to become a partner of the dynasty in governing the empire and near absolute master of the crownland of Galicia. The Ruthenian nation, with its less diversified social structure, had no class that could rival the Polish nobility as the dynasty's ruling partner. In this way the legacy of historicity and nonhistoricity helped to determine the balance of power between these two nationalities in Galicia. Furthermore, historicity/nonhistoricity showed up in the urban/rural distributions of the two nations. The cities, thanks to the heritage of the old Polish Commonwealth, had a predominantly Polish character even in ethnically Ruthenian Eastern Galicia. Thus the industrial middle class, the artisans, tended to be Polish, not Ruthenian. These differences between a historical nation and nonhistorical people also manifested themselves in differences between the Polish and Ruthenian socialist movements.

Right from the beginning of the socialist movements, in 1878, significant differences were apparent. The starting point of the Polish socialist movement was a radical *artisan* movement; the starting point of the Ruthenian socialist movement was a radical *student* movement. In the late 1870s, Polish *workers* and Ruthenian *intellectuals* formed the socialist movement grouped around the newspaper *Praca*. That Polish socialism started as a workers' movement and Ruthenian socialism as a movement of intellectuals was a circumstance deeply rooted in the differing social structures of the two nations.

The popular constituency of the Polish socialist movement was the artisan population of Lviv and Cracow. Artisans, because of the urban environment in which they lived and because, too, of their higher educational level, were able independently to come to an understanding of the need for a *political* defense of their interests. The Lviv artisans had, it is true, been encouraged to enter political life by the Polish

Democrats; the Democrats had also endowed them with institutions (voluntary artisan associations and the press) that enabled them to take initiatives. But, thanks to their travels and reading, the Lviv artisans were able to benefit from the example of artisans and workers outside of Galicia and therefore to arrive *independently* of their Democratic patrons at the militant ideology and strategy of the all-Austrian workers' movement. No Democrat had encouraged the artisans to strike, to establish trade unions, to publish Fourierist and Lassallean brochures. The artisans had done these things on their own. Thus Polish socialism started with a mass base that already displayed some degree of class consciousness.

The popular constituency of the Ruthenian socialist movement, however, was the peasantry. Without sustained leadership from the intelligentsia, the peasants, illiterate and confined to the villages, were incapable of accomplishing the same sort of militant transformation as the artisans had. Thus Polish artisans could provide the starting point for a socialist movement, but Ruthenian peasants could not.

The difference between an artisan-based and peasant-based movement explains only half of the problem posed by the difference in starting points between Polish artisan socialism and Ruthenian student socialism. The other half of the problem is: why were Ruthenian students apparently more inclined to social radicalism than were Polish students?

Polish students could look forward to a comfortable career in autonomous Galicia, providing that they adjusted themselves to the goals and values of the Polish nobility. Their predisposition to radicalism was accordingly very weak. Ruthenian students, however, were in an entirely different situation. The son of a Ruthenian peasant or country parson knew that his place in the future was already determined and that his assigned station would certainly be below that of the son of a Polish nobleman or government official. Moreover, to nurture one's Ruthenian national consciousness in Polish-dominated Galicia was in itself to engage in a form of radicalism vis-à-vis the *status quo* in Galicia as a whole.

Within their own society, too, Ruthenian students were less inclined than were their Polish counterparts to assimilate to the goals and values of their traditional elite. The circumstance that led the Polish intelligentsia to pay homage to the Polish nobility was immediate and obvious: the Polish nobility held power in Galicia and on its approval depended one's advancement in Galician society. The Ruthenian intelligentsia also had cause to assimilate to the goals of the Ruthenian traditional elite, the Greek Catholic clergy. This was so because the village clergy was the only bridge between the intelligentsia and the peasantry. The need to defer to the clergy, however, was not an obvious principle. After all, the clergy did not hold power in Galicia. The national populist intelligentsia had been quite secular and even anticlerical in the early 1860s. Only the practical experience of the constitutional era dictated that the Ruthenian intelligentsia had to work out a compromise with the clergy. The unspoken compromise of the Ruthenian secular intelligentsia with the Greek Catholic clergy occurred in the late 1860s and in the 1870s. Ruthenian students of the late 1870s, 1880s and 1890s would less readily see the need to compromise with the clergy than had their elders. So Ruthenian students were less predisposed to yield to their traditional elite than were Polish students to theirs.

The differences in social structure between the Poles and Ruthenians also had repercussions on the ideological development of their socialist movements. Polish socialism was, on the whole, Marxist in allegiance, while Ruthenian socialism was Drahomanovist. As both Drahomanov and Pavlyk pointed out, classic Marxism was best suited to the "state" (historical) nations and less suited to the "stateless" (nonhistorical) peoples.

The Ruthenians were not satisfied with a socialist doctrine that put the industrial proletariat at the center of the socialist revolution. Indisputably, a Ruthenian industrial proletariat did not exist. The Polish socialists in Galicia, however, though they lacked an industrial proletariat in the real sense of the concept, worked with a class that *appeared* (to them) to be an industrial proletariat — the journeyman artisans. According to Marx, however, the artisan just as much as the peasant is a representative of the petty bourgeoisie, not the proletariat. This nicety was lost on the Polish socialists in Galicia, who in practice encouraged journeyman "proletarians" against master "capitalists." By engaging in such a template interpretation of Marxism, Polish socialists in Galicia lost sight of the real class nature of their movement and their potential for ideological development was stunted. The Ruthenians, however, were forced by circumstances to come to grips with the real class nature of their movement and their ideological development was accordingly more interesting. Franko in particular spent much effort analyzing the agrarian question and developing a strategy for bringing the peasantry to social consciousness. When socialist political parties emerged in 1890, the Polish socialists did not even bother to formulate a distinct program, contenting themselves with a statement that they adhered to social democratic principles. The Ruthenian-Ukrainian Radical Party, on the other hand, formulated a detailed political program. The vitality of ideological thinking in the Ruthenian party was further reflected in the significant ideological divergences between the party's factions.

In spite of these various differences between Polish and Ruthenian socialism, there were some striking structural similarities between the two movements. Both the Polish and Ruthenian socialist movements built upon the foundation of the national movements. The Polish Democrats, in their struggle for Galician autonomy, had introduced the journeymen to political life and had given them institutions that developed their own momentum. The Ruthenian national populists in their struggle for a popular base of support, had done the same with the peasantry. In both cases, the entrance of the working classes into national politics presaged their entrance into *class* politics. Nationally-oriented institutions — artisan associations in the case of the Poles and reading clubs in the case of the Ruthenians — evolved into socially-oriented institutions. In both cases, too, a new intelligentsia had emerged, ready to make common cause with the radicalized working classes. In both cases, again, the socialist movements that had been formed by the 1890s represented alliances between the secular intelligentsia and the masses, without dependence upon and in opposition to the traditional elite. Thus, in a sense, partnerships were formed that the Polish and Ruthenian intelligentsias had sought to establish ever since the start of the constitutional era, when they hoped to organize the working classes primarily for national purposes. It is not altogether surprising, then, that after 1890 both the Polish and Ruthenian-Ukrainian socialist leaderships gave ever more primacy to national rather than social liberation.

In comparing Polish and Ruthenian socialism, one must keep in mind that Polish socialism itself had two paths of development. Polish socialism in Cracow was quite different from Polish socialism in Lviv.

Polish socialism in Cracow was an imported phenomenon in the 1870s and 1880s. It was introduced there by Russian Poles who took advantage of the absence of leadership and organization to transplant a Russian-style socialist movement into Austria. The Lviv movement, however, was indigenous. It rested on a pre-existing infrastructure of artisan associations, leaders and press. It was therefore better fitted for survival than the Cracow movement. The late 1880s, when strikes and assemblies flourished in Lviv and the journeymen were silent in Cracow, were entirely consistent with the late 1870s and early 1880s, when legal socialism had predominated in Lviv and conspiratorial socialism held sway in Cracow. Ultimately, the difference between Lviv's and Cracow's socialism went back to the start of the constitutional era, when the Democratic intelligentsia organized demonstrations in Lviv, but not in Cracow, when the Democratic intelligentsia established strong artisan associations and a press for artisans in Lviv, but again — not in Cracow.

It was the Lviv movement, therefore, which was most closely analogous to the Ruthenian movement. Polish socialism in Lviv shared with Ruthenian socialism an initial phase in which the nonsocialist, nationally-oriented intelligentsia first introduced the masses into political life and provided them with institutions that they eventually used to struggle for their own class interests. Cracovian socialism did not share in this phase and its pattern of development — in relation to both Polish socialism in Lviv and Ruthenian socialism — was anomalous. The anomaly of Cracow's socialist movement and its short life only underscore the basic similarity between the patterns of development of Ruthenian socialism and Polish socialism (the indigenous, Lviv variety).

The final points to be made in these concluding remarks concern a comparison in time between the 1860s and 1890. The 1860s were marked by two major events: the introduction of the constitution and the Stańczyks' assumption of power. Historically, these two events were closely connected with one another, because the new constitution restructured the empire and in the restructuring of the empire the Polish nobility took power in Galicia. In reality, however, these two events contradicted one another. The constitution provided the framework for undermining the very foundations of the nobility's rule in Galicia. By 1890, when a Polish socialist party emerged and Ruthenian society had undergone profound changes, time was running out for the Stańczyk dominion.

As Drahomanov was fond of pointing out, the Austrian constitution was an important force for democratization not because it enabled the masses to participate in the electoral process, but because it guaranteed such civil liberties as freedom of association, assembly, speech and press. Although the Galician authorities abused their powers to restrict civil liberties, there was still a great deal of extraparliamentary political and social activity in the crownland. The late 1860s put Galicia into the hands of the nobility, but they also put a weapon in the hands of the emerging elite, the intelligentsia. This weapon made it possible to organize the masses.

The most striking contrast between the 1860s and 1890s was evident in Galician Ruthenia. In 1860, the Ruthenians formed an inchoate mass of atomized villagers. By 1890, however, this mass had become a nation. The Ruthenians had undergone the decisive stage of national formation that transforms a people, an ethnically differentiated folk, into a conscious and organized nation. Socially, the Ruthenian national movement grew from the affair of a small group of intellectuals into an institutionalized mass movement with periodicals, organizations and large-scale peasant participation. Ideologically, it passed from historical, literary, ethnographic and religious concerns to the formulation of the goal of an independent Ruthenian state (Budzynovsky, 1890). The Polish nobility confronted entirely different Ruthenians in the 1860s and in the 1890s.

When the Stańczyks took power in Galicia in the late 1860s, they established the last stronghold of the Polish nobility. Never again was the traditional Polish elite to gain such a powerful position in national life. Already by 1890, we can see the foundations of their power shaken. The Ruthenians, relatively passive at the Stańczyks' assumption of power, had grown into a double threat to the Stańczyks, because they had both national and social objections to the rule of the Polish nobility. They were much better equipped, too, to make those objections felt. But also within the Polish nation itself, forces were coming to life that challenged Stańczyk supremacy. This study only briefly mentioned Bolesław Wysłouch. In the 1890s, however, Wysłouch was to bring into being a powerful peasant party that threatened the rule of the Polish nobility. The emergence of a Polish socialist party in 1890 was also a factor that loosened the Stańczyks' hold on Galicia. In the decades following 1890, the socialist party was to turn the brunt of its attack against the *szlachta* power monopoly. Although in 1890 the changes within the Polish nation were incomplete, they were nonetheless underway.

In sum, then, Galicia from the 1860s to the 1890s underwent a transition from a society securely dominated by the traditional elite of the Polish nation into a more complex polity. The Ruthenians had crossed the threshold into nationhood and thus made of the single

Galician polity two national societies. Within these societies, both the intelligentsia and the working classes were playing an increasingly important role.

Notes

Introduction

1. Galicia occupied 78,497 square kilometers; the next largest crownland, Bohemia, occupied 51,947. Galicia had 5,444,689 inhabitants in 1869 (20,396,630 in all of Austria) and 6,607,816 in 1890 (23,895,413 in all of Austria). *Österreich-Ungarn 1914: Reproduktion einer Freytag & Berndt-Karte aus dem Jahre 1914* (Vienna, 1975). *Bevölkerung und Viehstand der im Reichsrathe vertretenen Königreiche und Länder . . . 1869* (Vienna, 1871). "Die Ergebnisse der Volkszählung vom 31. December 1890," *Österreichische Statistik*, Bd. 32, Heft 1 (Vienna, 1892), pp. 124 and 130.

2. For an introduction to Jewish socialism, see Jacob Bross, "The Beginning of the Jewish Labor Movement in Galicia," *YIVO Annual of Jewish Social Science* 5 (1950): 55–84. Jewish socialism also emerged later than Polish socialism in the Congress Kingdom. Norman M. Naimark, *The History of the "Proletariat": The Emergence of Marxism in the Kingdom of Poland* (Boulder, Colo., 1979), pp. 202 and 291.

3. Miroslav Hroch, *Die Vorkämpfer der nationalen Bewegung bei den kleinen Völkern Europas: Eine vergleichende Analyse zur gesellschaftlichen Schichtung der patriotischen Gruppen* (Prague, 1968), pp. 15–17. Stefan Kieniewicz's review of Hroch's work in *Przegląd Historyczny*, 1970, no. 1, p. 150. Józef Chlebowczyk, *Procesy narodotwórcze we wschodniej Europie środkowej w dobie kapitalizmu (od schyłku XVIII do początków XX w.)* (Warsaw, 1975), pp. 15–18. Ivan L. Rudnytsky, "The Role of the Ukraine in Modern History," in *The Development of the USSR*, ed. Donald W. Treadgold (Seattle, 1964), pp. 211–12. See the interesting exchange between Ivan L. Rudnytsky and George G. Grabowicz in *Harvard Ukrainian Studies* 5 (1981): 358–88.

4. Józef Buzek, *Stosunki zawodowe i socyalne ludności w Galicyi według wyznania i narodowości, na podstawie spisu ludności z 31. grudnia 1900 r.* (Lviv, 1905), pp. 42–43.

5. Konstanty Grzybowski, *Galicja 1848–1914. Historia ustroju politycznego na tle historii ustroju Austrii* (Cracow, 1959), pp. 48–49.

6. Wilhelm Feldman, *Stronnictwa i programy polityczne w Galicyi 1846–1906*, 2 vols. (Cracow, 1907), 1:120–21.

7. Grzybowski, *Galicja*, p. 75.

8. *Wiadomości statystyczne o mieście Lwowie* 2 (1876): 74–75.

9. Grzybowski, *Galicja*, pp. 78–79.

Chapter One

1. According to the 1869 census, of Galicia's total population of five and a half million, only 180,000 were employed in industry. This figure does not include the 9,000 engaged in "non-productive industries," mainly tavern-keeping. Of the 179,626 employed in industry, 65,601 were counted as independent entrepreneurs (*selbständige Unternehmer*) or industrialists (*przemysłowcy*), a category including master artisans, 2,959 as clerks and 111,606 as workers. *Bevölkerung und Viehstand von Galizien nach der Zählung vom 31. Dezember 1869*, herausgegeben von der k. k. statistischen Central-Commission (Vienna, 1871), pp. 42–49.

Galician statistics for this period, and especially statistics on the working class, are unreliable. See the thorough discussion in Walentyna Najdus, "Źródła statystyczne do dziejów klasy robotniczej w Galicji," *Polska klasa robotnicza. Studia historyczne*, vol. 3 (Warsaw, 1972), pp. 367–85.

In the thirty-three districts of the Lviv Chamber of Commerce there were 32,640 people engaged in traditional crafts out of a total industrial population of 67,632 (excluding "non-productive industries," but including mining and metallurgy). The Lviv Chamber of Commerce region had 45.85 percent of Galicia's total population and 45.75 percent of its industrial population (including mining and metallurgy). *Bericht der Handels- und Gewerbekammer in Lemberg über den Handel und die Industrie . . . für die Jahre 1866 in 1870* (Lviv, 1873), pp. lxxxii–cvi. The figures given by the *Bericht* and *Bevölkerung . . . 1869* are not in full agreement. I have taken the proportion indicated by the *Bericht* and applied it to the absolute number given in *Bevölkerung . . . 1869*.

2. See Walentyna Najdus, "Galicja," *Polska klasa robotnicza. Zarys dziejów*, vol. 1, part. 1: *Od przełomu XVIII i XIX w. do 1870 r.*, ed. by Stanisław Kalabiński (Warsaw, 1974), p. 553, table 8.

3. *Bericht*, p. 269.

4. See H. I. Koval'chak, "Rozvytok kapitalistychnoi promyslovosti v Skhidnii Halychyni u 70–80-kh rokakh XIX st.," *Z istorii zakhidnoukrains'kykh zemel'*, vyp. 3 (Kiev, 1958), pp. 3–22. Ie. A. Iatskevych, *Stanovyshche robitnychoho klasu Halychyny v period kapitalizmu (1848–1900) (Narys)* (Kiev, 1958), p. 18. Ia. S. Khonihsman, "Sotsial'na struktura naselennia Halychyny na pochatku XX st.," *Ukrains'ke slov"ianoznavstvo*, no. 6 (1972), p. 68.

5. Iatskevych, *Stanovyshche*, p. 69. For the daily wages of construction workers in Cracow and Lviv, see Marian Górkiewicz, *Ceny w Krakowie w latach 1796–1914* (Poznań, 1950), pp. 225–30, and Stanisław Hoszowski, *Ceny we Lwowie w latach 1701–1914* (Lviv, 1934), p. 144.

6. A Lviv typesetter, married, with four small children, worked six days a week, ten hours a day. His weekly income averaged out to 15 gulden 42 kreuzers, but his weekly expenditures to 17 g. 77 kr. (1878):

Dues to benefit fund	79 kr.
Rent and local taxes	3 g. 15 kr.
Food for six people	8 g. 40 kr.
School supplies for one son	50 kr.
Clothing	2 g. 50 kr.
Tobacco and alcohol	48 kr.
Household goods	30 kr.
Household help	1 g. 55 kr.
Entertainment and gifts	10 kr.
Total	17 g. 77 kr.

I[osyp] D[anyliuk = Daniluk], "Zaribky i zhyt'e l'vivs'koho zetsera," *Molot* (Lviv, 1878), p. 145. It has been suggested that this article was written by Ivan Franko on the basis of facts prepared by Daniluk. The article is reprinted with commentary in M. F. Nechytaliuk, *Publitsystyka Ivana Franka (1875–1886 rr.)*. *Seminarii* (Lviv, 1972), pp. 52–59.

7. In 1880 a journeyman carpenter at the large shop (seventy workers) of the Wczelak brothers in Lviv earned a little less than 6 g. weekly; a journeyman cobbler in the same city could earn 6 g. 50 kr. a week by working fourteen hours daily; apprentices in print shops were paid 2 g. a week. *Praca*, 2 January 1880, p. 5, 10 February 1880, p. 13.

For more on craftsmen's wages and budgets, see Ivan Franko, "Promyslovi robitnyky v Skhidnii Halychyni i ikh plata r. 1870. Statystychna studiia," *Tvory*, 20 vols. (Kiev, 1950–56), 19:220–26; Iatskevych, *Stanovyshche*, pp. 67–68; Khonihsman, "Sotsial'na struktura," p. 71; and Hoszowski, *Ceny we Lwowie*, p. 145.

8. "Kaiserliches Patent vom 20. December 1859 . . . Gewerbe-Ordnung," *Reichs-Gesetz-Blatt fuer das Kaisertum Oesterreich*, 1859, pp. 619–44.

9. Ia. P. Kis', *Promyslovist' L'vova u period feodalizmu (XIII–XIX st.)* (Lviv, 1968), p. 68; see also p. 60 for a discussion of other early Austrian legislation limiting the privileges and breaking up the monopoly of the guilds.

10. Quoted in Kazimierz Wyka, *Teka Stańczyka na tle historii Galicji w latach 1849–1869* (Wrocław, 1951), p. 69. A Polish Democrat remarked in 1867: "Today everyone is opposed to the guilds, everyone, that is, except many of our artisans, who swear by them." Alfred Szczepański, *Cechy i stowarzyszenia. Posłanie pierwsze* (Cracow, 1867), p. 12.

11. "Przemysłowe stowarzyszenia," *Rękodzielnik*, 1869, no. 14, pp. 109–10. A Polish Democrat described the situation in Lviv: "In the artisan class, supreme tension reigns as a result of the lack of supervision and lack of authority, which alone can keep this host of several thousands in order. A sufficiently autonomist law has been lying ready for five years and is only awaiting implementation. Only a few isolated corporations with energetic leaders have succeeded in organizing themselves; two thirds of the artisans, however, remain in total disorganization, which has a most injurious influence on artisan youth and the state of craft industry." "Sprawy miejskie," *Praca*, 22 April 1865, no. 35, p. 1.

12. *O potrzebie stowarzyszeń przemysłowych czyli rzemieślniczych* (Lviv, 1864).

13. The brochure was printed in its entirety in at least two Galician papers, *Praca* and *Gazeta Narodowa*; summaries also appeared in German and French papers. "O potrzebie stowarzyszeń przemysłowych czyli rękodzielniczych," *Praca,* 1864, no. 19, pp. 1–4, no. 20, pp. 2–7. A Polish émigré in Paris translated the brochure into French and circulated it among Fourierists. One of the latter, Laurence Heronville, sent a letter praising the work to a Lviv newspaper. "Zdanie robotników paryzkich," *Gazeta Narodowa,* supplement, 8 December 1864, no. 281, p. 1.

14. Szczepański, *Cechy i stowarzyszenia.* Tadeusz Romanowicz, *O stowarzyszeniach* (Lviv, 1867).

15. J. S., "Ruch kooperacyjny," *Gazeta Narodowa,* 8–12 March 1867. Tadeusz Skałkowski, *Warsztaty i fabryki a postęp przemysłowy* (Lviv, 1869). Ruthenian national populists also held that the measures required to rescue the artisanal class were "associations, societies, i.e, equalized capital, because small amounts of capital cannot survive by themselves." A. D., "Dopysy. Zi L'vova," *Osnova,* 26 April 1872, no. 30, p. 2.

16. The average number of associations of all types founded annually in Lviv was 1.0 in 1851–60, 4.5 in 1860–67 and 8.6 in 1868–74. *Wiadomości statystyczne o mieście Lwowie* 2 (1876): 49–50.

17. See John-Paul Himka, "Voluntary Artisan Associations and the Ukrainian National Movement in Galicia (the 1870s)," *Harvard Ukrainian Studies* 2 (1978): 235–50.

18. The Jewish artisan association Yad Kharuzim was founded in Lviv in 1870 with the aim of "educating workers of the Mosaic confession and helping them in case of illness, unemployment and the like." In 1874 it had 300 members, in 1875 — 360. *Wiadomości statystyczne o mieście Lwowie* 2 (1876): 60–61; 3 (1877): 73.

19. These associations are treated in detail in John-Paul Himka, "Polish and Ukrainian Socialism: Austria, 1867–1890" (Ph.D. dissertation, The University of Michigan, 1977), pp. 38–42, 49–61, 73–76, 80–81, 84.

20. Stefan Kieniewicz, *Adam Sapieha (1828–1903)* (Lviv, 1939), pp. 53–54. Stanisław Tarnowski, "Z 'Teki Stańczyka' a) List Sycyniusza," in Stefan Kieniewicz, ed., *Galicja w dobie autonomicznej (1850–1914). Wybór tekstów* (Wrocław, 1952), pp. 120–21 and Kieniewicz's notes to the text.

21. "'Czasowi,'" *Dziennik Lwowski,* 27 August 1868, no. 197, p. 1. Emphasis added.

22. Tarnowski, "Z 'Teki Stańczyka,'" pp. 120–21. "Nowiny z kraju i zagranicy," *Dziennik Lwowski,* 12 July 1868, no. 159, p. 3.

23. Tarnowski, "Z 'Teki Stańczyka,'" pp. 121–22.

24. Józef Szujski, "Wydobycie zwłok Kazimierza Wielkiego i przyszły ich pogrzeb," in Michał Bobrzyński, Władysław Jaworski and Józef Milewski, *Z dziejów odrodzenia politycznego Galicyi 1859–1873* (Warsaw, 1905), pp. 358–63.

25. The Democrat Mieczysław Darowski, who presided at the constituent

meeting, spoke to the assembled journeymen on the importance of the Third of May for all Poles and on the role the working class must play in national life. (The Third of May commemorated the promulgation of the Polish constitution of 1791.) *Gazeta Narodowa,* supplement, 3 May 1868, p. 2.

26. Stanisław Rachwał, *Mieczysław Darowski. Czyny i słowa* (Lviv, 1923), pp. 59–60.

27. *Gazeta Narodowa,* supplement, 8 March 1868, p. 2.

28. Romanowicz probably drew up Gwiazda's statutes; this is implied in ibid. He definitely drafted the statutes of the mutual aid society affiliated with Gwiazda. *Rękodzielnik,* 1869, no. 1, p. 7. These statutes were distributed as a supplement to *Rękodzielnik,* 1869, no. 3. Romanowicz also composed the statutes for the Society of Women's Labor, founded by his sister, among others, in Lviv in 1874. Zofja Romanowiczówna, *Cienie (Kilka oderwanych kart z mojego życia)* (Lviv, 1930), p. 105.

29. Rachwał, *Mieczysław Darowski,* pp. 63–65. Agaton Giller, "Alfred Młocki. Życiorys," in *Księga wspomnień Alfreda Młockiego,* ed. Agaton Giller and Piotr Zbrożek (Paris, 1884), p. lxxii. Tadeusz Romanowicz, *Dwie opinie* (Cracow, 1891), p. 28.

30. Gwiazda had 6,105 gulden in 1875. The mutual aid society associated with it had 13,127 g. in 1872 and 23,530 g. in 1875. The artisans themselves could only have contributed several thousand gulden. *Wiadomości statystyczne o mieście Lwowie* 3 (1877): 71, 73. *Rękodzielnik,* 1873, no. 1–2, p. 8. Cf. Himka, "Voluntary Artisan Associations," pp. 239, 245, 249.

31. *Polski Słownik Biograficzny* (Cracow-Wrocław, 1935–), s.v. "Darowski Weryha Mieczysław" by Marian Tyrowicz. Kis', *Promyslovist' L'vova,* p. 209. According to *Żywot ś. p. Mieczysława Darowskiego* (Cracow, [1889]), p. 17, the association had 800 members.

32. Konstanty Grzybowski, *Galicja 1848–1914. Historia ustroju politycznego na tle historii ustroju Austrii* (Cracow, 1959), pp. 33, 35. Words of the decree.

33. In December 1863 Romanowicz was sentenced to two years' imprisonment for his activities in support of the insurrection. S. M. Trusevych, *Suspil'no-politychnyi rukh u Skhidnii Halychyni v 50–70-kh rokakh XIX st.* (Kiev, 1978), p. 95.

34. This account is from Adam Eugeniusz Panasiewicz, a tinsmith imprisoned in 1863–64. His memoirs originally appeared in Józef Białynia Chołodecki, *Półwiekowa przeszłość Stowarzyszenia katolickiej młodzieży rękodzielniczej "Skała" we Lwowie* (Lviv, 1906), pp. 107–13. Portions are reprinted in Rachwał, *Mieczysław Darowski,* pp. 51–52, 58–60.

35. Adolf Aleksandrowicz, Szczęsny Bednarski, Józef Daniluk, Jan Hoszowski, Wincenty Kornecki, Antoni Mańkowski, Józef Seniuk. With the exception of Aleksandrowicz, all were printers.

36. "Lećcie me pieśni, niech wam towarzyszy,

   "Szczęśliwa gwiazda pod gościnne strzechy."

   (Fly, my songs! Let a lucky star
   Accompany you 'neath hospitable thatched roofs.)

37. Wiktor Hahn, *Karol Libelt we Lwowie w roku 1869. Wspomnienie w setną rocznicę urodzin* (Lviv, 1907), pp. 12–13.

38. In the original account (ibid.), Gwiazda was mentioned second, immediately after the university and technical students. The other associations mentioned by name were the Circle of Merchant Youth and the gymnastic society Sokół.

39. *Rękodzielnik*, 1869, no. 8, pp. 62–63. This account mentions that Libelt made a special visit to Gwiazda's premises during his stay in Lviv.

40. When Gwiazda was founded in 1868, 661 artisans signed up. Only 421 members were left by January 1869, but most of the decline represented journeymen struck from the membership rolls for not paying dues. Analogy with other Galician artisan associations would suggest that members who failed to pay dues were still permitted to take part in the association's functions. In 1872 Gwiazda had 945 members. If Gwiazda had expanded at a steady rate from 1868 to 1872, it would have had over seven hundred members when Libelt came to Lviv. The membership figures are from: *Rękodzielnik*, 1869, no. 3, p. 22 (cf. also no. 1, p. 8, no. 11, p. 82); *Sprawozdanie z czynności wydziałów . . . "Gwiazda" . . . 1872* ([Lviv, 1873]).

Also, an organization like Gwiazda could serve as "the moral and organizational center" for all Lviv's journeymen, members or not. William H. Sewell makes this point about French mutual-aid societies: *Work and Revolution in France: The Language of Labor from the Old Regime to 1848* (Cambridge, 1980), p. 165.

41. Stanisław Koźmian, "Z 'Teki Stańczyka,' b) List Brutusika (eks-ministra)," in Kieniewicz, *Galicja*, p. 123. Emphasis added.

42. Wyka, *Teka Stańczyka*, p. 165.

43. In 1869 Lviv had a population of 87,159, Cracow — 49,835; Lviv had 8,614 journeyman artisans, Cracow — 4,016. Władysław Rapacki, *Ludność Galicji* (Lviv, 1874), pp. 30–34. Najdus, "Galicja," p. 542.

44. *Rękodzielnik*, 1869, no. 14, p. 112.

45. Police reports on Cracow's Gwiazda are in the Archiwum Państwowe m. Krakowa i woj. Krakowskiego [APKr], Starostwo Grodzkie w Krakowie [StGKr], 762.

46. See above, note 40; also *Wiadomości statystyczne o mieście Lwowie* 2 (1876).

47. "Whoever has peeked into the wretched living quarters of a journeyman, often burdened by a large family; whoever has had a look at this life without hope of bettering one's lot, without hope of peaceful bread in old age or at least of insuring one's family's future; whoever has looked at the life of a journeyman, always aware that at any moment unemployment or drawn-out illness will force him to seek refuge in charity; whoever, seeing this horrible state of affairs, reflects on it . . . will admit that among us, too, exists the social question of capital's exploiting labor, that we, too, must work against it." Romanowicz, *O stowarzyszeniach*, pp. 20–21.

48. See, for example, the article "Proletariat krajowy," *Dziennik Lwowski*, 1 September 1867, p. 2, discussed by Walentyna Najdus,

"Oddźwięk Komuny Paryskiej i I Międzynarodówki w Galicji," *Z Pola Walki,* 1965, no. 3, pp. 3–4.

49. *Gazeta Narodowa,* supplement, 8 March 1868, p. 2.

50. Tadeusz Romanowicz in a speech to Gwiazda on the occasion of the four-hundredth anniversary of Copernicus' birth (19 February 1873). Romanowicz's speech was described with approval by the none-too-radical socialist Bolesław Limanowski in *Bluszcz,* 1873, no. 11, p. 86.

51. S., "Teraźniejsze socjalistyczne dążności," *Gazeta Narodowa,* 23 April 1870, p. 1. This "S." was also the "J. S." who wrote an article on cooperatives for *Gazeta Narodowa* in 1867 (see note 15 above).

52. Cited in Marian Żychowski, "Społeczeństwo Galicji i Królestwa Polskiego wobec Pierwszej Międzynarówki w latach 1864–1876," *Małopolskie Studia Historyczne* 8 (1965): 55–56.

53. APKr, StGKr, 749:265/1872.

54. Karol Libelt, *Koalicya kapitału i pracy* (Poznań, 1868). Kazimierz Szulc, *Kwestja socjalna i sposób jej załatwienia równie korzystny dla robotników jak i właścicieli* (Lviv, 1871). Szulc's views are discussed in Najdus, "Oddźwięk," pp. 14–15.

55. *Polski Słownik Biograficzny,* s.v. "Groman Karol" by Czesław Lechicki.

56. *Czcionka,* 1872, no. 6, pp. 21–22, no. 7, p. 28, no. 8, pp. 29–30.

57. Stefan Pawlicki, "Lassalle i przyszłość socyalizmu," *Przegląd Polski,* 1874, no. 8, pp. 167–68. In this very strange article, Pawlicki makes an equivocal hero, but a hero all the same, of Lassalle, whom he views as a spiritual ally in the struggle against the liberal bourgeoisie. Pawlicki saw the world divided into two irreconcilably opposed camps: liberalism and Christianity (or rather, Catholicism). Socialism shares liberalism's great faults (materialism and pantheism), but at least is not hypocritical, since it carries liberal postulates to their conclusion. Liberals are pharisees. They are Protestants instead of Catholics, when logically they should throw the church out altogether. Freedom is their motto, but they use the police force and capital to enforce their volition. Liberals want a good life, a paradise on this earth, but only the socialists are ready to attempt its introduction. The root of socialism is liberalism. The only antidote to socialism is the Catholic church and the war against liberalism.

58. *Gazeta Narodowa,* 13 February 1868, p. 3, 16 February 1868, p. 2. *Rękodzielnik,* 20 February 1870, no. 4, pp. 25–27.

59. [Herman] Schulze-Delitsch, *Prawa i obowiąki społeczne. Wykład miany 14 lutego 1866 r. w Berlinie,* Wiedza, zbiór popularnych odczytów z literatury i nauk (Warsaw, 1868). This twenty-page brochure consists of a philosophical disquisition making no mention of the workers' movement *per se.*

60. Walentyna Najdus, *Powstanie związku zawodowego drukarzy w Galicji (Wyjątek z Księgi Pamiątkowej Związku Zawodowego Pracowników Poligrafii wydanej w 1960 roku z okazji jubileuszu 90-lecia Związku)* (n.p., [1960]), p. 40. "Kept in constant dependence on the masters and having grown used to the guild hierarcy, [the Galician worker] has a single ambition: *to become a master!*" "Z kraju i o kraju. Korespondencyja," *Równość,* 1880, no. 4, p. 18.

61. Bolesław Limanowski, "Wspomnienia z pobytu w Galicyi (Zaczątki obecnego ruchu socyalistycznego)," *Z pola walki. Zbiór materyałów tyczących się polskiego ruchu socyalistycznego* (London, 1904), p. 2. Żychowski, "Społeczeństwo Galicji," pp. 66–67.

62. Najdus, "Oddźwięk." Żychowski, "Społeczeństwo Galicji." Henryk Dobrowolski, "Pierwsza Międzynarodówka w zasobie aktowym Archiwum Państwowego w Krakowie," *Małopolskie Studia Historyczne* 8 (1965): 111–17. M. M. Kravets', "Vidhuky na Paryz'ku Komunu v Skhidnii Halychyni," *Visnyk L'vivs'koho . . . universytetu . . . Seriia istorychna*, no. 7 (1971), pp. 14–20. V. Makaiev, *Robitnychyi klas Halychyny v ostannii tretyni XIX st.* (Lviv, 1968), pp. 74–83. Makaiev considers the International a major influence on the Galician workers' movement, but fails, in my opinion, to document his assertions adequately.

63. Szulc depicted the Commune as "an undivine comedy" in which "people [*ludzie*] changed into predatory and blood-thirsty beasts, and women [!] into furies and witches." Szulc, *Kwestja socjalna,* pp. 3, 6.

64. Maksymilian Machalski, *Wykład o stowarzyszeniu miedzynarodowém (L'internationale)* (Cracow, 1872), p. 20.

65. In *Rękodzielnik,* 1871, nos. 8 and 9. See Kravets', "Vidhuky," p. 27.

66. "Międzynarodowe Stowarzyszenie robotników a obecne zmowy w Genewie," *Rękodzielnik,* 1869, no. 7, pp. 52–53.

67. Factories perhaps not. But workers in breweries and distilleries worked (in season) fourteen to twenty-one hours a day! Franko, "Promyslovi robitnyky," p. 224. Locksmiths in Cracow never worked less than thirteen or fourteen hours daily. K. Dłuski and W. Piekarski, "Mistrz Wścieklica i Spółka," in *Pierwsze pokolenie marksistów polskich. Wybór pism i materiałów źródłowych z lat 1878–1886,* ed. Alina Molska, 2 vols. (Warsaw, 1962), 1:616.

68. *Rękodzielnik,* 1869, no. 11, pp. 81–82.

69. B[olesław] L[imanowski], "Czasopisma lwowskie," *Niwa,* 1873, no. 30, p. 134.

70. These articles were collected and published, at the cost of the noble Alfred Młocki, as a brochure: *Warsztaty i fabryki.* Bolesław Limanowski, the self-proclaimed socialist, wrote that most important in *Rękodzielnik* are "the articles dealing with economics, and the best of these are from the pen of Tadeusz Skałkowski." Limanowski, "Czasopisma," p. 134.

71. "Razem," *Rękodzielnik,* 1869, no. 1, pp. 5–7, no. 2, pp. 10–12, no. 3, pp. 19–21, no. 4, pp. 27–29, no. 5, pp. 33–36.

72. Najdus, *Powstanie związku,* p. 58.

73. Limanowski, "Czasopisma," p. 134.

74. This was the first printers' benefit fund in the entire empire, the next having been founded in Linz in 1824. In 1857 two smaller mutual aid societies formed the Mutual Aid Society of Lviv Printers with eighty-three members. In Cracow, a printers' mutual aid society had existed since 1849. The organizational development of the printers' movement is treated in Najdus' thorough study, *Powstanie związku.* A wealth of source materials is in Adam Wiktor Bober, *Historja drukarń i stowarzyszeń drukarskich we Lwowie* (Lviv, 1926).

75. There were 134 typesetters, machinists and pressmen in Lviv in 1878, not including 81 apprentices. Of the 134, 63 percent belonged to the printers' mutual aid society and 62 percent to the educational trade-union society Ognisko. 75 percent belonged to at least one of the two organizations. *Praca*, 1878, no. 11, p. 43.

76. Daniluk, "Zaribky," p. 145.

77. Romanowicz, *O stowarzyszeniach*, p. 64.

78. These thoughts largely stem from a discussion with Professor Walentyna Najdus.

79. The statutes of Vienna's Progressive Society were confirmed in 1864. Its goal was "the elevation and propagation of education among its members as well as the unremitting defense of their material interests." Active in the Austrian workers' movement, the society in late 1867 underwent an evolution in ideology from Schulze-Delitsch to Lassalle. Najdus, *Powstanie związku*, pp. 45–46.

80. Hoszowski was a veteran of the 1863 insurrection, during which he had fought in the ranks of the Reds. Before his return to Lviv in 1869, he had worked in England, Italy, Germany and Austria, where he came into close contact with the workers' movement. Thus, well acquainted with West European workers' organizations, Hoszowski had been able to criticize Romanowicz's draft of the statutes of Gwiazda's mutual aid society (March 1869) and was a logical candidate to draw up the statutes for Lviv's Progressive Society. *Polski Słownik Biograficzny*, s.v. "Hoszowski Jan" by Helena Szwejkowska. *Rękodzielnik*, 1869, no. 6, p. 44.

81. Najdus, *Powstanie związku*, pp. 46–47. Bober, *Historja drukarń*, pp. 35–36. Both Bober and Najdus refer to Józef Wiśniewski as Antoni Wiszniewski. My usage is based on Wiśniewski's obituary in *Praca*, 1878, no. 6, p. 23.

82. Bober, *Historja drukarń*, pp. 59–62. Bednarski wrote, nearly twenty years later, by which time he had already renounced his earlier radicalism, that the Left-Wing Circle dissolved itself in April 1870. Szczęsny Bednarski, *Materyały do historyi o drukarniach lwowskich i prowincyonalnych* (Lviv, 1888), p. 111.

83. V. O. Borys, "Do pytannia pro pochatok robitnychoho rukhu v Halychyni (1848–1850 rr.)," *Dopovidi ta povidomlennia L'vivs'koho derzhavnoho universytetu*, no. 8, pt. 1 (1958), p. 67.

84. Bober, *Historja drukarń*, pp. 65–67. Price-list agitation and the course of the strike in Lviv was reported in the organ of Vienna's Progressive Society. M. P., "Lemberg," *Vorwärts*, 13 January 1870, p. 7. Der Ausschuss des Buchdrucker-Fortbildungsvereins in Lemberg, "Lemberg," *Vorwärts*, 20 January 1870, p. 11. [Leon Zubalewicz], "Lemberg," *Vorwärts*, 17 February 1870, p. 27.

85. "Prawo zmowy," *Rękodzielnik*, 1869, no. 10, pp. 76–77. Here *Rękodzielnik* defended the right to strike as essential to a constitutional state.

86. M. M. Kravets', "Pochatok robitnychoho rukhu v Skhidnii Halychyni," *Z istorii zakhidnoukrains'kykh zemel'*, vyp 3 (1958), p. 29. Bolesław Limanow-

ski, *Socyjalizm jako konieczny objaw dziejowego rozwoju* (Lviv, 1879), p. 90. *Gazeta Narodowa*, 10 June 1870, p. 2.

87. Kravets', "Pochatok," p. 29. On Augustyn and his close relations with the Galician workers, see Emil Haecker, *Historja socjalizmu w Galicji i na Śląsku Cieszyńskim* (Cracow, 1933), pp. 104–05, and *Rękodzielnik*, 1871, no. 4, p. 16.

88. Bober, *Historja drukarń*, p. 69.

89. Kravets', "Pochatok," p. 29. Najdus, *Powstanie związku*, p. 50. In 1861 the administration of the Lviv Printers' Mutual Aid Society passed a ruling forbidding Jews, and Christians who worked for Jewish print shops, to join the society. This did not apply to those who were already members. The ruling was re-affirmed, against the opposition of Antoni Mańkowski and Antoni Trompeteur, in 1886, when Naftali Telz (later active in the Polish socialist movement) applied for membership. Bober, *Historja drukarń*, pp. 30, 48. An anti-Semitic Polish printer from Lviv described his Jewish colleagues in A. P., "Lemberg," *Vorwärts*, 3 March 1870, p. 35.

90. Kravets', "Pochatok," p. 29. *Rękodzielnik*, 1871, no. 4, p. 16.

91. "Kronika. Zmowa stelmachów," *Dziennik Polski*, 6 June 1871, p. 2.

92. Najdus, "Oddźwięk," p. 8.

93. Najdus, *Powstanie związku*, p. 51.

94. On the significance of the fixed price-list or tariff in nineteenth-century artisan movements, see Sewell, *Work and Revolution in France*, p. 181.

95. [Antoni Mańkowski], "Przed 25 laty — a dziś," *Ognisko*, 1897, no. 25, pp. 1–2.

96. *Czcionka*, 1872, no. 38, p. 150.

97. Ibid., p. 153.

98. L'vivs'kyi oblasnyi derzhavnyi arkhiv [LODA], 350/1/2328, pp. 2–3.

99. Ibid., pp. 6, 9–9v, 10, 17. Najdus, *Powstanie związku*, p. 50.

100. *Czcionka*, 1873, no. 3, pp. 9–11.

101. Ibid., 1873, no. 5, p. 17, no. 6, p. 21. Mańkowski, "Przed 25 laty," pp. 1–2. LODA, 350/1/2328, pp. 19–21.

102. APKr, StGKr, 762: 1198–99/1872, 488/1874, 67/1875. Najdus, *Powstanie związku*, pp. 51–52.

103. Bober, *Historja drukarń*, p. 61.

104. Szczepański, *Cechy i stowarzyszenia*, p. 39.

105. [Tadeusz Skałkowski], "Zmowa towarzyszy sztuki drukarskiej we Lwowie," *Rękodzielnik*, 1870, no. 3, p. 17.

106. [Leon Zubalewicz], "I. Związkowa drukarnia we Lwowie," *Czcionka*, 1873, no. 10, pp. 37–39. Najdus, *Powstanie związku*, p. 48. *Wiadomości statystyczne o mieście Lwowie* 2 (1876): 82–83; 3 (1877): table 56.

107. *Czcionka*, 1873, no. 6, pp. 21–23.

108. Ibid., 1873, no. 8, pp. 31–32. A sarcastic review of the employers' organ *Oesterreichische Buchdrucker Zeitung*.

109. Haecker, *Historja socjalizmu*, p. 126.

110. *Czcionka*, 1873, no. 8, pp. 29–31.

111. Ibid., 1873, no. 10, pp. 37–39.

112. Kravets', "Pochatok," p. 28.

113. Najdus, *Powstanie związku,* p. 60.

114. *Czcionka,* 1873, no. 39, an issue devoted entirely to the Piller anniversary, contains excerpts from the banquet speeches, but does not settle the question of who objected to capital and labor toasting each other's friendship. That there were objections is indicated by the summary of Zubalewicz's speech: "Zubalewicz does not share the opinion of those honorable speakers who claimed that labor and capital have nothing in common. . . ." Ibid., p. 155. Haecker, *Historja socjalizmu,* pp. 126–29, suggests that Zubalewicz was referring to Limanowski's speech. Limanowski himself, writing decades after the event, does not remember any polemics at the Piller anniversary, least of all directed against himself. He implies that the tailor Franciszek Głodziński might have said something anti-capitalist at the banquet. Bolesław Limanowski, *Pamiętniki. (1870–1907)* (Warsaw, 1958), p. 88. Najdus plausibly suggests that Mańkowski delivered the speech in question, though it seems she has misread the latter source. Walentyna Najdus, "Klasowe związki zawodowe w Galicji," *Przegląd Historyczny* 51 (1960): 135.

115. Haecker, *Historja socjalizmu,* p. 129. Kravets', "Pochatok," p. 30, note 2. Bednarski, *Materyały,* p. 87.

116. Szczęsny Bednarski, trans. *Głosy robotników! Podług broszury F. Schönhofer'a: "Was wollen, was sollen die Arbeiter!"* (Lviv, 1873), pp. 1–2, 15–17.

117. Najdus, *Powstanie związku,* pp. 53–54. Kravets' "Pochatok," p. 30. *Wiadomości statystyczne o mieście Lwowie* 3 (1877): 72.

118. Bober, *Historja drukarń,* p. 77.

119. Ibid., p. 44. Chapter Two will discuss the 1878 trial. The police were probably looking for propaganda brochures (published by Petr Lavrov's *Vpered*) that Drahomanov was to send to Mańkowski. Elżbieta Hornowa, *Ukraiński obóz postępowy i jego współpraca z polską lewicą społeczną w Galicji 1876–1895* (Wrocław, 1968), p. 22.

120. Głodziński, on the occasion of his marriage in 1879, was characterized by the socialist paper *Praca* as a "master and owner of a tailor shop" who "belongs to that unfortunately small number of masters who deny neither money nor enthusiasm to Gwiazda and other associations and who have not withdrawn from participation in all patriotic work." *Praca,* 1879, no. 3, p. 12. Głodziński was a curator of Gwiazda in 1879. He was among those who took care of Mańkowski's family when Mańkowski was imprisoned as a socialist for eight months in 1879. *Praca,* 1879, no. 19, p. 80. For his activity on behalf of artisan associations, Głodziński was named an honorary member of the Catholic journeymen's association Skała in 1886. He died in 1888. Chołodecki, *Półwiekowa przeszłość,* p. 164.

121. Franciszek Głodziński, *Odezwa do współkolegów Towarzystwa "Gwiazda" w dniu uroczystości poswięcenia jej chorągwi* (Lviv, 1871).

122. [Bolesław Limanowski], "Wielka rodzina," *Dziennik Polski,* 4 July 1871, p. 2. This article got Limanowski into trouble with the paper's editors. Limanowski, *Pamiętniki,* p. 58. Limanowski's opinion of Głodziński's project

was not unequivocally positive. In his memoirs, Limanowski mentions, but does not explain, his "coming out against Głodziński's little brochure." Ibid., p. 88.

123. Limanowski's activities in Galicia are well covered in Kazimiera Cottam, *Boleslaw Limanowski (1835–1935): A Study in Socialism and Nationalism* (Boulder, Colo., 1978), pp. 46–63. His role in the development of Galician socialism should not be exaggerated, as it is by Norman M. Naimark: "Limanowski influenced and shaped an entire generation of Lwów socialists through his immense intellectual gifts and constant publicist activities." *The History of the "Proletariat": The Emergence of Marxism in the Kingdom of Poland, 1870–1887* (Boulder, Colo., 1979), p. 85.

124. Bolesław Limanowski, *O kwestji robotniczej* (Lviv, 1871).

125. Limanowski, "Wspomnienia," pp. 3–4.

126. Szulc, *Kwestja socjalna*, pp. 77–78.

127. Marian Żychowski, *Bolesław Limanowski 1835–1935* (Warsaw, 1971), pp. 150–51.

128. Ibid., pp. 152–53. Limanowski had been planning to publish a "Library of the Social Sciences" in 1876. Brzeziński and W. Rapacki corresponded with Limanowski about the project, which resulted in the publication of Lassalle's works. Centralne Archiwum Komitetu Centralnego PZPR [CA], 5/II–2, pp. 15–16. The works by Lassalle were: *Program robotników; Pośrednie podatki i położenie klas pracujących*; and *Kapitał i praca czyli Pan Bastiat-Szulce z Delicza, Julian Ekonomiczny*. All came out in Lviv in 1878.

129. CA, 5/II–2, p. 16.

130. Ibid. Żychowski, *Bolesław Limanowski*, pp. 154–55.

Chapter Two

1. In the mid-1860s, Klymkovych had been editor of the Ukrainophile journal *Meta* in Lviv. After the journal collapsed, he was in such straits that he had to pawn his clothing to pay for moving back to the village. Illia Vytanovych, *Volodymyr Navrots'kyi (1847–1882)* (Lviv, 1934), p. 28. On funding for Galician Russophilism, see *Zarubezhnye slaviane i Rossiia. Dokumenty arkhiva M. F. Raevskogo 40–80 gody XIX veka* (Moscow, 1975), pp. 144–45, 158–59, 227, 372, 375, 432, 451; and Jan Kozik, "Moskalofilstwo w Galicji w latach 1848–1866 na tle odrodzenia narodowego Rusinów" (M.A. dissertation, Jagellonian University, 1958), pp. 155–73.

2. Iuliian Bachyns'kyi, *Ukraina irredenta* (Lviv, 1895), pp. 43–44, was one advocate of the simple formula that Russophilism was a clerical movement while national populism was secular. This falls short of the truth not only because Russophilism has a claim to consideration as a secular movement, but also because national populism inevitably fell under strong clerical influence.

3. [Ivan Franko], "Po zjeździe radykałów ruskich," *Kurjer Lwowski*, 12 October 1891, supplement to no. 284, p. 1. Kornylo Ustiianovych was prompted to become a Russophile in reaction to the Old Ruthenians' "Austrianism" and "clericalism." Kornylo N. Ustiianovych, *M. F. Raievskii i rosiiskii panslavyzm* (Lviv, 1884), p. 16.

4. (D.), "Sambór," *Dziennik Polski,* 22 May 1872, no. 138, p. 2. "Jeszcze o p. Kaczkowskim w Samborze," ibid., 26 May 1872, no. 142, p. 3. According to the memoirs of a Polish civil servant in Galicia, repeating — by his own admission — the gossip of "evil tongues," Kachkovsky's love for Ruthenian peasants was also sexual: "The Ruthenian Kachkivsky [sic], a fanatic and old bachelor, . . . would regularly visit the market and buy various items from the village women. He would order the articles brought to his quarters and would only pay the women then . . . not only for the purchased goods, but also for certain other matters." This is reminiscent, of course, of the sort of slander spread about white civil rights activists in America in the 1960s ("niggerlovers"). Józef Doboszyński, "Pamiętnik," in *Pamiętniki urzędników galicyjskich,* ed. Irena Homola and Bolesław Łopuszański (Cracow, 1978), p. 379. In Soviet historiography Kachkovsky generally figures as a reactionary because of his adhesion to the Russophile movement; a recent Soviet work, however, notes that Kachkovsky read Herzen. S. M. Trusevych, *Suspil'no-politychnyi rukh u Skhidnii Halychyni v 50–70-kh rokakh XIX st.* (Kiev, 1978), p. 60.

5. M. P. Dragomanov, "Literaturnoe dvizhenie v Galitsii," *Politicheskiia sochineniia,* ed. I. M. Grevs and B. A. Kistiakovskii, vol. I: *Tsentr i okrainy* (Moscow, 1908), p. 386. M. Pavlyk, "Ukraina Avstriis'ka," *Hromada,* rik V (1881), no. 1, p. 96.

6. According to Ivan Franko, the Ruthenian intelligentsia had the choice "either to rely solely on their own powers and to set to work on their own ground to create here a center of progress and civilizing development, and slowly, but persistently, to win that which they could not win at once, on the road of diplomacy; or else, wrapping themselves in the cloak of national exclusivity and fanaticism, to wash their hands of all compromise work and to create in northeastern Austria a Muscovite irredenta." "Po zjeździe," p. 1.

7. Ostap Terlets'kyi, *Halyts'ko-rus'ke pys'menstvo 1848–1865 rr. na tli tohochasnykh suspil'no-politychnykh zmahan' halyts'ko-rus'koi inteligentsii. Nedokinchena pratsia* (Lviv, 1903), p. 97.

8. Mykhailo Pavlyk, "Pro rus'ko-ukrains'ki narodni chytal'ni," *Tvory* (Kiev, 1959), pp. 476–77. Oleksander Barvins'kyi, *Spomyny z moho zhytia,* part 1 (Lviv, 1912), pp. 59–60.

9. Terlets'kyi, *Halyts'ko-rus'ke pys'menstvo,* p. 98, citing Shashkevych.

10. This Ukrainophile circle had thirty members, all Polish; it disbanded in 1864 when many of the Kievan students, owing to the proclamation of martial law, were obliged to abandon Galicia. On the 1863 insurrection and Galician national populism, see Barvins'kyi, *Spomyny,* 1:41–43; Osyp Nazaruk and Olena Okhrymovych, "Khronika rukhu ukrains'koi akademychnoi molodizhy u L'vovi," in *1868–1908. "Sich". Al'manakh v pamiat' 40-ykh rokovyn osnovania tovarystva "Sich" u Vidni,* ed. Zenon Kuziela and Mykola Chaikivs'kyi (Lviv, 1908), pp. 392–94; Cyryl Studziński, *Powstańcy polscy z roku 1863 w redakcji ukraińskiej "Mety"* (Lviv, 1937); Trusevych, *Suspil'no-politychnyi rukh,* pp. 108–10.

11. The following anecdote, which turns on the double meaning of the

Ukrainian word *narid,* reflects the democratic spirit prevalent among some Ukrainophile youth in the mid-1860s. Volodymyr Navrotsky and Ostap Terletsky were going to school. Ahead of them walked a mutual acquaintance dressed as a cossack (as was then the fashion among some of the Ukrainophile youth). Terletsky remarked that he, too, would like to buy a cossack outfit and dress "po narodn'omu." "Po narodn'omu!" exclaimed Navrotsky. "De vy vydily narid, shchoby tak ubyravsia? . . . Se poprostu smikh tai hodi. . . . Koly khochemo buty zovsim konsekventnymy narodovtsiamy i nosytysia po narodn'omu, to nosimsia zovsim po muzhyts'ky." Vytanovych, *Volodymyr Navrots'kyi,* pp. 25–26.

12. Terlets'kyi, *Halyts'ko-rus'ke pys'menstvo,* pp. 115–16.

13. Antin Kobylians'kyi and Kost' Horbal', *Holos na holos dlia Halyčyny* (Chernivtsi, 1861), cited in Pavlyk, "Pro rus'ko-ukrains'ki narodni chytal'ni," pp. 484–86. *Holos na holos* was printed in the Latin alphabet, though in the Ukrainian language.

14. I have argued this interpretation in several studies of the social composition and class relationships within the Ruthenians' national movement: "Voluntary Artisan Associations and the Ukrainian National Movement in Galicia (the 1870s)," *Harvard Ukrainian Studies* 2 (1978): 235–50; "Priests and Peasants: The Greek Catholic Pastor and the Ukrainian National Movement in Austria, 1867–1900," *Canadian Slavonic Papers* 21 (1979): 1–14; "The Membership of the Popular Education Society Prosvita, 1868–74," in "Polish and Ukrainian Socialism: Austria, 1867–1890" (Ph.D. dissertation, The University of Michigan, 1977), pp. 126–42.

15. Mykhailo Drahomanov, "Perednie slovo do 'Hromady,'" *Vybrani tvory* (Prague, 1937), p. 121; see also pp. 140–44, and M. P. Drahomanov, "Avtobiograficheskaia zametka," *Literaturno-publitsystychni pratsi,* 2 vols. (Kiev, 1970), 1:59, 61, 65. For a general introduction to Drahomanov, see Ivan L. Rudnytsky, ed., *Mykhaylo Drahomanov: A Symposium and Selected Writings* (New York, 1952).

16. In the previous year, largely thanks to Drahomanov's efforts, the Russian Ukrainophiles had been a source of financial and literary support for national populism in Galicia. The national populists, threatened with a boycott on the part of the Russian Ukrainophiles, entered into negotiations with Drahomanov to repair the ruptured connection. These negotiations failed, and Drahomanov, in 1875, published a running commentary on the defects of the Galician Ukrainophiles in the newspaper *Kievskii telegraf.* M. Drahomanov, "Deshcho pro l'vivs'kykh narodovtsiv i sotsiializm v Halychyni," *Hromada,* no. 4 (1879): 364–66. For the text of the open letter, see "Odkrytyi lyst z Ukrainy do redaktsii 'Pravdy,'" *Pravda,* 1873, no. 19, pp. 660–64; reprinted in M. P. Drahomanov, "Avstro-rus'ki spomyny," *Literaturno-publitsystychni pratsi,* 2:217–19 (see also 2:181, 194–98). Drahomanov, "Avtobiograficheskaia zametka," 1:57, errs in giving the number of signatories as forty-five. The editors of *Pravda* noted that the letter bore thirty-one signatures. An additional forty-five were appended later. "Novynky," *Pravda,* 1873, no. 20, p. 699. For samples of Drahomanov's criticism of Galician affairs in *Kievskii telegraf,* see

"Pominki Shevchenka v L'vove i Vene," *Kievskii telegraf,* 18 April 1875, p. 1; "Galitskiia otnosheniia kievskago otdela Slavianskago blagotvoritel'nago komiteta," ibid., 25 May 1875, p. 2.

17. Drahomanov, "Avtobiograficheskaia zametka," 1:55. Dragomanov, "Literaturnoe dvizhenie," 1:375–77. M. P. Dragomanov, "Vostochnaia politika Germanii i obrusenie," *Politicheskiia sochineniia,* 1:121.

18. M. P. Drahomanov, "Literatura rosiis'ka, velykorus'ka, ukrains'ka i halyts'ka," *Literaturno-publitsystychni pratsi,* 1:80–220.

19. Drahomanov to Navrotsky, 27 December 1872: "You tell me: We have here our own Russia, i.e., the St. George party, with whom we have no choice but to fight." Tsentral'nyi derzhavnyi istorychnyi arkhiv u L'vovi [TsDIAL], 152/2/14417, p. 35.

20. "Vidpovid' p. M. P. Drahomanovu. (S prychyny napadiv v 'Hromadi')," *Pravda,* 1879, no. 6. This was the national populists' reply to Drahomanov's "Deshcho pro l'vivs'kykh narodovtsiv."

21. Hnat Onyshkevych [Halychanyn], "Novoie napravleniie ukrainskoi literatury," *Druh,* 1874, no. 17, p. 385.

22. Drahomanov, "Galitskiia otnosheniia," p. 2. Drahomanov, "Deshcho pro l'vivs'kykh narodovtsiv," p. 363.

23. "Odkrytyi lyst," p. 661.

24. Kachala's letter to the editorial board of *Druh,* 7 August 1876, in *Perepyska Mykhaila Drahomanova z Mykhailom Pavlykom. (1876–1895),* ed. Mykhailo Pavlyk, 7 vols., numbered 2–8 (Chernivtsi, 1910–12), 2:79–80. (Hereafter referred to as Pavlyk, *Perepyska.*)

25. Drahomanov, "Avstro-rus'ki spomyny," 2:249. Drahomanov frequently repeated this story, for instance in "Deshcho pro l'vivs'kykh narodovtsiv," p. 365. Sushkevych declared that Drahomanov's account of this incident was *absolutely untrue.* V. Barvins'kyi, "Vidpovid' p. M. P. Drahomanovu," p. 380.

26. [M. P. Drahomanov], *Vydumki "Kievlianina" i pol'skikh gazet o malorusskom patriotizme* (Kiev, 1874). Elżbieta Hornowa, "Prześladowania ukraińskiej kultury przez rząd carski za panowania Aleksandra II," *Zeszyty Naukowe Wyższej Szkoły Pedagogicznej w Opolu,* Seria A: *Filologia Rosyjska,* no. 9 (1972), pp. 113–31. Roman Sol'chanyk, "Lex Jusephovicia 1876," *Suchasnist',* 1976, no. 5 (185), pp. 36–68. Svitozar M. Drahomanov, "Pro zvil'nennia Mykhaila Drahomanova z posady dotsenta Kyivs'koho universytetu," *Novi dni,* no. 322 (November 1976), pp. 6–9.

27. Letter of Drahomanov to Buchynsky, 17 February 1873, in M. Pavlyk, ed., *Perepyska Mykhaila Drahomanova z Melitonom Buchyns'kym 1871–1877* (Lviv, 1910), p. 281.

28. Terletsky to Buchynsky, 17 September 1874, TsDIAL, 152/2/14417, p. 74.

29. Terletsky's "Halyts'ko rus'kyi narid i halyts'ko-rus'ki narodovtsi" appeared in *Pravda,* 1874, nos. 17 and 18.

30. The four brochures were: [S. Podolyns'kyi], *Parova mashyna* (Vienna, 1875); [S. Podolyns'kyi], *Pro bidnist'* (Vienna, 1875); [V. Varzar and S. Podo-

lyns'kyi], *Pravda* (Vienna, 1875); [F. Volkhovs'kyi], *Pravdyve slovo khliboroba* (Vienna, 1876). Podolynsky was an anti-Semite and this is reflected in some of the brochures.

31. Onyshkevych, "Novoie napravleniie," *Druh,* 1874, no. 17, pp. 384–89, no. 18, pp. 411–16.

32. Drahomanov, "Galitskiia otnosheniia," p. 2.

33. M. P. Drahomanov, "Pershyi lyst do redaktsii 'Druha,'" *Literaturno-publitsystychni pratsi,* 1:397–401. The letter originally appeared in *Druh,* 1 (13) June 1875, no. 11, pp. 265–70. Drahomanov signed the letter "Ukrainets."

34. M. P. Drahomanov, "Druhyi lyst do redaktsii 'Druha.' Ukrainshchina ili rutenshchina?" and "Tretii lyst Ukraintsia do redaktsii 'Druha,'" *Literaturno-publitsystychni pratsi,* 1:402–27. The normal word for Ruthenians in Ukrainian was *rusyny*; when Drahomanov referred to *rutentsi,* from the German *Ruthenen,* he wanted to emphasize the peculiar "Austrianism" of the Galician Ruthenians. I am using the word "Ruthene" to translate *rutenets'*; this preserves Drahomanov's distinction, although it does not convey the same nuances.

35. [Hnat Onyshkevych], "Otpovid' na pys'mo h. Ukraintsa v ch. 11 nashoi chasopysy," *Druh,* 1875, no. 12, p. 292.

36. On Dovbush, see E. J. Hobsbawm, *Primitive Rebels* (New York: The Norton Library, 1965), pp. 13–29. On the Pavlyk family, see Ivan Denysiuk, *Mykhailo Pavlyk* (Kiev, 1960), p. 11, and TsDIAL, 663/1/110, p. 38.

37. In his story "Yurko Kulykiv," Pavlyk describes how Yurko defended a servant girl from a malicious mistress, the daughter of a priest. The priest then beat Yurko and called him "an outlaw" and "an *opryshok.*" Pavlyk, *Tvory,* p. 60.

38. Denysiuk, *Mykhailo Pavlyk,* p. 12. TsDIAL, 663/1/108, p. 280.

39. Letter of Pavlyk to Drahomanov, 20 April 1876, cited in Mykhailo Lozyns'kyi, *Mykhailo Pavlyk. Ioho zhyttie i diial'nist'* (Vienna, 1917), pp. 5–6.

40. TsDIAL, 663/1/110, p. 141. The Kachkovsky Society was a Russophile association devoted to the education of the peasantry.

41. Pavlyk, "Pro rus'ko-ukrains'ki narodni chytal'ni," p. 529. Lozyns'kyi, *Mykhailo Pavlyk,* p. 6.

42. There is no satisfactory biography of Ivan Franko. The following, however, can be read with profit: I. Bass, *Ivan Franko. Biografiia* (Moscow, 1957); M. Lozyns'kyi, *Ivan Franko. (Z portretom)* (Vienna, 1917); Jurij Lawrynenko, "Ševčenko's Role in Ivan Franko's Self-Realization," in *Taras Ševčenko 1814–1861: A Symposium,* ed. Volodymyr Mijakovs'kyj and George Y. Shevelov (The Hague, 1962), pp. 217–52.

43. Ivan Franko, "Schönschreiben," *Vybrani tvory,* 3 vols. (Kiev, 1973), 2:127.

44. Ivan Franko, "Otets' humoryst," ibid., 2:387.

45. Ibid., 2:372.

46. Ivan Franko, "Spomyny iz moikh gimnaziial'nykh chasiv," *Zhytie. (Neperiodychne vydavnytstvo prysviachene spravam ukrains'koi molodizhy)* (Lviv, 1912), no. 4, pp. 156–62.

47. TsDIAL, 663/1/108, pp. 225, 418.

48. Ivan Franko, *Tvory,* 20 vols. (Kiev, 1950–56), 20:6, 8–9, 13–14.

49. O. I. Dei, *Ukrains'ka revoliutsiino-demokratychna zhurnalistyka. Problema vynyknennia i stanovlennia* (Kiev, 1959), p. 45.

50. Letter of 20 April 1876, cited in Lozyns'kyi *Mykhailo Pavlyk*, p. 7.

51. Dei, *Ukrains'ka revoliutsiino-demokratychna zhurnalistyka*, pp. 112–13. M. Pavlyk, "Ukraina Avstriis'ka," *Hromada*, rik V (1881), no. 1, p. 98. The preoccupation with the Bosnian revolt is evident from Vol. Orlyk, "Chornohora," *Druh*, 1876, no. 1, pp. 10–11, and Ivan Franko [Dzhedzhalyk], "Pisnia zadunaiskaia," *Druh*, 1876, no. 3, pp. 33–34.

52. Dei, *Ukrains'ka revoliutsiino-demokratychna zhurnalistyka*, pp. 61–66. M. Bernshtein "Diial'nist' I. Franka — krytyka u zhurnali 'Druh,'" in O. I. Bilets'kyi, ed., *Slovo pro velykoho kameniara*, 2 vols. (Kiev, 1956), 2:162.

53. Letter of Ivan Belei to a hromada (student club) outside Lviv, 13 July 1876, in TsDIAL, 152/2/14400, p. 5.

54. Dei, *Ukrains'ka revoliutsiino-demokratychna zhurnalistyka*, p. 82. Pavlyk was correct that peasants would be impressed by printed collections of folklore. In the mid-1880s Vasyl Fedorovych, a peasant from Dobrostany (Horodok district), came upon a book of Ruthenian folk songs from Bukovyna. He wrote a letter to the popular newspaper *Bat'kivshchyna* urging that more such collections be published. "In this way we peasants would get to know one another more intimately; we would get to know our cultural life and our history." *Bat'kivshchyna*, 1885, no. 3, p. 21.

55. M. Pavlyk [Khmara], "Akademycheske obshchestvo," *Druh*, 1875, no. 19, pp. 455–56.

56. Denysiuk, *Mykhailo Pavlyk*, p. 13.

57. [Antin Dol'nyts'kyi], "Vstupna besida," *Druh*, 1876, no. 12, pp. 188–89.

58. Dei, *Ukrains'ka revoliutsiino-demokratychna zhurnalistyka*, pp. 161–63. "Shcho diiaty?" *Druh*, 1877, nos. 1–5.

59. On "scientism," see Alina Molska, *Model ustroju socjalistycznego w polskiej myśli marksistowskiej lat 1878–1886* (Warsaw, 1965), pp. 46–94. The students of *Druh* foresaw a great role for science in "the improvement of people's lives, especially of the lives of the working masses, our People [*liud*]." Dei, *Ukrains'ka revoliutsiino-demokratychna zhurnalistyka*, p. 110.

60. Dei, *Ukrains'ka revoliutsiino-demokratychna zhurnalistyka*, p. 174. Antin Dolnytsky, a member of the kruzhok, recalled Pavlyk's attitude towards priests in a memoir written a half century later. Pavlyk's "one-sidedness bordered on the maniacal"; "he would have liked to eradicate them [priests] from the face of the earth." Dolnytsky felt Pavlyk was "a forerunner of the Bolsheviks" in his anticlericalism. Cited by Bernshtein, "Diial'nist' I. Franka," p. 167.

61. Dei, *Ukrains'ka revoliutsiino-demokratychna zhurnalistyka*, pp. 114–15.

62. "Tandem! (Poiednan'e akademycheskykh Tovarystv)," *Druh*, 1876, no. 13, p. 206. A similar union of Russkaia osnova (Russian Foundation) and Sich, simultaneously planned in Vienna, did not come to fruition. Myron Korduba, "Istoriya 'Sichy,'" in Myron Korduba et al., ed., *1868–1898. "Sich". Al'manakh v pamiat' 30-ykh rokovyn osnovania tovarystva "Sich" u Vidni* (Lviv, 1898), pp. 17–18.

63. In the mid-1870s, just as in the mid-1860s, Ukrainophile students in gymnasia throughout Galicia formed secret societies called "hromadas." These patriotic clubs corresponded with one another; individually, the hromadas gathered for talks on Ukrainian history and literature and commemorated national heroes such as Shevchenko and Markiian Shashkevych at musical and declamatory evenings and at memorial liturgical services. Hromadas were active in the gymnasia in Ternopil, Przemyśl, Stanyslaviv, Berezhany and Sambir. A Ukrainophile hromada also existed, despite discouragement from the Russo-phile administration, at the Greek Catholic seminary in Lviv. At Lviv University, a "central hromada," identical with the legally registered student club Druzhnii lykhvar, functioned as the communications center of the network of hromadas. That the radicalized, united Akademicheskii kruzhok-Druzhnii lykhvar continued in this function is evident from Ivan Belei's letter, 13 July 1876, in TsDIAL, 152/2/14400, pp. 5–6. Natalia Kobrynska recalled in her autobiography that Franko and Pavlyk gave her brothers (then gymnasium students in Lviv) the following authors to read: Chernyshevsky, Belinsky, Dobroliubov, Pisarev, Drahomanov, Limanowski, Lassalle and Marx. Natalia Kobryns'ka, "Avtobiohrafiia," *Vybrani tvory* (Kiev, 1958), p. 375.

64. Letter of Belei, p. 6. Prosvita, like the Kachkovsky Society, was a popular educational association, only Ukrainophile in orientation.

65. Dei, *Ukrains'ka revoliutsiino-demokratychna zhurnalistyka*, p. 66.

66. S[tepan Labash], "Nichto ob odnoi chasopysi," *Slovo,* 1876, nos. 71–77. The articles appeared in July.

67. "Korespondentsii 'Slova'. Ot Vostoka. (Nichto o 'Druzi' i ieho 'krytykakh')," *Slovo,* 13 (25) July 1876, no. 79, p. 3.

68. "Novynky. O nashykh akademychnykh tovarystvakh," *Ruskii Sion,* 1876, no. 14, p. 469.

69. Illia Mardarovych, "Iz Volchyntsa," *Ruskii Sion,* 1876, no. 13, pp. 424–26. The article was reprinted in *Slovo,* 1876, no. 78, pp. 2–3.

70. Pavlyk, *Perepyska,* 2:79–80.

71. Ibid., cited in Dei, *Ukrains'ka revoliutsiino-demokratychna zhurnalistyka,* p. 146.

72. Dei, *Ukrains'ka revoliutsiino-demokratychna zhurnalistyka,* pp. 94–95.

73. Ibid., pp. 103–04. Bernshtein, "Diial'nist' I. Franka," pp. 188–90.

74. Ivan Verkhrats'kyi, *Odvit p. O. Partytskomu . . . i dekotri inshi zamichan'ia, imenno o literaturnii stiinosty i tendentsii "Druha"* (Lviv, 1876), p. 40. According to Dei, *Ukrains'ka revoliutsiino-demokratychna zhurnalistyka,* p. 145, Verkhratsky sent his brochure to priests subscribing to *Druh.*

75. M. Drahomanov [Ukrainets'], "Opiznaimo sia. (Lyst v redaktsiiu 'Pravdy')," *Druh,* 1877, no. 1, pp. 12–14, no. 2, pp. 28–31. Drahomanov, "Deshcho pro l'vivs'kykh narodovtsiv," pp. 366–67.

76. Dei, *Ukrains'ka revoliutsiino-demokratychna zhurnalistyka,* p. 150.

77. Ibid., pp. 150–51.

78. Cited in ibid., pp. 176–77.

79. S. V. Shchurat, "Ivan Franko i rosiis'ki revoliutsiini narodnyky," in *Doslidzhennia tvorchosti Ivana Franka,* no. 2 (Kiev, 1959), pp. 93–95. Mykhai-

lo Hrushevs'kyi, *Z pochyniv ukrains'koho sotsiialistychnoho rukhu* (Vienna, 1922), p. 55.

80. Haus-, Hof- und Staatsarchiv [HH], Informationsbüro des k. k. Ministeriums des Äussern [Informationsbüro], 322, 576, 765, 865, 874/1877. Volodymyr Levyns'kyi, "Drahomaniv i drahomanivtsi u svitli avstriis'kykh tainykh dokumentiv," *Z mynuloho. Zbirnyk,* vol. I (Warsaw, 1938), pp. 11–12 (= vol. XLVIII of *Pratsi Ukrains'koho naukovoho instytutu*). V. I. Kalynovych, *Politychni protsesy Ivana Franka ta ioho tovaryshiv* (Lviv, 1967), pp. 24–32. On Liakhotsky, see Yury Boshyk, "A Chapter from the History of the Ukrainian Diaspora: M. Drahomanov's *Hromada,* the Ukrainian Printing House in Geneva, and A. M. (Kuzma) Liakhotsky," *Journal of Ukrainian Graduate Studies,* no. 5 (1978), pp. 25–39.

81. HH, Informationsbüro, 1960, 1982, 2174, 2262, 3306, 4559/1877. TsDIAL, 663/1/103, 108–09; 152/2/14412; 309/1/336. Danylo Taniachkevych [O. Obachnyi], *Sotsiialisty mezhy seminarystamy?! Studiia na nashim tserkovno-narodnim poli* (Lviv, 1877). Bolesław Limanowski, *Pamiętniki (1870–1907)* (Warsaw, 1958), pp. 169–81. Kalynovych, *Politychni protsesy,* pp. 33–96.

82. For an account of the trial I have used the transcript in TsDIAL, 152/2/14417, pp. 130–80. Useful, too, are the detailed reports in *Slovo,* "Sotsialisty. Iz sudovoi sali," which appeared in installments almost simultaneously with the trial. The trial is also well covered in Emil Haecker, *Historja socjalizmu w Galicji i na Śląsku Cieszyńskim* (Cracow, 1933), pp. 144–50, and Kalynovych, *Politychni protsesy,* pp. 33–96.

83. Franko to Drahomanov, 26 April 1890 (a *curriculum vitae*), in *Lystuvannia I. Franka i M. Drahomanova* (Kiev, 1928), p. 325.

84. So he told Limanowski. Bolesław Limanowski, "Wspomnienia z pobytu w Galicyi (Zaczątki obecnego ruchu socyalistycznego)," in *Z pola walki. Zbiór materyałów tyczących się polskiego ruchu socyalistycznego* (London, 1904), p. 7.

85. Kobryns'ka "Avtobiohrafiia," p. 376.

86. The destruction of all cities as a key element of socialist belief was repeated by *Nauka* in 1885. "Rozhovor Mykhaila i Pylypa o sotsialistakh," *Nauka,* 1885, no. 10, pp. 604–09. The Galician socialists never advocated such radical deurbanization. Father Naumovych, editor of *Nauka,* probably learned of this doctrine, associated with Babouvism, from Kazimerz Szulc, *Kwestja socjalna i sposób jej załatwienia, równie korzystny dla robotników jak i właścicieli* (Lviv, 1871), p. 14.

87. *Nauka,* 1878, no. 1, p. 24.

88. "Vira i nevirstvo. (Rozhovor ottsa s synom)," *Nauka,* 1878, no. 2, pp. 25–28.

89. TsDIAL, 152/2/14417, p. 145.

90. M. P. Drahomanov, "Shevchenko, ukrainofily i sotsializm," *Literaturno-publitsystychni pratsi,* 2:15–16.

91. Cited in ibid., 2:16.

92. Omelian Partytsky cited in ibid., 2:19.

93. "Slovo v spravi sotsiializmu," *Ruskii Sion,* 1877, no. 18, pp. 569–72.

94. To appreciate the potential malignancy of Pavlyk's gangrene, the reader should be aware of the following facts about Galicia's otherwise "healthy body." In all of Austria, there averaged (1874) one physician per 2,707 inhabitants; in Galicia, one per 7,092. Savage epidemics visited the population: in 1873, for example, 91,308 Galicians died of cholera. In the late 1880s it was estimated that 50,000 Galicians died annually of hunger. *Statistische Monatschrift* 5 (1879): 67; 1 (1875): 136. Stanisław Szczepanowski, *Nędza Galicyi w cyfrach i program energicznego rozwoju gospodarstwa krajowego* (Lviv, 1888), pp. 55–57.

95. A. S., "Novynky. Sotsiializm. Protses vo L'vovi," *Ruskii Sion,* 1878, no. 2, p. 62.

96. Ivan Franko, "Iak tse stalosia," in O. I. Dei and N. P. Korniienko, eds., *Ivan Franko u spohadakh suchasnykiv* (Lviv, 1956), p. 552.

97. J. F[ranko], "Rutećny. Typy i portrety galicyjskich 'ludzi,'" *Tydzień literacki, artystyczny, naukowy i społeczny,* 1878, nos. 57–58, 63.

98. Limanowski, *Pamiętniki,* p. 182.

Chapter Three

1. Bolesław Limanowski, *Pamiętniki (1870–1907)* (Warsaw, 1958), pp. 198–99. Kazimiera Janina Cottam, *Boleslaw Limanowski (1835–1935): A Study in Socialism and Nationalism* (Boulder, Colo., 1978), p. 62.

2. Adam Wiktor Bober, *Historja drukarń i stowarzyszeń drukarskich we Lwowie* (Lviv, 1926), p. 80. Emil Haecker, *Historja socjalizmu w Galicji i na Śląsku Cieszyńskim* (Cracow, 1933), p. 170.

3. Among others, Ignacy Daszyński, in a letter to Viktor Adler, 15 October 1892 (Verein für Geschichte der Arbeiterbewegung, Vienna, Adler-Archiv, 105/2), Józef Kozłowski, *Pieśń Bolesława Czerwieńskiego* (Warsaw, 1966), p. 24, and Feliks Tych, in his edition of *Polskie programy socjalistyczne 1878–1918* (Warsaw, 1975), p. 72, attribute the transformation of *Praca* to the efforts of Ludwik Waryński. Indeed, Ludwik Waryński was concerned about broadening the scope of *Praca* to make it a socialist organ. So too was the Galician socialist Adolf Inlaender. Jerzy Targalski, ed., "Krakowska sprawa socjalistów polskich. Materiały śledztwa z lat 1878–1880 (Wybór), Część 1," *Z Pola Walki,* 1974, no. 4, pp. 156–58, 167. But Pavlyk, in a report prepared for (but not published in) the *Jahrbuch für Sozialwissenschaft und Sozialpolitik* (1880), states unequivocally that he himself convinced Daniluk to change *Praca* from a printers' paper to a working class paper. Mykhailo Pavlyk, ed., *Perepyska Mykhaila Drahomanova z Mykhailom Pavlykom. (1876–1895),* 7 vols., numbered 2–8 (Chernivtsi, 1910–12), 3:185–86. Hereafter abbreviated as Pavlyk, *Perepyska.*

4. "Kilka słów o pracy," *Praca,* 1878, no. 3, p. 9.

5. M. M. Kravets', "Pochatok robitnychoho rukhu v Skhidnii Halychyni," *Z istorii zakhidnoukrains'kykh zemel',* vyp. 3 (1958), p. 38.

6. H. D. Verves, "Ivan Franko v robitnychii hazeti 'Praca,'" in *I. Ia. Franko iak istoryk* (Kiev, 1956), pp. 114–38. Franko's articles in Praca are listed in M. O. Moroz, *Ivan Franko. Bibliohrafiia tvoriv 1874–1964* (Kiev, 1966),

pp. 158–63. Some have been reprinted in Ukrainian translation in volume 19 of Ivan Franko, *Tvory,* 20 vols. (Kiev, 1950–56).

7. M. Pavlyk, "Ukraina Avstriis'ka," *Hromada,* rik V (1881), no. 1, pp. 115–19.

8. "Przegląd polityczny," *Czas,* 25 August 1881, no. 193, p. 2. Excerpts and a response are printed in "Hajże na socjalistów!" *Praca,* 1881, no. 12, pp. 44–45. *Czas* questioned *Gazeta Narodowa* as to why the Democratic paper allowed *Praca* to be published in its printshop.

9. "*Praca* is collapsing." Franko to Pavlyk, *ca.* 16 April 1879, in Pavlyk, *Perepyska,* 3:12. "*Praca,* in my opinion, is no force at all, and if it should stop coming out today not so much as a dog would bark among the workers." Franko to Pavlyk, 11 April 1881, ibid., 3:427.

10. *Praca,* 1880, no. 15, p. 59.

11. "Z kraju i o kraju. Korrespondencyja," *Równość,* 1880, no. 4, p. 18. See also: "Stowarzyszenie rękodzielników pod nazwą 'Gwiazda' we Lwowie," *Praca,* 5 September 1883, no. 12, p. 48; and above, chapter one, note 60.

12. "Nasze stosunki i środki zaradcze" and "W sprawie projektu Towarzystwa wzajemnej pomocy," *Praca,* 1 April 1879, no. 7, pp. 26–27, and 5 June 1879, no. 10, p. 37.

13. "Stowarzyszenia robotnicze angielskie (Trade-Unions, ich cele i organizacja)," *Praca,* 1879, nos. 8 and 9.

14. Walentyna Najdus, "Klasowe związki zawodowe w Galicji," *Przegląd Historyczny* 51 (1960): 132. "Różności," *Praca,* 19 December 1881, no. 16, p. 62.

15. "Różności," *Praca,* 19 December 1881, no. 16, p. 62 and 1 February 1882, no. 2, pp. 7–8.

16. "Wiec szewców samoistnych," *Praca,* 10 October 1879, no. 15, p. 58. "Zgromadzenie samoistnych przemysłowców," ibid., 20 November 1879, no. 17, pp. 69–70. "Zgromadzenie majstrów," ibid., 15 February 1882, no. 3, p. 11. "Reforma ustawy przemysłowej," ibid., 6 March 1882, no. 4, pp. 13–14. "Różności," ibid., 6 March 1882, no. 4, p. 15, and 3 April 1882, no. 5, p. 20. "Reforma ustawy przemysłowej," *Sztandar Polski,* 1 April 1882, no. 1, pp. 5–6.

17. "Nowa ustawa przemysłowa," *Praca,* 20 October 1883, no. 14, p. 53.

18. "Warsztaty i fabryki," *Praca,* 18 April 1882, no. 6, p. 21.

19. "Robotnicy czescy o ustawie przemysłowej," *Praca,* 22 December 1879, no. 19, p. 79.

20. "Wolne Zgromadzenie robotników," *Praca,* 1880, nos. 1–3.

21. "Nasze żądania," reprinted in Tych, *Polskie programy socjalistyczne,* pp. 81–85.

22. "Rezolucje przedstawione Wolnemu Zgromadzeniu robotników," *Praca,* 2 January 1880, no. 1, pp. 2–3.

23. "Różności," *Praca,* 1 March 1880, no. 4, p. 18.

24. "Lwowskie zgromadzenie robotników," *Praca,* 10 February 1881, nos. 2–3, pp. 6–8. "Zgromadzenie robotników," ibid., 9 July 1881, no. 9, pp. 32–34. "Zgromadzenie robotników," ibid., 25 July 1883, no. 10, p. 38.

"Wolne Zgromadzenie robotników," ibid., 5 September 1883, no. 12, pp. 46–47.

25. Tych, *Polskie programy socjalistyczne*, pp. 135–37.

26. M. Pavlyk, "Ukraina Avstriis'ka," *Hromada*, rik V (1881), no. 1, pp. 112–13.

27. Reported by M. Pavlyk, "Novynky z Avstriis'koi Ukrainy," *Hromada*, rik V (1881), no. 2, p. 229.

28. "Pierwsze zgromadzenie robotnicze we Lwowie," *Równość*, January 1880, no. 4, p. 2.

29. "Zgromadzenie robotników," *Praca*, 9 July 1881, no. 9, pp. 32–34.

30. Tsentral'nyi derzhavnyi istorychnyi arkhiv URSR u L'vovi [TsDIAL], 146/4/224/3690, p. 173.

31. Police statement cited in *Praca*, 29 October 1881, no. 14, p. 51.

32. "1883 marzec 29, Lwów. — Akt oskarżenia . . . przeciwko socjalistom M. Drabikowi . . . i innym," *Źrodła do dziejów klasy robotniczej na ziemiach polskich*, vol. 2 (Warsaw, 1962), p. 782.

33. *Praca*, 3 May 1882, no. 7, p. 28.

34. "Głosy prasy burżoaznej," *Praca*, 3 August 1882, no. 12, p. 45.

35. On the theoretical concerns of Polish socialists from the Russian partition, see Alina Molska, ed., *Pierwsze pokolenie marksistów polskich. Wybór pism i materiałów źródłowych z lat 1878–1886*, 2 vols. (Warsaw, 1962); Alina Molska, *Model ustroju socjalistycznego w polskiej myśli marksistowskiej lat 1878–1886* (Warsaw, 1965); Norman M. Naimark, *The History of the "Proletariat": The Emergence of Marxism in the Kingdom of Poland, 1870–1887* (Boulder, Colo., 1979), pp. 81–106, 115–24.

36. See below, pp. 110–12.

37. Franko, "Pro sotsializm," *Tvory*, 19:16. Only one copy of the original brochure, *Co to jest socjalizm*, exists. Though printed in Lviv, the brochure bears the imprint "8 August 1878, Leipzig"; the false place of publication was intended to deceive the censors and police. The catechism seems to have enjoyed some popularity among craftsmen. See Kravets', "Pochatok," p. 36, and Naimark, *History of the "Proletariat"*, pp. 74, 271.

38. Mieczysław Romański, trans., *Wiara socjalistów przez Ludwika Blanka* (Lviv, 1868). A pile of the brochures lay unsold and unread for ten years in a Lviv bookshop until the January 1878 trial awakened an interest in socialism. Limanowski, *Pamiętniki*, p. 199.

39. Bolesław Limanowski, *Socyjalizm jako konieczny objaw dziejowego rozwoju* (Lviv, 1879). In spite of the date on the title page (1879), the brochure came out in September 1878. The Galician authorities ordered it confiscated after most copies had already been distributed.

40. Ibid., p. 12. Stanisław Mendelson, in a letter to Ludwik Waryński (17 October 1878): "What sort of definition of socialism is *that*?" Targalski, "Krakowska sprawa," p. 163. The definition is incorrectly cited by Cottam, *Boleslaw Limanowski*, p. 59.

41. *Program socjalistów galicyjskich* (Geneva [1881]). Reprinted in Tych, *Polskie programy socjalistyczne*, pp. 97–120.

42. *Program Galicyjskiej Partyi Robotniczej* (n.p., [1881]). Reprinted in Tych, *Polskie programy socjalistyczne,* pp. 120–37.

43. Tych, *Polskie programy socjalistyczne,* pp. 73 and 78. Ivan Franko, editorial note to M. Lozyns'kyi, "Z suchasnoho robitnys'koho rukhu," *Literaturno-naukovyi visnyk* 28 (1904), p. 179.

44. Tych, *Polskie programy socjalistyczne,* pp, 108, 114.

45. Kozłowski, *Piesń Bolesława Czerwieńskiego,* p. 105.

46. Limanowski, *Socyjalizm,* p. 61.

47. Franko, "Pro sotsializm," 19:14–15.

48. "Program socjalistów galicyjskich," in Tych, *Polskie programy socjalistyczne,* p. 116.

49. "Program Galicyjskiej Partii Robotniczej," in ibid., p. 127.

50. "Program socjalistów galicyjskich," in ibid., pp. 116–17.

51. Franko, "Choho vymahaiemo," *Tvory,* 19:213–14. This article originally appeared in *Praca* in 1879.

52. "Program socjalistów galicyjskich," in Tych, *Polskie programy socjalistyczne,* p. 114.

53. "Program Galicyjskiej Partii Robotniczej," in ibid., pp. 126–27.

54. Franko, "Pro sotsializm," *Tvory,* 19:15. "Program socjalistów galicyjskich," in Tych, *Polskie programy socjalistyczne,* p. 116.

55. "Program Galicyjskiej Partii Robotniczej," in ibid., p. 135.

56. Limanowski, *Socyjalizm,* p. 61. Franko, "Choho my khochemo?" [*Praca,* 1979], *Tvory,* 19:217. "Program socjalistów galicyjskich," in Tych, *Polskie programy socjalistyczne,* p. 118. "Program Galicyjskiej Partii Robotniczej," in ibid., p. 133. See also above, p. 35.

57. "Program socjalistów galicyjskich," in Tych, *Polskie programy socjalistyczne,* p. 103 (see also p. 113). Cf. Franko, "Pro sotsializm," 19:12, and "Choho vymahaiemo?" 19:214.

58. [Tadeusz Romanowicz?], "Socyalizm w Polsce," *Tydzień literacki, artystyczny, naukowy i społeczny,* vol. V, 1 July 1877, no. 43, p. 673.

59. "1883 marzec, etc.," *Źródła,* 2:779.

60. Limanowski, *Socyjalizm,* p. 90.

61. "Program socjalistów galicyjskich," in Tych, *Polskie programy socjalistyczne,* p. 102. Yet the January program also said that the primary reason for the relatively stunted development of the Galician socialist movement was the crownland's complicated ethnic structure! Ibid., pp. 97–98.

62. Ibid., p. 110. Karl Marx, "Preface to the First German Edition," *Capital,* 3 vols. (New York, 1967), 1:8–9.

63. Ibid., pp. 111–12. See also Limanowski, *Socyjalizm,* pp. 87–88; Franko, "Pro pratsiu" [*Praca,* 1881], *Tvory,* 19:233; "Program Galicyjskiej Partii Robotniczej," in Tych, *Polskie programy socjalistyczne,* p. 128.

64. Emphasis in the original, "Program Galicyjskiej Partii Robotniczej," in ibid., p. 126. Earlier, Franko had made a distinction between the *szlachta* and the bourgeoisie. "Choho vymahaiemo?" 19:211.

65. "Program Galicyjskiej Partii Robotniczej," in Tych, *Polskie programy socjalistyczne,* p. 128.

66. See above, p. 13.

67. "Program Galicyjskiej Partii Robotniczej," in Tych, *Polskie programy socjalistyczne*, p. 122.

68. As Franko wrote in December 1881, the May program "put its main emphasis on urban, not rural, workers." "Choho khoche 'Halyts'ka robitnyts'ka Hromada'?" *Tvory*, 19:57.

69. Franko, "Pro pratsiu," *Tvory*, 19:231.

70. Limanowski, *Socyjalizm*, pp. 92–93; "Program socjalistów galicyjskich," in Tych, *Polskie programy socjalistyczne*, pp. 108–09. The Ukrainian socialist Serhii Podolynsky held similar views in 1876 about the peasantry in Russian Ukraine. See N. T. Assonova, *Sotsialistychni pohliady ukrains'kykh revoliutsioneriv-demokrativ (kinets' XIX – pochatok XX st.)* (Kiev, 1977), pp. 95–96.

71. The Russian populists did much the same. "Everything Lassalle said about the working class we transferred to our peasantry. . . . We replaced the worker with the peasant, and the West European bourgeoisie with our own privileged class." Vladimir Debogorii-Mokrievich, *Vospominaniia*, 3 vols. in one (Paris, 1894–98), pp. 14–15.

72. S. V. Budzinovskii, *Kul'turnaia nuzhda avstriiskoi Rusi* (Lviv, 1891). Iuliian Bachyn'skyi, *Ukraina irredenta* (Lviv, 1895). These were the first modern political programs to call for Ukrainian independence.

73. Cottam, *Boleslaw Limanowski*, p. 60. Drahomanov had almost identical views. See above, p. 46, and M. P. Drahomanov, *Vybrani tvory* (Prague, 1937), pp. 71, 140.

74. Franko, "Pro sotsializm," 19:16; "Program socjalistów galicyjskich," in Tych, *Polskie programy socjalistyczne*, pp. 106–07; "Program Galicyjskiej Partii Robotniczej," in ibid., p. 124.

75. Ibid., pp. 123–24, 129; Franko, "Choho khoche 'Halyts'ka robitnyts'ka Hromada'?" 19:58.

76. Franko, "Pro sotsializm," 19:16; "Program socjalistów galicyjskich," in Tych, *Polskie programy socjalistyczne*, p. 114; "Program Galicyjskiej Partii Robotniczej," in ibid., pp. 129–30.

77. "Program socjalistów galicyjskich," in ibid., pp. 107, 115.

78. Ibid., p. 117.

79. Franko, "Pro sotsializm," 19:16–17.

80. By the end of 1881, a few Polish socialists in Galicia had adopted the patriotic program of Limanowski's émigré socialist party, Lud Polski (The Polish People), which aimed at the restoration of the Polish state. The Lviv representatives approached Daniluk in 1881 and tried to convince him to give them control of *Praca*, but Daniluk refused, since he knew that the Ruthenian socialists would object. Pavlyk to Drahomanov, 31 January 1883, in Pavlyk, *Perepyska*, 4:135–36. For more on Lud Polski in Galicia, see "Z Kraju," *Przedświt*, 1881, no. 6–7, pp. 6–7. The program of Lud Polski is reprinted in Tych, *Polskie programy socjalistyczne*, pp. 141–46. See also Limanowski's *Patryjotyzm i socyjalizm* (Geneva, 1881). For Drahomanov's critique of Limanowski's views, see "Sotsialistychnyi patriotyzm v Pol'shchi," *Lystok hromady*, 1878, no. 1, pp. 21–22.

81. "Program socjalistów galicyjskich," in Tych, *Polskie programy socjalistyczne,* pp. 108–09.

82. Wladimir Lewinsky, "Das erste Jahrzehnt der ukrainischen Sozialdemokratie in Oesterreich," *Der Kampf* (1910): 316. Hans Mommsen, *Die Sozialdemokratie und die Nationalitätenfrage im habsburgischen Vielvölkerstaat,* vol. I (Vienna, 1963), p. 241.

83. "Program socjalistów galicyjskich," in Tych, *Polskie programy socjalistyczne,* p. 108.

84. Limanowski, *Pamiętniki,* p. 266.

85. Franko, *Tvory,* 20:144. Curiously, in both Franko's account and in Limanowski's the titles are once again mangled: Franko erred in describing the final version ("Eastern Galicia" did not remain in the title) and Limanowski in describing the original version (which contained the words "Polish and Ruthenian"). This is the incident Naimark has in mind when he refers to "the negative reaction of Ukrainian socialists to the [January 1881] program." Naimark, *History of the "Proletariat,"* p. 274, note 14.

86. Pavlyk [M. T.], "Nadesłane," *Praca,* 1 July 1880, no. 10, p. 41.

87. "M. Pavlyk do khrystiians'koho tai zhydivs'koho liudu na Ukraini," in Pavlyk, *Perepyska,* 3:437–46.

88. See Ivan L. Rudnytsky, "Mykhailo Drahomanov and the Problem of Ukrainian-Jewish Relations," *Canadian Slavonic Papers* 11 (1969): 182–98.

89. "Korespondencje. Kraków," *Praca,* 16 January 1880, no. 2, p. 10. By early 1880 a socialist movement had already appeared in Cracow, but all its leaders and a good part of its rank and file were in jail.

90. The story is told in English by Lucjan Blit, *The Origins of Polish Socialism: The History and Ideas of the First Polish Socialist Party 1878–1886* (Cambridge, 1971), and more analytically by Naimark, *History of the "Proletariat."* See also: Józef Buszko, *Narodziny ruchu socjalistycznego na ziemiach polskich* (Cracow, 1967). Wilhelm Feldman, *Dzieje polskiej myśli politycznej 1864–1914,* 2nd ed. (Warsaw, 1933). Ulrich Haustein, *Sozialismus und nationale Frage in Polen* (Cologne, 1969). Feliks Perl [Res], *Dzieje ruchu socjalistycznego w zaborze rosyjskim,* vol. I (Warsaw, 1910). I. Wołkowiczer, *Początki socjalistycznego ruchu robotniczego w Królestwie Polskim lata 1876–1879* (Warsaw, 1952). For memoirs re-creating the atmosphere of childhood, adolescence and young manhood, see especially Edmund Brzeziński, "Wspomnienia z mojego życia," *Niepodległość* 4 (1931), no. 1 (7), pp. 44–57. Also: Kazimierz Dłuski, "Wspomnienia z trzech lat (1875–1878)," *Niedpodległość* 1 (1929/30): 220–35.

91. Brzeziński, "Wspomnienia," *Niepodległość* 4 (1931), no. 2 (8), p. 216. Dłuski, "Wspomnienia," p. 227. Szczepan Mikołajski, "Pierwszy posiew socjalizmu w Galicji," *Niepodległość* 12 (1935): 342–63.

92. Letter of Mendelson to Waryński and letter of Kazimierz Dłuski to Waryński, both letters undated, but intercepted by the Lviv police on 20 October 1878, printed in Leon Baumgarten, ed., "Nowe dokumenty o początkach polskiego ruchu socjalistycznego," *Z Pola Walki,* 1969, no. 3 (47), pp. 146, 148.

93. Pavlyk's report written for (but not published in) the *Jahrbuch für Sozialwissenschaft und Sozialpolitik* (1880), in Pavlyk, *Perepyska,* 3:187–90.

94. "Sprawy sądowe. Rozprawa główna przed sądem przysięgłych przeciw Ludwikowi Waryńskiemu i 34 wspólnikom o zbrodnie zaburzenia spokojności publicznej," *Czas,* supplement, 21 February 1880, no. 42, p. 1. This source is an almost stenographic transcript of the Cracow trial of Waryński and his thirty-four co-defendants.

95. Ibid., supp. 18 February 1880, no. 39, p. 2; supp. 19 February 1880, no. 40, p. 1. The police found out about Waryński in the process of investigating Jewish socialism. At this time Aron Liberman, an émigré from the Russian empire and lone pioneer of Jewish socialism, was publishing Hebrew propaganda in Vienna. The police noted that two Polish socialists from Russia, Szymon Dickstein and Mendelson, were also Jewish. Furthermore, the pharmacist-socialist Adolf Inlaender in Lviv was, the police dutifully recorded, Jewish. Ryszard Cossa, an ambitious police officer who hoped to make a splendid career by suppressing the socialist danger, began illegally to intercept Inlaender's mail. Since Waryński received his correspondence at Inlaender's address, the police discovered that he was in Lviv and were determined to catch him. But Waryński made a speedy getaway. On Aron Liberman and his activities, see John Bunzl, *Klassenkampf in der Diaspora: Zur Geschichte der jüdischen Arbeiterbewegung* (Vienna, 1975), pp. 49–51.

96. "Sprawy sądowe," *Czas,* 18 March 1880, no. 64, p. 2. Testimony of former secretary of Gwiazda.

97. Piekarski to "Moje drogie," 23 March 1879, in Centralne Archiwum KC PZPR [CA], 5/II-1, "Wielki Proletariat. Materiały procesu krakowskiego 1880 r.," "Listy znalezione przy rewizji Ludwika Straszewicza i do niego w toku śledztwa nadeszłe," p. 3.

98. Piekarski to "Bartek," 20 March 1879, in ibid., p. 9.

99. "*Swołocz.*" Letter of Witold Piekarski to his father, Teodozy Piekarski, 23–24 October 1879, in Witold Piekarski, *Listy z więzienia (1879),* ed. Jerzy Zathey (Wrocław, 1953), p. 55. Emphasis in original.

100. "Sprawy sądowe," *Czas,* supp. 19 February 1880, no. 40, p. 2.

101. Ibid., 3 March 1880, no. 51, p. 3.

102. Mikołajski, "Pierwszy posiew," pp. 344–48.

103. "Program organizacji," in Baumgarten, "Nowe dokumenty," pp. 151–56.

104. The cells are described in "Sprawy sądowe," *Czas,* supp. 19 February 1880, no. 40, p. 2.

105. When the police arrested Adam Dąbrowski, they took from him a large stiletto and an explosive fuse. In the possession of Jan Drozdowski they found a revolver with 41 rounds of ammunition. Ibid., supp. 19 February 1880, no. 40, p. 2; supp. 21 February 1880, no. 42, p. 1.

106. Ibid., supp. 20 February 1880, no. 41, p. 1.

107. Ibid. Also, 29 February 1880, no. 49, p. 3.

108. Ibid., supp. 19 February 1880, no. 40, pp. 1–2.

109. Bogucki described the tactics of the police in ibid., 4 March 1880, no. 52, p. 2. Evidently, the socialists were not following their own strict

conspiratorial rules fully, or Bogucki would not have been able to give the police as helpful an account as he did.

110. Mikołajski, "Pierwszy posiew," p. 357.

111. Witold to Teodozy Piekarski, 2 September 1879, in Piekarski, *Listy*, p. 27. "Sprawy sądowe," *Czas*, 25 February 1880, no. 45, p. 4; 27 February 1880, no. 47, p. 2.

112. Leon Baumgarten, ed., *Krakowski komisarz policji na służbie carskiego wywiadu. Korespondencja komisarza Jana Kostrzewskiego . . . 1882–1884* (Cracow, 1967), pp. 75–76.

113. Haus-, Hof- und Staatsarchiv [HH], Informationsbüro des k. k. Ministeriums des Äussern [Informationsbüro], 2657/1879. "Sprawy sądowe," *Czas*, 7 March 1880, no. 55, p. 2. Witold to Teodozy Piekarski, 2 September 1879, in Piekarski, *Listy*, p. 28.

114. Jerzy Zathey, "Wstęp" to Piekarski, *Listy*, p. 18.

115. Witold to Teodozy Piekarski, 5 September 1879, ibid., p. 34.

116. Brzeziński, "Wspomnienia," *Niepodległość* 4 (1931), z. 2 (8), pp. 214–15. Mikołajski, "Pierwszy posiew," p. 359.

117. Copies of *Zgrzyt*, 22 April 1879, no. 1, and 3 May 1879, no. 2, are in CA (P. 14020).

118. The accused were: Stanisław Barabasz, Stanisław Bogucki, Edmund Brzeziński, Walery Chaberski, Adam Dąbrowski, Jan Drozdowski, Józef Gozdecki, Zygmunt Hałaciński, Adolf Inlaender, Leonard Jabłoński, Konrad Klazar, Erazm Kobylański, Jan Kozakiewicz, Kazimierz Krasucki, Bronisław Lubiczankowski, Antoni Mańkowski, Mieczysław Mańkowski (Antoni's nephew), Stanisław Mendelson, Edmund Mikiewicz, Szczepan Mikołajski, Apolinary Nowicki, Józef Ostafin, Stanisław Ożarowski, Władysław Paurowicz, Witold Piekarski, Jan Schmiedhausen, Karol Schmiedhausen, Ludwik Straszewicz, Hieronym Truszkowski, Józef Uziembło, Ludwik Waryński, Stanisław Waryński (Ludwik's brother), Ludwik Wąsowicz, Józef Zawisza and Jan Zieliński. A list of the accused, with pertinent personal information, is given in the indictment, "1879 listopad 28, Kraków. — Akt oskarżenia . . . przeciw L. Waryńskiemu i towarzyszom . . . ," in *Źródła*, 2:748–51. Paurowicz's name is misspelled in *Źródła* as Taurowicz; two of the accused are listed in the indictment under aliases (Biesiadowski = Uziembło, and Koturnicki = Kobylański); Mieczysław Mańkowski is omitted because he was arrested in December 1879, after the indictment was drawn up. See Baumgarten, *Krakowski komisarz*, p. 62.

119. "Sprawy sądowe," *Czas*, supp. 18 February 1880, no. 39, p. 1.

120. Ibid. For a quotation from an anti-socialist brochure by Machalski, see above, p. 28.

121. "Sprawy sądowe," *Czas*, 2 March 1880, no. 50, p. 2; 3 March 1880, no. 51, p. 3.

122. See, for instance, the caricature reproduced opposite p. 225 in Brzeziński, "Wspomnienia," *Niepodległość* 4 (1931), z. 2 (8).

123. "Sprawy sądowe," *Czas*, 7 March 1880, no. 55, p. 3.

124. Baumgarten, *Krakowski komisarz*, p. 78.

125. The authorities decided not to prosecute the law student, Leopold Poźniak, after Poźniak explained that by "taki zasrany Cesarz" he meant the tsar of Russia. APKr, Sąd Krajowy Karny w Krakowie [SKKKr], 83/II/11761.

126. "Sprawy sądowe," *Czas*, 3 March 1880, no. 51, pp. 3–4; 5 March 1880, no. 53, p. 2; 7 March 1880, no. 55, p. 2; 9 March 1880, no. 56, p. 3.

127. Ibid., supp. 21 February 1880, no. 42, p. 2.

128. In the revolutionary cells, the members were taught that there was no way to dispense with "the spilling of blood." Ibid., supp. 20 February 1880, no. 41, p. 1.

129. Ibid., supp. 21 February 1880, no. 42, p. 2.

130. Ibid., supp. 22 February 1880, no. 43, p. 1.

131. Ibid., supp. 21 February 1880, no. 42, p. 2.

132. Letters to his father, 1879, in Piekarski, *Listy*, pp. 25, 28, 41, 58.

133. See the classic statements of Dickstein, Dłuski, Mendelson and Waryński at the fiftieth anniversary of the November insurrection (1881), in Molska, *Pierwsze pokolenie*, 1:375–424.

134. "Sprawy sądowe," *Czas*, 25 March 1880, no. 70, p. 3.

135. "Intencya na miesiąc Marzec," *Apostolstwo Serca Jezusowego*, nakładem X. Michała Mycielskiego T. J. (Cracow, 1879), pp. 94–95, reprinted in *Hromada*, rik V (1881), no. 2, p. 189.

136. "Sprawy sądowe," *Czas*, supp. 20 February 1880, no. 41, p. 2.

137. Ibid., supp. 21 February 1880, no. 42, p. 1. Mikiewicz's denial in 10 March 1880, no. 57, p. 3.

138. Ibid., supp. 21 February 1880, no. 42, p. 2.

139. Ibid., 3 March 1880, no. 51, p. 3.

140. Ibid., supp. 13 April 1880, no. 84, p. 1.

141. Ibid., supp. 16 April 1880, no. 87, p. 1.

142. "Plädoyer des Verteidigers Josef Rosenblatt," in *Berühmte Verteidigungsreden 1860–1918*, ed. Max Neuda and Leo Schmelz (Vienna, 1921), pp. 194–216. Max Neuda was a very prominent Austrian defense attorney. Edmund Mikiewicz translated the speech from Polish to German.

143. The verdict is reprinted in *Źródła*, 2:755–71.

144. "Kraków 16 kwietnia," *Czas*, 17 April 1880, no. 88.

145. Paweł Popiel, *Choroba wieku* (Cracow, 1880). The brochure relied heavily upon Rev. Stefan Pawlicki's earlier work on Lassalle. (See above, pp. 26–27 and 186, note 57.)

146. Baumgarten, *Krakowski komisarz*, pp. 80–81. HH, Informationsbüro, 2842/1881. "Z kraju. Nowa sprawa krakowska," *Przedświt*, 1881, no. 5, pp. 3–4.

147. L'vivs'kyi oblasnyi derzhavnyi arkhiv [LODA], 350/1/2391, p. 17. HH, Informationsbüro, 2810, 2999/1881 and 585/1883, p. 9. *Źródła*, 2:801.

148. See the leftist periodicals *Robotnik* (Worker) and *Przyszłość* (Future) which came out in Cracow at this time, and Baumgarten, *Krakowski komisarz*, passim. A fuller discussion of socialism in Cracow in the early 1880s is in John-Paul Himka, "Polish and Ukrainian Socialism: Austria, 1867–1890" (Ph.D. dissertation: The University of Michigan, 1977), pp. 298–306.

149. "Odezwa Socyalistów polskich Zachodniej Galicyi," in CA, AM, 877/II, podt. 11.

150. APKr, SKKKr, 196, c 1049/1884, p. 3. *Źródła*, 2:785, 798.

151. The records of the the trial of Onufrowicz and company are preserved in APKr, SKKKr, 197, c 131/1885. Records of the police investigation can be found in HH, Informationsbüro, 3217/1883, 124–25/1884. The indictment is summarized in Leon Baumgarten, ed., *Kółka socjalistyczne, gminy i Wielki Proletariat. Procesy polityczne 1878–1888. Źródła* (Warsaw, 1966), pp. 555–62. The verdict has been published in *Źródła*, 2:787–96. The best account of the activities of Onufrowicz *et al.* in Galicia is that of Leon Baumgarten, *Dzieje Wielkiego Proletariatu* (Warsaw, 1966), pp. 313–16.

152. *Źródła*, 2:797–803. See HH, Informationsbüro, 1077/1884 for negotiations with the Russian consulate in Vienna about the extradition of Piechowski, Gostyński and Onufrowicz.

153. Baumgarten, *Kółka*, pp. 562, 1075–76, 1104, 1107.

154. Baumgarten, "Wstęp," *Krakowski komisarz*, pp. 16–17.

155. Sułcewski testified that he was recruited to the socialist introductory circles early in 1884 and that he only attended four or five meetings before the attempt to assassinate Kostrzewski took place. APKr, SKKKr, 197, c 1168/1885, p. 70. Malankiewicz had attended just three or four meetings of the introductory circle before attempting to execute Kostrzewski. Ibid., p. 58.

156. Ibid., p. 9. "Co się dzieje w kraju?" *Przedświt*, 1884, no. 7, p. 4. See also HH, Informationsbüro, 2256/1884 about the hunt for Piechowski.

157. APKr, SKKKr, 197, c 1168/1885, pp. 52–146. "Co się dzieje w kraju?" p. 4. As a result of the assassination attempt, Malankiewicz lost one eye and the other was badly injured. He left prison at the age of twenty-three a complete invalid. He was forced, upon release, to return to the community where he was born. In this community, Jaskowice, he was without friends or family, since his father had left Jaskowice when Malankiewicz was a small child. He lived here under constant police supervision and without employment. Even to visit his doctor in Cracow, Malankiewicz had to leave in secret. He went abroad for a short time, but this failed to improve his situation. He returned to Galicia in 1893 and in the next year was once again escorted back to Jaskowice. Walentyna Najdus, "Początki socjalistycznego ruchu robotniczego w Galicji (Lata siedemdziesiąte — osiemdziąte XIX w.)," *Z Pola Walki*, 1960, no. 1, pp. 25–26.

158. APKr, SKKKr, 196 c 1049/1884; 197 c 136/1885. "Przegląd," *Praca*, 25 July 1885, no. 5, p. 19.

159. The Galician authorities did, as we have frequently seen, arrest and prosecute socialists, generally on the charge of belonging to a secret society. Such was the case in 1884 in Cracow where Maria Zofia Onufrowicz stood trial. When the prosecutor asked her if she professed socialist doctrines, Onufrowicz was formally correct in replying: "This is not what I am accused of." APKr, SKKKr, 197, c 131/1885, p. 16. Cf. "Ustawa antisocjalna w Austrji," *Praca*, 1891, no. 11, p. 1. An anti-anarchist law was, however, promulgated on 25 June 1886. Konstanty Grzybowski, *Galicja 1848–1914. Historia ustroju politycznego na tle historii ustroju Austrii* (Cracow, 1959), pp. 82–83.

160. "Z kraju i o kraju. Korrespondencyja," *Równość,* 1880, no. 4, p. 19. See also the letter from Franko to Pavlyk, 26 March 1879, in Pavlyk, *Perepyska,* 3:7. Also: [Ivan Franko], "Pierwszy zjazd galic. partji socjalno-demokratycznej," *Kurjer Lwowski,* 1 February 1892, supplement to no. 33, p. 1.

161. Najdus, "Początki," p. 18.

162. Ibid., p. 25. Some socialists were prosecuted more than once. Jan Schmiedhausen, for example, was prosecuted three times. In the total of eighty-eight defendants, Schmiedhausen has been counted three times.

163. M. Drahomanov, "Nauka z poperednykh opovidan'n'," *Hromada,* rik V (1881), no. 2, p. 215.

164. Emil Haecker, *Historja socjalizmu w Galicji i na Śląsku Cieszyńskim* (Cracow, 1933), p. 255.

165. Najdus, "Początki," p. 19. M. M. Volianiuk, "Pershi nelehal'ni robitnychi hurtky u L'vovi," *L'vivs'kyi filial Tsentral'noho muzeiu V. I. Lenina. Naukovi zapysky* 1 (1959): 29.

166. The Cracow police heard from a good source that Waryński was seen in Cracow on 11 March 1881; they warned the police in Lviv that he took a train bound for that city. TsDIAL, 146/4/224/3690, p. 78. HH, Informationsbüro, 410/1882. "Proces Anny Sieroszewskiej i wsp.," *Praca,* 18 April 1882, no. 6, pp. 22–23.

167. *Źródła,* 2:783. Volianiuk, "Pershi nelehal'ni robitnychi hurtky," p. 28.

168. *Źródła,* 2:783.

169. Mykhailo Drabyk, ethnically Ruthenian, first became involved with the socialist movement in Lviv in 1880. In that same year, Drabyk moved to Przemyśl where he engaged in socialist agitation for one month until his arrest in July 1880. He returned to Lviv after release from prison in May 1881, and was active in the preparations for the congress of workers to found a socialist party. Volianiuk, "Pershi nelehal'ni robitnychi hurtky," pp. 38–39.

170. Ibid., pp. 40–41.

171. "Z Izby Sądowej," *Praca,* 27 May 1883, no. 8, p. 30.

172. Volianiuk, "Pershi nelehal'ni robitnychi hurtky," p. 41.

173. V. Makaiev, *Robitnychyi klas Halychyny v ostanii tretyni XIX st.* (Lviv, 1968), pp. 92–93.

174. Volianiuk, "Pershi nelehal'ni robitnychi hurtky," p. 36. APKr, SKKKr, 194, c 22873/1883, p. 5.

175. On the Ruthenian cell, see LODA, 350/1/4849, p. 80v. On the Ukrainophile orientation of *Strażnica Polska* and its editor, Jan Gniewosz, see "Redaktor-zavediia," *Bat'kivshchyna,* 29 (17) April 1887, no. 17, p. 103, as well as copies of the paper (which, to save money on taxes, alternately appeared under another title, *Sztandar Polski* [Polish Flag]). That Hapii and Stronsky were conscious Ruthenians is indicated by the fact that Volodymyr Simenovych recruited them to work among Ruthenian immigrants in Pennsylvania; but only Hapii, apparently, went to America. Pavlyk, *Perepyska,* 5:289, 291.

176. Volianiuk, "Pershi nelehal'ni robitnychi hurtky," p. 42. Makaiev, *Robit-*

nychnyi klas, pp. 92–93. Ie. A. Iatskevych, *Stanovyshche robitnychoho klasu Halychyny v period kapitalizmu (1848–1900) (Narys)* (Kiev, 1958), pp. 81–82. Najdus, "Początki," p. 21. A handwritten copy of the leaflet, "Gmina socyalistyczna Lwów do Robotników," is in CA, AM, 877/I, podt. 11. The date on the leaflet is not 22 November 1882, but 2 November 1882. 2 November is also the date given by Najdus. That the date 2 November is an error for 22 November is indicated by the reference to the recent arrests in Lviv and by the date of dissemination. The leaflet was reprinted in *Przedświt,* 1883, no. 11, according to Jan Kozik, "Współpraca Ukraińców z Polakami w ruchu robotniczym Galicji do 1890 r. (Artykuł materiałowy)" (unpublished manuscript), p. 44.

177. "Różności," *Praca,* 25 January 1883, no. 2, p. 8.

178. A copy of the leaflet, "Towarzysze!" is in the possession of Dr. Marian Tyrowicz in Cracow. Mykhailo Pavlyk censured the leaflet's terrorist import. Elżbieta Hornowa, *Ukraiński obóz postępowy i jego współpraca z polską lewicą społeczną w Galicji 1876–1895* (Wrocław, 1968), pp. 58–59. Pavlyk was, in general, an opponent of the terrorist sentiments that came to the fore in Lviv in 1883. "In the mid-1880s a terrorist tendency began to grow among the Lviv workers, mainly owing to the influence of the late [Marian] Udałowicz, a carpenter, an exceptionally likable and energetic person. I opposed this tendency decisively and successfully. Once, for instance, Udałowicz wanted to use powder or dynamite to destroy police headquarters. He had found, he told me, a route through the sewers that led right underneath the building. I just about had to use force to stop him." Mykhailo Pavlyk, *Moskvofil'stvo ta ukrainofil'stvo sered avstro-rus'koho narodu* (Lviv, 1906), p. 55.

179. "Z Izby Sądowej," *Praca,* 27 May 1883, no. 8, p. 30.

Chapter Four

1. Mykhailo Pavlyk, ed., *Perepyska Mykhaila Drahomanova z Mykhailom Pavlykom. (1876–1895),* 7 vols., numbered 2–8 (Chernivtsi, 1910–12), 3:185. Hereafter abbreviated as Pavlyk, *Perepyska.*

2. Ibid.

3. V. Dmytruk, *Narys z istorii ukrains'koi zhurnalistyky XIX st.* (Lviv, 1969), p. 95.

4. "Bibliohrafiia. Molot," *Pravda,* 1879, vyp. 2, p. 127.

5. Ibid., p. 135.

6. Haus-, Hof- und Staatsarchiv [HH], Informationsbüro des k. k. Ministeriums des Äussern [Informationsbüro], 3087/1878.

7. O. I. Dei, *Ukrains'ka revoliutsiino-demokratychna zhurnalistyka. Problema vynyknennia i stanovlennia* (Kiev, 1959), pp. 198–203. M. L. Butryn, "Tsenzurna istoriia zbirky 'Molot' (1878)," *Ukrains'ke literaturoznavstvo,* no. 12 (1971), pp. 46–50.

8. HH, Informationsbüro, 1345/1878.

9. "Korespondentsii 'Slova'. Iz L'vova. (Sotsialisticheskoe)," *Slovo,* 5 October 1878. The story of Pavlyk's birds is also told in Ludwik Krzywicki,

Wspomnienia, 3 vols. (Warsaw, 1957–59), 1:322, and Bolesław Limanowski, *Pamiętniki (1870–1907)* (Warsaw, 1958), p. 181.

10. "Izvestiia i zametki," *Vol'noe slovo*, 15 September 1882, no. 45, p. 16. Tsentral'nyi derzhavnyi istorychnyi arkhiv URSR u L'vovi [TsDIAL], 663/1/111.

11. I. Bass, *Ivan Franko. Biografiia* (Moscow, 1957), pp. 109–15.

12. On the *Dribna biblioteka* series, see Dei, *Ukrains'ka revoliutsiino-demokratychna zhurnalistyka*, pp. 286–331.

13. Ivan Franko, "Mysli o evoliutsii v istorii liuds'kosti," *Vybrani suspil'no-politychni i filosofs'ki tvory* (Kiev, 1956), pp. 187–245. O. T., "Robitnyts'ka plata i rukh robitnyts'kyi v Avstrii v poslidnykh chasakh," *S'vit*, 1881, no. 4, pp. 78–79.

14. Quoted in Dei, *Ukrains'ka revoliutsiino-demokratychna zhurnalistyka*, pp. 469–70.

15. Pavlyk, *Perepyska*, 4:140, 156.

16. Bass, *Ivan Franko*, pp. 172–75, 189–90.

17. O. I. Dei, "Zhurnal 'Tovarysh' (Epizod iz zhurnalistychnoi diial'nosti I. Franka)," *Doslidzhennia tvorchosti Ivana Franka*, vyp. 2 (Kiev, 1959), pp. 103–32.

18. Krzysztof Dunin-Wąsowicz, "Iwan Franko a polskie siły postępowe" (mimeographed) (Warsaw, 1958). H. D. Verves, *Ivan Franko i pytannia ukrains'ko-pol's'kykh literaturno-hromads'kykh vzaiemyn 70–90-kh rokiv XIX st.* (Kiev, 1957).

19. On Wysłouch, see Peter Brock, "Bolesław Wysłouch, Founder of the Polish Peasant Party," *Slavonic and East European Review* 30 (1951), no. 74, pp. 139–74.

20. Quoted in Wilhelm Feldman, *Dzieje polskiej myśli politycznej 1864–1914*, 2nd ed. (Warsaw, 1933), p. 257.

21. *Lystuvannia I. Franka i M. Drahomanova*, Zbirnyk Istorychno-filolohichnoho viddilu VUAN, no. 52 (Kiev, 1928), p. 271.

22. Ibid., pp. 478–79.

23. Letter of Teofil Okunevsky to Drahomanov, 19 February 1888, in Mykhailo Pavlyk, ed., *Perepyska Mykhaila Drahomanova z drom Teofilem Okunevs'kym (1883, 1885–1891, 1893–1895)* (Lviv, 1905), p. 99.

24. See S. M. Vozniak, "Revoliutsiini demokraty Ukrainy druhoi polovyny XIX — pochatku XX st. — pobornyky idei vozz"iednannia ukrains'koho narodu," *Ukrains'kyi istorychnyi zhurnal*, 1979, no. 8, p. 248.

25. Pavlyk [M.T.], "Klein-Russland," *Jahrbuch für Sozialwissenschaft und Sozialpolitik*, 1879, pp. 305–11. Eduard Bernstein mistakenly ascribed this article to a Serbian socialist. Eduard Bernstein, "Spomyny pro Mykhaila Drahomanova i Serhiia Podolyns'koho," in M. Hrushevs'kyi, *Z pochyniv ukrains'koho sotsiialistychnoho rukhu. Mykh. Drahomanov i zhenevs'kyi sotsiialistychnyi hurtok* (Vienna, 1922), pp. 154–61. Pavlyk acknowledged himself as the author of the 1879 article on p. 372 of the 1880 volume of the *Jahrbuch*. For the reaction of Polish socialists in Geneva, see Limanowski, *Pamiętniki*, p. 232. For the reaction of a Lviv socialist (Franko? Ludwik Inlaender?), see "Z kraju i o kraju. Korrespondencyja," *Równość*, 1880, no. 4 (January), p. 17.

26. Pavlyk, *Perepyska*, 4:134, 167. Elżbieta Hornowa, *Ukraiński obóz postępowy i jego współpraca z polską lewicą społeczną w Galicji 1878–1895* (Wrocław, 1968), p. 62.

27. Piekarski was so annoyed by the article that he also attacked Pavlyk for posing as a Polish socialist and accused him of not being able to write proper Polish. W. Piekarski, "'Federalistyczna' krytyczność w '*polskiej skórze*,'" *Przedświt*, 1883, no. 16, p. 1. Reprinted in Alina Molska, ed., *Pierwsze pokolenie marksistów polskich. Wybór pism i materiałów źródłowych z lat 1878–1886*, 2 vols. (Warsaw, 1962), 2:49–55. Even Drahomanov, though offended by Piekarski's response, recognized that Pavlyk had committed a gross breach of tact and a number of factual errors. "Izvestiia i zametki," *Vol'noe slovo*, 1 May 1883, no. 60, p. 16.

28. "Karol Marx," *Praca*, 10 April 1883, no. 6, p. 21.

29. Drahomanov's views on the different socialisms of the state and stateless nations are best expressed in his foreword to the first issue of *Hromada* (1878), reprinted in *Vybrani tvory* (Prague, 1937); see especially pp. 140–44. See also *Modern Encyclopedia of Russian and Soviet History*, s.v. "Drahomanov, Mykhailo Petrovych," by John-Paul Himka.

30. Drahomanov to Franko, 26 September 1884, *Lystuvannia*, p. 86.

31. Drahomanov to Franko, 25 October 1884, ibid., p. 95.

32. Drahomanov to Franko, 11 April 1886, ibid., pp. 178–80.

33. Franko to Drahomanov, n.d., ibid., p. 171.

34. Reprinted in ibid., pp. 209–12.

35. Bass, *Ivan Franko*, p. 152.

36. Ivan Franko, "Hlukhi visty," in M. F. Nechytaliuk, *Publitsystyka Ivana Franka (1875–1886 rr.). Seminarii* (Lviv, 1972), p. 202.

37. Ivan Franko, "Nash pohliad na pol's'ke pytannia," in ibid., pp. 185–86.

38. Bass, *Ivan Franko*, pp. 171, 175–78, 185–86.

39. Teofil Okunevsky to Drahomanov, 19 February 1888, in Pavlyk, *Perepyska Drahomanova z Okunevs'kym*, p. 99.

40. Pavlo Iashchuk, *Mykhailo Pavlyk. Literaturno-krytychnyi narys* (Lviv, 1959), p. 98.

41. I have also discussed the Boryslav workers in "The Background to Emigration: The Ukrainians of Galicia and Bukovyna, 1848–1914," in *A Heritage in Transition: Essays in the History of Ukrainians in Canada*, ed. Manoly R. Lupul (Toronto: McClelland and Stewart, 1982), p. 17.

42. Ie. A. Iatskevych, *Stanovyshche robitnychoho klasu Halychyny v period kapitalizmu (1848–1900) (Narys)* (Kiev, 1958), p. 38. See pp. 31–32 for an explanation of why there were more oil workers than recorded inhabitants in Boryslav.

43. Emil Haecker, *Historja socjalizmu w Galicji i na Śląsku Cieszyńskim* (Cracow, 1933), p. 138. The brutal atmosphere of Boryslav had a similar effect on the Polish socialist Ignacy Daszyński. See his *Pamiętniki*, 2 vols. (Cracow, 1925–26), 1:22–23.

44. Bass, *Ivan Franko*, pp. 18–28.

45. Ibid., pp. 71–73, 127–28, 141. Some of Franko's "Boryslav Cycle" is

available in English: Ivan Franko, *Boa Constrictor and Other Stories* (Moscow, n.d.). Unfortunately, the translation, by Fainna Solasko, is not from the original, but from Russian.

46. *Praca,* 19 October 1880, no. 15, p. 59.

47. Bass, *Ivan Franko,* pp. 144, 175. Franko was also interested in establishing a base in Drohobych because of "the mass of Jews [there], many of whom are progressive; and among the youth there are even socialist elements." Letter to Pavlyk, 12 November 1882, in Pavlyk, *Perepyska,* 4:95.

48. V. Makaiev, *Robitnychyi klas Halychyny v ostannii tretyni XIX st.* (Lviv, 1968), p. 82.

49. *Praca,* 1881, no. 7. Iatskevych, *Stanovyshche robitnychoho klasu,* pp. 34, 84.

50. Iatskevych, *Stanovyshche robitnychoho klasu,* p. 27.

51. "Robitnytska sprava v Boryslavi," *Bat'kivshchyna,* 15 (3) August 1884, no. 33, p. 203. On Jewish workers in Boryslav, see Raphael Mahler, "The Economic Background of Jewish Emigration from Galicia to the United States," *YIVO Annual of Jewish Social Science* 7 (1952), pp. 261–62, 267.

52. Ivan Franko, "Deshcho pro Boryslav," *Vybrani statti pro narodnu tvorchist'* (Kiev, 1955), pp. 145–46. Ivan Franko, "Spravy suspil'no-politychni v ustakh rus'koho liudu v Halychyni," *V naimakh u susidiv* (Lviv, 1914), pp. 83–84.

53. "Robitnytska sprava," describes the background to the riots. Franko, "Deshcho," pp. 144, 146, 148 describes — with reference to local folklore — the economic changes in Boryslav in the early 1880s, as Galician Jewish capital was absorbed by large foreign capital.

54. William Lathrop Harwood, "Ignacy Daszynski: The Making of an Austro-Polish Statesman, 1866–1918" (Ph.D. dissertation: The University of Illinois at Urbana-Champaign, 1977), pp. 153–58.

55. M-on, "Pis'ma iz Galitsii," *Vol'noe slovo,* 15 November 1882, no. 49, pp. 8–9.

56. *Praca,* 11 December 1880, no. 17, p. 67.

57. From a folk song transcribed by Franko in the early 1880s:
Oi pidu ia v Buryslavku hroshyi zarobliaty,
Iak sia vernu z Buryslavky, budu gazduvaty.

(Oy, I'll go to Buryslavka to make some money,
When I return from Buryslavka, I'll be farming my own land.)

58. Ivan Franko, "Zemel'na vlasnist' u Halychni," *Tvory,* 20 vols. (Kiev, 1950–56), 19:296–97.

59. Ibid., 19:278.

60. Ibid., 19:285–86. For a more thorough study confirming the proliferation and concomitant diminution of peasant holdings, see Wincenty Styś, *Rozdrabnianie gruntów chłopskich w byłym zaborze austrjackim od roku 1787 do 1931* (Lviv, 1934).

61. Ivan Franko, "Halyts'ka indemnizatsiia," *Tvory,* 19:456–87.

62. Franko, "Zemel'na vlasnist'," 19:288.

63. M. M. Kravets' *Ivan Franko — istoryk Ukrainy* (Lviv, 1971), p. 106.

64. Franko, "Zemel'na vlasnist'," 19:280.

65. Ibid., 19:295. See also: Franko, "Niech giną jak pędraki," *V naimakh,* pp. 188–89. Franko, "Podil'nist' chy nepodil'nist' selians'kykh gruntiv," ibid., pp. 210–21.

66. Franko, "Zemel'na vlasnist'," 19:297–98.

67. By the turn of the century parcellation had become a special branch of trade run by speculators, merchants and lawyers. In about 65 percent of the cases, such middlemen — and not the owners of the manorial estates — were behind the plans to parcel the estates. The middlemen put up the capital to buy estates from the financially inept nobility and then sold the estates in pieces to the peasants. Generally, there was a 25–50 percent difference between the purchase and sale price of an estate. In 1902–04, the peasants paid 8–15 million crowns annually for the services of the parcellation intermediaries. Fr. Bujak, "Parcelacja," in Stefan Kieniewicz, ed., *Galicja w dobie autonomicznej (1850–1914). Wybór tekstów* (Wrocław, 1952), pp. 329–32.

68. Franko, "Zemel'na vlasnist'," 19:301. Franko, "Uderzhavlenie zemli," *V naimakh,* pp. 196–202. Franko, "Agitatsiia za unarodovlenie zemli v Nimechchyni," ibid., pp. 26–29. All of these originally appeared in Wysłouch's press, 1886–88.

69. Franko, "Zemel'na vlasnist'," 19:299–304.

70. This is only a brief sketch of a topic important in its own right as well as to the argument of this study. I have developed some of the themes touched on here in "Background to Emigration"; "Priests and Peasants: The Greek Catholic Pastor and the Ukrainian National Movement in Austria, 1867–1900," *Canadian Slavonic Papers,* 1979, no. 1, pp. 1–14; and "Hope in the Tsar: Displaced Naive Monarchism among the Ukrainian Peasants of the Habsburg Empire," *Russian History* 7 (1980), pp. 125–38. The Canadian Institute of Ukrainian Studies has given me a grant to explore the topic further.

71. Jews, of course, were not the only tavern keepers and lenders in the village. Especially in the early twentieth century more and more Ruthenian peasants came into control of local taverns. However, in common Ruthenian parlance of the period, the stratum of lenders-innkeepers was almost invariably referred to as the "Jews" (*zhydy*). The Russophiles, national populists and even the radicals identified the "Jews" as the enemies of the peasantry. The radicals sometimes took pains to point out that the majority of Jews were not exploiters, but this did not prevent them from generally referring to the lenders-innkeepers as the "Jews."

72. The following complaint, submitted by a reading-club partisan to a popular newspaper, is typical: "Our chief also for some reason doesn't like to hear about a reading club. But how could a chief like ours like it if people read newspapers in a reading club, because from newspapers people would find out how our chief voted in the elections. And our chief, who was an elector in the recent elections to the Diet, . . . paid no attention to the national cause, but only paid attention to who was giving out kielbasa and other treats. So he voted for Pan Sznel and not for the Ruthenian candidate." Shchyryi druh I., "Poriadky v Sknylovi," *Bat'kivshchyna,* 27 April (9 May) 1890, p. 235.

73. See, for example, M. Pavlyk, *Drukovanyi lyst Mykhaila Pavlyka do l'udei* (Geneva, 1880).

74. Franko to Pavlyk, 11 April 1881, in Pavlyk, *Perepyska*, 3:427.

75. TsDIAL, 663/1/110, pp. 178–79, 255. "Sotsialisty. Iz sudovoi sali," *Slovo*, 11 (23) January 1878, p. 3; 14 (26) January 1878, p. 3. These must have been the Vienna pamphlets.

76. "Sotsialisty," *Slovo*, 14 (26) January 1878, p. 3.

77. V. I. Kalynovych, *Politychni protsesy Ivana Franka ta ioho tovaryshiv* (Lviv, 1967), pp. 41, 85, 88.

78. Pavlyk, *Perepyska*, 3:13, 125–26.

79. TsDIAL, 663/1/110, pp. 38, 326–29.

80. Styś, *Rozdrabnianie*, p. 352. See also Andrii Kos [N.S.], "Zhyt'e, dokhody i bazhan'a komarn'ans'kykh tkachiv," *Dzvin* (Lviv, 1878), pp. 269–71.

81. TsDIAL, 663/1/110, pp. 221–23, 225–26. The Kosiv police found radical literature by Franko and Pavlyk in Pistuniak's workshop. Ibid., p. 11.

82. Ibid., pp. 226–28.

83. TsDIAL, 663/1/111, pp. 347–406.

84. M. Pavlyk, *Drukovanyi lyst*, pp. 10–11. Anna Pavlyk, "Moi i l'uts'ki hrikhy, a pans'ka ta popivs'ka pravda," *Hromada*, 1881, no. 2, p. 201. The literature found hidden in Dmytro Fokshei's home was: *Hromads'kyi druh*, *Dzvin*, *Pro khliborobstvo*, *Pro bahatstvo ta bidnist'* and a Polish translation of the latter, *Opowiadanie starego gospodarza*.

85. M. Pavlyk, *Drukovanyi lyst*, pp. 11–14.

86. The trial and events leading up to it are described in Kalynovych, *Politychni protsesy*, pp. 97–119.

87. A. Pavlyk, "Moi i l'uts'ki hrikhy," p. 202.

88. Ibid., pp. 153–205. An earlier version appeared in *Dzvin* (Lviv, 1878), pp. 273–85. The memoirs were also to appear in German, in a translation by Hryhorii Kupchanko, but only the beginning appeared in *Czernowitzer Chronik*; the Chernivtsi prosecutor stopped publication because the memoirs might have moved others to hate and scorn state authority. Kupchanko's translation was entitled "Zwei Huzulinnen." When the Chernivtsi prosecutor forbade further publication, Kupchanko intended to publish the memoirs in *Auf der Höhe*, a Leipzig journal published by the Galician émigré Leopold von Sacher-Masoch. Kupchanko also planned to publish the memoirs separately as a brochure. Neither of these plans was carried out. M. Pavlyk, ed., "Perepyska M. Drahomanova z Hr. Kupchankom," *Dilo*, 1904, no. 126, p. 1; no. 140, p. 2; no. 146, p. 1.

89. Paraska Pavlyk, "Ot khto robyt por'adok mezhy l'ud'my!" *Hromada*, 1881, no. 2, pp. 205–13. Anna to Mykhailo Pavlyk, 6 December 1881, in M. Pavlyk, *Perepyska*, 3:507.

90. A. Pavlyk, "Moi i l'uts'ki hrikhy," pp. 202–03.

91. TsDIAL, 663/1/124, *passim*, and 146/4/224/3686, p. 248.

92. M. Pavlyk, *Drukovanyi lyst*, p. 30.

93. TsDIAL, 663/1/110, pp. 106–08. Ironically, another Melnyk, Panas Melnyk of Volia Yakubova, became Anna's suitor after reading about her

-

exploits in one of the 1878 anthologies. Ignacy Daszyński to Ivan Franko, 4 February 1884, Instytut literatury Akademii nauk URSR, Viddil rukopysiv [IL], fond 3, odynytsia zberezhennia 1603, p. 109.

94. A. Pavlyk, "Moi i l'uts'ki hrikhy," p. 197. When Mykhailo Pavlyk tried to join the Monastyrske reading club in 1883, the officers of the club unanimously rejected his application. TsDIAL, 146/4/224/3686, p. 60v.

95. L'vivs'kyi oblasnyi derzhavnyi arkhiv [LODA], 350/1/2423, pp. 2–4.

96. Ibid.

97. [Documents of the Lviv police relating to Józef Daniluk and socialist leaflets in Lviv, 1883–84], "Teki ikonobiograficzne XIX–XX w.," vol. 2 (collection of Dr. Marian Tyrowicz).

98. Maksymiak to Franko, 27 October 1883, IL, f. 3, od. zb. 1618, p. 141.

99. Maksymiak to Franko, 18 August 1883, ibid., p. 87.

100. Maksymiak to Franko, 27 October 1883.

101. Maksymiak to Franko, IL, f. 3, od. zb. 1603, pp. 43–44.

102. LODA, 350/1/2423, pp. 16–17, 23.

103. E. L. Solecki [El.], "Wojna o 'jura stolae,'" *Gazeta Naddniestrzańska,* 15 June 1886, p. 2.

104. Iv. Franko, "Znadoby do vyvchenia movy i etnohrafii ukrains'koho naroda, IV. Sud hromads'kyi v seli Dobrivlianakh," *S'vit,* 25 September 1882, no. 20–21 (8–9), pp. 346–48.

105. *Klasova borot'ba selianstva Skhidnoi Halychyny (1772–1849). Dokumenty i materialy* (Kiev, 1974), pp. 99–100, 236 and 531, note 19.

106. Hryhorii Rymar [Tam.], "Pys'mo vid Drohobycha," *Bat'kivshchyna,* 1881, no. 19, pp. 153–54.

107. Hryhorii Rymar [R.], "Pys'mo z-pid Drohobycha," ibid., 1882, no. 8, p. 62.

108. Bezstoronnyi [pseud. V. Nahirny?], "Pys'mo z Drohobytskoho," ibid., 1886, no. 36–37, p. 215. That Rymar was a smallholder (*malozemel'nyi hospodar*) is known from Petro Berehuliak, "Spomyny Petra Berehuliaka pro Ivana Franka," in O. I. Dei, ed., *Ivan Franko u spohadakh suchasnykiv. Knyha druha* (Lviv, 1972), p. 43.

109. Panas Mel'nyk [Pryiatel' hromady], "Pys'mo vid Drohobycha," *Bat'-kivshchyna,* 1881, no. 23, p. 186.

110. Solecki, "Wojna," p. 3.

111. [Panas Mel'nyk], "Novynky i vsiachyna," *Bat'kivshchyna,* 1882, no. 2, p. 16.

112. Panas Mel'nyk [Pryiatel' hromady], "Pys'mo vid Drohobycha," ibid., 1882, no. 3, p. 21.

113. Mel'nyk, "Pys'mo," 1881, no. 23, p. 186.

114. Panas Mel'nyk [Chytal'nyk], "Pys'mo vid Drohobycha," *Bat'kivshchyna,* 1885, no. 27, p. 198. Mel'nyk, "Novynky i vsiachyna," p. 16.

115. Mel'nyk, "Novynky i vsiachyna," p. 16.

116. Mel'nyk, "Pys'mo," 1882, no. 3, p. 21.

117. [Panas Mel'nyk], "Pys'mo z pid Drohobycha," *Bat'kivshchyna,* 1884, no. 31, p. 194.

118. Ibid.

119. Panas Mel'nyk [A. M.], "Volia Iakubova," *Gazeta Naddniestrzańska,* 15 May 1885, p. 2.

120. Bezstoronnyi, "Pys'mo," 1886, no. 38, p. 224. Only councilmen voted for the chief.

121. Mel'nyk, "Pys'mo vid Drohobycha," 1885, no. 27, p. 198.

122. Daszyński, *Pamiętniki,* 1:26.

123. Mel'nyk, "Novynky i vsiachyna," p. 16.

124. Mel'nyk, "Pys'mo," 1882, no. 3, p. 21.

125. Mel'nyk, "Pys'mo z pid Drohobycha," 1884, no. 31, p. 194.

126. Rev. Mykhailo Harbinsky was having trouble with his son Iliarii, whom the priest expelled from his home. For a time Iliarii joined the reading club, gave out radical literature and intended to take up communal farming with Melnyk, Anna Pavlyk and the Polish socialist Ignacy Daszyński. In mid-1884, however, he was reconciled with his father and became a vociferous foe of the reading club. Parts of Iliarii's story can be reconstructed from: Semen Vityk, "Iz moikh spohadiv pro Franka," in Dei, *Ivan Franko u spohadakh . . . kn. druha,* pp. 51–53. Daszyński to Franko, 4 February 1884, IL, f. 3, od. zb. 1603, p. 109. Bezstoronnyi, "Pys'mo," 1886, no. 38, p. 224. Mel'nyk, "Pys'mo z pid Drohobycha," 1884, no. 31, p. 194.

127. Mel'nyk, "Pys'mo z pid Drohobycha," 1884, no. 31, p. 194.

128. Solecki, "Wojna," p. 3.

129. Hromadski, "Volia Iakubova v Tsvitni 1886," *Gazeta Naddniestrzańska,* 1 May 1886, p. 2.

130. Panas Mel'nyk [M], "Z Voli Iakubovoi," *Gazeta Naddniestrzańska,* 1 February 1885, p. 3. Mel'nyk, "Pys'mo z pid Drohobycha," 1884, no. 31, p. 194.

131. Panas Mel'nyk [Chytal'nyky], "Pys'mo vid Drohobycha," *Bat'kivshchyna,* 1885, no. 3, pp. 20–21.

132. Solecki, "Wojna," p. 2. Bezstoronnyi, "Pys'mo," 1886, no. 36–37, pp. 214–15. [Edmund Solecki], "Kronika. Ksiądz Antoni Czapelski," *Gazeta Naddniestrzańska,* 15 February 1885, p. 5.

133. Berehuliak, "Spomyny," p. 46. Bezstoronnyi, "Pys'mo," 1886, no. 36–37, p. 215.

134. Solecki, "Wojna," pp. 2–3.

135. Bezstoronnyi, "Pys'mo," 1886, no. 36–37, p. 215.

136. Berehuliak, "Spomyny," pp. 44–46.

137. Ibid., pp. 43–45.

138. See O. I. Dei's note to Berehuliak's memoirs in Dei, *Ivan Franko u spohadakh . . . kn. druha,* p. 308. Copies of the leaflets can probably be found in the acts of the trial of 31 May – 3 June 1886, held in Sambir. Both LODA and TsDIAL maintained in 1976 that they did not possess these acts.

139. Franko, "Znadoby do vyvchenia." Ivan Franko [Redaktsiia], "Do istorii halyts'ko-rus'koho selianstva. I. Bunt ahrarnyi v Iakubovii Voli v r. 1819," *Zhytie i slovo,* t. 1, kn. 1, pp. 66–68 (I have only consulted a [partial?] reprint of this in *Klasova borot'ba selianstva,* pp. 99–100). Franko also wrote a short

history of the reading club in "Dobra volia": Ivan Franko [Myron***], *Rozmova pro hroshi i skarby z peredmovoiu o zalozheniu Dobrovil's'koi chytal'ni* (Lviv, 1883), pp. 3–24. I have not consulted this brochure.

140. Daszyński to Franko, 26 March 1884, IL, 3/1629, p. 288. Mel'nyk to Franko, 13 April 1884, IL, 3/1603, pp. 141–43. Mel'nyk to Franko, 12 November 1886, IL, 3/1615, p. 596.

141. Berehuliak, "Spomyny," pp. 45–46. For confirmation that Franko was in Dobrivliany in the summer of 1885, see Mariia Bilets'ka, "Kartyna z zhyttia Ivana Franka," in O. I. Dei and N. P. Korniienko, eds., *Ivan Franko u spohadakh suchasnykiv* (Lviv, 1956), p. 157.

142. Daszyński to Franko, 4 February 1884, IL, 3/1603, p. 109. Daszyński to Franko, 26 March 1886, p. 288. Daszyński, *Pamiętniki,* 1:26.

143. Mel'nyk, "Pys'mo z pid Drohobycha," 1884, no. 31, p. 194.

144. Hromadski, "Volia Iakubova." Solecki, "Wojna," p. 3. Bezstoronnyi, "Pys'mo," 1886, no. 38, p. 224.

145. "Protses o bohokhul'stvo i sotsialistychnu vorokhobniu," *Bat'kivshchyna,* 1886, no. 24, pp. 141–42. Bezstoronnyi, "Pys'mo," 1886, no. 36–37, p. 215; no. 38, p. 224. [E. L. Solecki], "Nic to 'Wam' nie pomoże," *Gazeta Naddniestrzańska,* 15 March 1886, pp. 1–2. Vityk, "Iz moikh spohadiv," p. 53.

146. Bezstoronnyi, "Pys'mo," 1886, no. 38, p. 224.

147. "Protses o bohokhul'stvo," p. 141.

148. "Psevdo-diiateli," *Novyi prolom,* 31 May (12 June) 1886, p. 1.

149. "Korespondencya 'Czasu'. Lwów 7 czerwca," *Czas,* 9 June 1886, p. 1.

150. "Spys chleniv ruskoho politychnoho tovarystva 'Narodna Volia' v Kolomyi," *Khliborob,* 1893, no. 16, p. 112; no. 17–18, p. 124.

151. "Novynky. Z Kupnovych," *Hromads'kyi holos,* 1899, no. 13, pp. 113–14.

152. Vityk, "Iz moikh spohadiv." Stepan and Mykhailo Novakivsky, the Radical and social democratic activists, hailed from Torky in Przemyśl district.

153. Uchasnyk, "Vicha v seli Morozovychakh," *Hromads'kyi holos,* 1899, no. 3, pp. 19–21.

154. Daszyński, *Pamiętniki,* 1:26. Vityk, "Iz moikh spohadiv," p. 53.

155. Franko in 1881 wrote that socialists will "send books, written in the spirit of our ideas, to all existing reading clubs." "Choho khoche 'Halyts'ka robitnyts'ka Hromada'?" *Tvory,* 19:61.

Chapter Five

1. "Kronika spółczesna. Echa galicyjskie," *Przegląd Społeczny,* 1886, z. IV (April), pp. 320–21. Ernest Breiter [J. L. Prawdzic], *Krótki rys ruchu socyalistycznego we Lwowie w ostatnim 25-leciu* (Lviv, 1895), p. 7. Ie. A. Iatskevych, *Stanovyshche robitnychoho klasu Halychyny v period kapitalizmu (1848–1900). (Narys)* (Kiev, 1958), p. 87.

2. Z. Seweryn, "Strejk robotników piekarskich we Lwowie," *Praca,* no. 4–5, pp. 13–15. *Die socialdemokratische und anarchistische Bewegung im*

Jahre 1888 (Vienna, 1889), p. 3 (an internal publication of the Austrian government).

3. Osyp Makovei, "Iz shchodennyka," in *Ivan Franko u spohadakh suchasnykiv*, ed. O. I. Dei and N. P. Korniienko (Lviv, 1956), p. 217. It is possible that Makovei was simply confused (but in a diary?) and was really referring to the July 1888 strike.

4. Ibid. Centralne Archiwum Komitetu Centralnego PZPR [CA], 289/II — poz. 2, "Emil Haecker — spuścizna," p. 11. Pages 11–13v of this source contain notes to an interview with Mykola Hankevych conducted *ca.* 1910. Hankevych had a bad memory for dates, a better memory for people.

5. *Praca*, 1890, no. 4, pp. 11–12; no. 5, p. 3; no. 11, p. 1. *Robotnik*, 1890, no. 3, pp. 4–5; no. 4, p. 4; no. 5, pp. 3–4.

6. *Praca*, 1890, nos. 9–11. *Arbeiter-Zeitung*, 1890, no. 27, p. 11; no. 30, p. 9.

7. *Praca*, 1890, no. 13, pp. 2–3.

8. "Z pod trzech zaborów," *Pobudka*, June 1889, no. 6, p. 27.

9. "Zur Lohnbewegung. Kolomea," *Arbeiter-Zeitung*, 25 June 1890, no. 30, p. 8.

10. "Z Kraju," *Pobudka*, January 1889, no. 1, p. 25.

11. "Sprawy drukarskie," *Praca*, 3 May 1889, no. 2, p. 8. "Zgromadzenie korporacyjne," ibid., 13 August 1890, no. 13, pp. 2–3. "Czy nam juz dobrze?" ibid., 21 February 1889, no. 1, p. 3. "Zgromadzenie robotników lwowskich," ibid., 14 June 1889, no. 3, pp. 9–10.

12. K. Sierp., "Robotnicy galicyjscy i izby robotnicze w Austryi," *Pobudka*, March 1889, no. 3, p. 24. "Dnia 6. lutego," *Praca*, 12 February 1887, no. 2, p. 7. Mykhailo Pavlyk addressed the assembly in Ukrainian. Mykhailo Pavlyk, ed., *Perepyska Mykhaila Drahomanova z Mykhailom Pavlykom. (1876–1895)*, 7 vols., numbered 2–8 (Chernivtsi, 1910–12), 5:149. Hereafter abbreviated as Pavlyk, *Perepyska*. "W sprawie Izb robotniczych," *Praca*, 18 March 1887, no. 3, p. 9.

13. According to the Lviv police, in a report to the viceroy, over one hundred and fifty workers participated in the assembly. According to the socialist paper *Praca*, about four hundred workers were in attendance. L'vivs'kyi oblasnyi derzhavnyi arkhiv [LODA], 350/1/2461, pp. 4, 5v. "Izby robotnicze," *Praca*, 21 February 1889, no. 1, pp. 2–3.

14. "Izby robotnicze," *Praca*, 12 February 1889, no. 1, p. 2.

15. The Daniluk faction objected that Mańkowski and Tabaczkowski had been picked to attend the inquiry in an undemocratic manner and by nonworkers. The assembly nonetheless confirmed Mańkowski's and Tabaczkowski's appointment. Ibid. Daniluk's charge was true. Under pressure from parliamentary deputy Stanisław Szczepanowski to provide immediately the names of two workers to represent Lviv in the inquiry, Franciszek Głodziński, master tailor and president of Gwiazda, submitted the names of Mańkowski and Tabaczkowski. LODA, 350/1/2461, pp. 8v–9.

16. Sierp, "Robotnicy galicyjscy," p. 27. "Izby robotnicze," *Praca*, 3 May 1889, no. 2, p. 6.

17. "O krok dalej," *Praca,* 3 May 1889, no. 2, pp. 6–7. "Śledztwo," *Kurjer Lwowski,* 22 March 1889, no. 81, p. 4. "Sprawozdanie ekspertów," *Praca,* 6 August 1889, no. 4, p. 15.

18. "Jęk boleści pp. majstrów," *Praca,* 15 May 1888, no. 3, pp. 9–10.

19. "Bolesław Czerwieński," *Praca,* 15 May 1888, no. 3, p. 9.

20. "Petycja do Rady Państwa," *Praca,* 6 August 1889, no. 4, p. 13.

21. *Robotnik,* 1890, no. 2, p. 4.

22. "Wieczorek Lassallowski," *Praca,* 13 September 1890, no. 15, pp. 2–3.

23. *Robotnik,* 1890, no. 15, p. 4. "Różności. Obchód," *Praca,* 13 November 1890, no. 17, p. 4. "Inland. Lemberg," *Arbeiter-Zeitung,* 10 October 1890, no. 41, pp. 3–4.

24. Bolesław Limanowski, "Rzecz o Galicyi ze stanowiska przywłaściowego niepodległości polskiej," *Pobudka,* June 1889, no. 6, p. 21. M. K. Ivasiuta, "Pershe sviatkuvannia 1 travnia na Ukraini," *Ukrains'kyi istorychnyi zhurnal,* 1965, no. 5, p. 133.

25. "Dzień pierwszego maja," *Robotnik,* 1890, no. 1, p. 1; no. 2, pp. 1–2; no. 3, pp. 1–2. "Co będzie w dniu 1. Maja," ibid., 1890, no. 4, pp. 1–2. "1. Maja 1890," *Praca,* 8 February 1890, no. 1, p. 1. J. Czech., "1. Maj w świetle stosunków galicyjskich," ibid., 28 February 1890, no. 2, p. 1; 13 March 1890, no. 3, p. 1. "Święćmy dzień 1. maja," ibid., 13 April 1890, no. 5, p. 1.

26. *Robotnik,* 1890, no. 2, p. 4; no. 3, pp. 2–3. (JC), "Krok naprzód," *Praca,* 28 March 1890, no. 4, pp. 9–10. Mykola Hankevych, "Pershe robitnyche sviato," *Narod,* 1890, no. 7, pp. 101–03.

27. *Robotnik,* 1890, no. 5, p. 2.

28. Wiktor Adam Bober, *Historja drukarń i stowarzyszeń drukarskich we Lwowie* (Lviv, 1926), p. 51.

29. Ivasiuta, "Pershe sviatkuvannia," p. 134.

30. Ignacy Daszyński [Żegota], *Krótka historya rozwoju partyi socyalistycznej w Galicyi* (Lviv, 1894), p. 7.

31. Brieter, *Krótki rys,* p. 14.

32. M. Drahomanov and M. Pavlyk [D. V. i P. K.], *Pro vicha* (Lviv, 1887), pp. 30–31. The police dissolved the Kosiv assembly. According to Teofil Okunevsky, "the dissolution of the assembly infuriated the people more than God knows what kind of revolutionary speeches could have done." Letter to Drahomanov, 1 November 1886, in Mykhailo Pavlyk, ed., *Perepyska Mykhaila Drahomanova z drom Teofilem Okunevs'kym (1883, 1885–1891, 1893–1895)* (Lviv, 1905), p. 47.

33. Severyn Danylovych, "Franko — dukhovnyi bat'ko Radykal'noi partii v Halychyni," in *Ivan Franko u spohadakh suchasnykiv* (1956), pp. 223–24.

34. Tsentral'nyi derzhavnyi istorychnyi arkhiv URSR u L'vovi [TsDIAL], 663/1/129, pp. 158–59. "Iliarii Harasymovych," *Hromads'kyi holos,* January 1902, no. 1, pp. 5–6.

35. Okunevsky to Drahomanov, 20 April 1886, in Pavlyk, *Perepyska Drahomanova z Okunevs'kym,* pp. 29–30.

36. 27 June 1886, ibid., p. 37.

37. Okunevsky to Drahomanov, 1 November 1886, ibid., p. 46.

38. For example, describing attendance at the Kolomyia assembly, Okunevsky noted that "a few members of our so-called intelligentsia" came, but "unless I am mistaken, they were more attracted by the dance that the committee arranged for the evening before the assembly than they were by the assembly itself." Ibid., p. 47.

39. Ibid., p. 48.

40. Ibid. See also: Sniatynchuk [Kyrylo Tryl'ovs'kyi?], "Pys'mo vid Sniatyna," Bat'kivshchyna, (6) 18 March 1887, no. 11, p. 64. After the experience of the Kolomyia assembly, Sniatynchuk proposed that each assembly set up a legal commission to give the peasants free legal advice.

41. Okunevsky to Drahomanov, 29 December 1886, in Pavlyk, Perepyska Drahomanova z Okunevs'kym, pp. 57–58.

42. Drahomanov to Okunevsky, 8 November 1886, ibid., p. 50. Okunevsky to Drahomanov, 29 December 1886, ibid., p. 57.

43. Pavlyk, "Peredne slovo," Perepyska Drahomanova z Okunevs'kym, p. xv.

44. "Dr. Kyrylo Tryl'ovs'kyi," Hromads'kyi holos, 1900, no. 27–28, pp. 227–28.

45. Okunevsky to Drahomanov, 31 August 1887, in Pavlyk, Perepyska Drahomanova z Okunevs'kym, pp. 77–80.

46. Severyn Danylovych, "O ekonomychnim stani selian v Halychyni," Dilo (30 December 1886) 11 January 1887, no. 145, p. 3. TsDIAL, 663/1/130, pp. 143–46.

47. Okunevsky to Drahomanov, 13 August 1889, in Pavlyk, Perepyska Drahomanova z Okunevs'kym, pp. 122–23.

48. For an essay on Przegląd Społeczny together with a selection of the journal's material, see Krzysztof Dunin-Wąsowicz, ed., Przegląd Społeczny 1886–1887 (Wrocław, 1955).

49. Wilhelm Feldman [Junius], "Współcześni politycy polscy. XX. Bolesław Wysłouch," Krytyka, rok XI — tom I (Dział polityczno-społeczny), z. vii–viii, July-August 1910, p. 35.

50. TsDIAL, 146/4/224/3684, p. 99.

51. The club in Ternopil had a socialist wing led by Yevhen Levytsky and including Mykola Hankevych among its members. Budzynovsky, Levytsky and Hankevych all became prominent members of the younger faction of the Radical party in the early 1890s. CA, 289/II — poz. 2, "Emil Haecker — spuścizna," p. 11.

52. TsDIAL, 146/4/224/3684, p. 105.

53. Ibid., p. 99. Ludwik Krzywicki, Wspomnienia, vol. I: 1859–1885 (Cracow, 1947), pp. 257–61.

54. Lucjan Blit, The Origins of Polish Socialism (Cambridge, 1971), p. 71. See also Wilhelm Feldman, Dzieje polskiej myśli politycznej 1864–1914, 2nd ed. (Warsaw, 1933), p. 241.

55. CA, 71/III–1, "Wspomnienia Jędrzeja Moraczewskiego. Ludzie, czasy i zdarzenia," część I: "Młodość i praca inżynierska. 1870–1907 r.," vol. I: "Lata nauki," pp. 20–21. The young socialist Wilhelm Feldman wrote in his

diary, 17 November 1886: "At the university the youth have come to life and set to work. The polytechnic especially is seething: many come there from the Congress Kingdom, effectively educated fellows, stalwart friends of progress." TsDIAL, 146/4/224/3684, p. 108.

56. Krzywicki, *Wspomnienia*, 1:268–69.

57. Ibid. LODA, 350/1/2435, p. 42.

58. Stanisław Padlewski had already been deported, from Cracow, in 1879. From Cracow he went to Zurich, then to Poznań where he was arrested in 1883 for socialist agitation. Released from prison in 1886, Padlewski returned to Russia to live with his mother. In May 1889, Padlewski stopped in Galicia on his way to Western Europe. In Lviv he stayed with Wilhelm Feldman and then moved on to Cracow where the police arrested him. On his person the police found chemicals for making invisible ink, socialist literature, a letter of introduction to Naftali Telz (originally from Lviv, then editor of the socialist periodical *Gleichheit* in Vienna) and an address book with the addresses of such known socialists as Karol Medwecki (Paris), Adolf Inlaender and Władysław Arciszewski (Vienna). HH, Informationsbüro, 1572, 1586, 1759/1889.

59. Arrested in Cracow, October 1888, and deported. Ibid., 1691/1889.

60. Stayed with Feldman and Padlewski in Lviv, roommate of Gizbert in Warsaw. Arrested in June 1889, deported in August. Ibid., 1691, 2032, 2420/1889.

61. Student at Dubliany Agricultural School. Letter of Artur Schleyen to Viktor Adler, 1890, in Verein für Geschichte der Arbeiterbewegung [Verein] (Vienna), Adler-Archiv, Mappe no. 168/1890, p. 18.

62. Student at Lviv Polytechnic. Ibid.

63. Izaak Kassjusz (alias Hausman, Słonimski) had been expelled from Zurich University and deported from Switzerland for involvement with a Polish socialist revolutionary group that experimented with bombs. From Zurich he went to Paris where he attended the founding congress of the Second Socialist International. He came to Lviv, where he roomed with Szpunt, in January 1890. Kassjusz was one of the founders of *Robotnik* and very active in agitation for Mayday. The Lviv police arrested him and handed him over to the Russian gendarmes in June 1890. It seems that Kassjusz, suffering from tuberculosis, died in the Peter-Paul fortress in Petersburg in 1891. Ibid. Daszyński, *Krótka historya*, p. 6. "Inland. Lemberg," *Arbeiter-Zeitung*, 13 March 1891, no. 11, p. 10. HH, Informationsbüro, 722, 896–97, 1371–72/1889, 1554/1890.

64. Letter of Count Edward Taafe (prime minister) to Count Gustav von Kálnoky (foreign minister), 15 May 1890, in HH, Informationsbüro, 1477/1890.

65. Konstanty Grzybowski, *Galicja 1848–1914* (Cracow, 1959), p. 139.

66. "Feliks Stanisław Daszyński," *Praca*, 13 July 1890, no. 11, p. 2. Ignacy Daszyński, *Pamiętniki*, 2 vols. (Cracow, 1925–26), 1:4–6. According to the brothers' cousin, in a deposition to the police (17 April 1889), Feliks was sentenced as a result of the trial. LODA, 350/1/2413, p. 32. But this would have been mentioned in police documents and is not.

67. Daszyński, *Pamiętniki*, 1:7–12. Ignacy Daszyński implies that the

sending of delegates and conversion to socialism occurred in 1882, after the arrest of several club members in the spring of that year. In choosing October 1881 as the time of conversion, I am guided by several facts: (1) Władysław Dzwonkowski had met Ivan Franko *before* March 1882 (TsDIAL, 146/4/ 224/3684, p. 55); (2) club member Leon Zatorski already had a copy of the program of Lud Polski by March 1882 (ibid., p. 54); and (3) Feliks Daszyński spent some weeks in Cracow in October 1881 (Archiwum Państwowe M. Krakowa i Woj. Krakowskiego [APKr], Starostwo Grodzkie w Krakowie [StGKr], 88/1883).

68. Daszyński, *Pamiętniki,* 1:11. TsDIAL, 146/4/224/3684, pp. 56, 62. HH, Informationsbüro, 1184, 1490/1882; 408, 2160/1883.

69. See above, p. 104.

70. Daszyński, *Pamiętniki,* 1:26–27. "Różności. Ucieczka z więzienia," *Praca,* 20 October 1883, no. 14, p. 52. The story in Krzywicki, *Wspomnienia,* 1:263–64, is garbled.

71. Krzywicki, *Wspomnienia,* 1:260.

72. Letter of Feliks to Ignacy Daszyński, 18 October 1888, in LODA, 350/1/2413, pp. 7v–8. Daszyński, *Pamiętniki,* 1:29–30. TsDIAL, 663/1/131, p. 186.

73. Daszyński, *Pamiętniki,* 1:29–30. An entry in Wilhelm Feldman's diary, 14 November 1886: "Daszyński, a cosmopolitan Marxist, converted everyone to the socialist faith. . . ." Feldman seems to be referring to Feliks. TsDIAL, 146/4/224/3684, pp. 103–04.

74. TsDIAL, 146/4/224/3684, pp. 99–108. "Kronika," *Kurjer Lwowski,* 4 December 1886, no. 336, p. 4. Austrian law forbade gymnasium students to form or belong to any organizations. Grzybowski, *Galicja,* p. 117.

75. TsDIAL, 146/4/224/3684, p. 100. See Ezra Mendelsohn, "Jewish Assimilation in Lvov: The Case of Wilhelm Feldman," *Slavic Review* 28 (1969), pp. 577–90.

76. Wilhelm F[eldman], "Z życia codziennego," *Praca,* 1884, nos. 9 and 10.

77. TsDIAL, 146/4/224/3684, p. 102.

78. Ibid., p. 101.

79. Viacheslav Budzynovs'kyi, "Avtobiografiia. (Fragment iz posmertnykh paperiv)," in his *Iak cholovik ziishov na pana* (Lviv, 1937), p. 12.

80. Other members of the club were Yuliian Bachynsky and Osyp Makovei. Osyp Makovei, *Istoriia odnoi studentskoi hromady* (Lviv, 1912). Makovei vividly describes the club in his short story, "Vesniani buri," *Vybrani tvory* (Kiev, 1954), pp. 48–77.

81. Letter of Seweryn to Ignacy Daszyński, 30 November 1886, in TsDIAL, 146/4/224/3684, p. 104.

82. CA, 71/III–1, "Wspomnienia Moraczewskiego," pp. 20–21. TsDIAL, 663/1/131, pp. 13, 18, 19, 30, 180.

83. Iw. Franko, "Z Rusi halickiej," *Kraj* (St. Petersburg), 21 October (2 November) 1888, no. 43, p. 9. Letter of Kozlovsky to Arciszewski, 9 November 1888, in TsDIAL, 663/1/134, p. 140.

84. TsDIAL, 663/1/131, p. 13.

85. TsDIAL, 663/1/134, pp. 140–41.

86. TsDIAL, 663/1/131, pp. 13–17, 26–27, 175; 663/1/135, p. 189.

87. TsDIAL, 663/1/135, pp. 12–19. CA, 71/III–1, "Wspomnienia Moraczewskiego," pp. 23–25. "Wiec akademicki," *Kurjer Lwowski,* 12 March 1889, no. 71, p. 5, and supplement 11 March 1889, no. 71, p. 1. W. Budzynowski, "Lwów. Marzec 1889. (Wiec akademicki)," *Ognisko,* April 1889, no. 1, pp. 20–22. Fr. Nowicki, "Pamiętniki," *Zjednoczenie* (Przemyśl), July 1906, no. 3, pp. 23–24. "Z pod trzech zaborów," *Pobudka,* May 1889, no. 5, p. 27.

88. "Walne zgromadzenie czytelni akademickiej," *Kurjer Lwowski,* 26 March 1889, no. 85, p. 3. "Wydział Tow. 'Akademiczne Bractwo,'" and "Skutki pyszałkowstwa i zarozumiałości," supplement to ibid., p. 1.

89. "W sprawie wiecu młodzieży szkół wyższych," ibid., 24 March 1889, no. 83, p. 4.

90. CA, 71/III–1, "Wspomnienia Moraczewskiego," p. 23.

91. "Z izby sądowej," *Kurjer Lwowski,* 1889, nos. 269–73. "Inland. Lemberg," *Arbeiter-Zeitung,* 11 October 1889, no. 7, p. 4.

92. Józef Białynia Chołodecki, *Półwiekowa przeszłość Stowarzyszenia katolickiej młodzieży rękodzielniczej "Skała" we Lwowie* (Lviv, 1906), p. 60.

93. Breiter, *Krótki rys,* p. 10. Letters of Kozlovsky to Arciszewski, 9 November 1888, 14 February 1889 and 6 July 1889 in TsDIAL, 663/1/134, pp. 142, 146–47; 663/1/131, pp. 151–52. Kozlovsky translated Paul Lafargue's "Proletarjat rzemieślniczy i umysłowy," seralized in *Praca* beginning with the 28 February 1890 issue.

94. TsDIAL, 663/1/131, pp. 151–53.

95. "O krok dalej," *Praca,* 3 May 1889, no. 2, p. 7.

96. Ignacy Daszyński, who came to Cracow to study in 1887, described the state of Cracovian journeymen: "Cracow's working class had sunk into darkest ignorance. Their drunkenness was horrifying, and masons, who constituted the largest profession, led a wanton and completely thoughtless life. Low wages and the lack of organization and education made of Cracow's working class guardians of clericalism. Once they beat some students bloody for wanting to demonstrate against a Jesuit who used the pulpit to damn and slander the insurrection of 1863! Up until 1890 the working class of Cracow was inimical to the progressive intelligentsia; it was devoted to bigotry and ignorant to the point of despair." Daszyński, *Pamiętniki,* 1:39.

97. Nowicki, "Pamiętniki," pp. 26–28.

98. For an account of the *Ognisko* group, see Stanisław Konarski's contribution to *Postępowe tradycje młodzieży akademickiej w Krakowie,* ed. Henryk Dobrowolski, et al. (Cracow, 1962), pp. 18–40.

99. Nowicki, "Pamiętniki," p. 25.

100. *Ognisko,* May 1889, no. 1, p. 1.

101. [Zygmunt Zgodziński], "Od Wydawnictwa," *Ognisko* (Lviv, 1890), pp. 3–4.

102. Ludwik Krzywicki, "Samokształcenie społecznoznawcze," *Ognisko* (Lviv, 1890), p. 5.

103. TsDIAL, 146/4/224/3684, pp. 114–15.

104. Instytut literatury Akademii nauk URSR, Viddil rukopysiv [IL], f. 3, od. zb. 1605, p. 261.

105. Redakcya, "Zamiast programu," *Ognisko,* April 1889, no. 1, pp. 1–3.

106. Ibid. Ziemowit, "Młoda Polska," *Ognisko* (Lviv, 1890), pp. 75–76. "'Przegląd Akademicki' o Rusinach," ibid., pp. 27–37. "Patryotyzm," *Ognisko,* May 1889, no. 1, pp. 1–4.

107. Budzynovs'kyi, "Avtobiografiia," p. 12.

108. The best analysis of the journal is O. I. Dei, "Zhurnal 'Tovarysh' (Epizod iz zhurnalistychnoi diial'nosti I. Franka)," *Doslidzhennia tvorchosti Ivana Franka,* vyp. 2 (Kiev, 1959), pp. 103–32.

109. Letter of Kozlovsky to Arciszewski, 9 November 1888, in TsDIAL, 663/1/134, p. 143.

110. Pavlyk to Drahomanov, 21–25 October 1888, in Pavlyk, *Perepyska,* 5:246–48. Osyp Makovei, "Iz shchodennyka," p. 217. Budzynovs'kyi, "Avtobiografiia," p. 13.

111. See my article, "Ukrains'kyi sotsiializm u Halychyni (do rozkolu v Radykal'nii Partii, 1899 r.)," *Journal of Ukrainian Graduate Studies,* no. 7 (1979), pp. 42–51.

112. TsDIAL, 663/1/134, p. 144. CA, 289/II-poz. 2, "Emil Haecker — spuścizna," pp. 11–11v. Osyp Nazaruk and Olena Okhrymovych, "Khronika rukhu ukrains'koi akademychnoi molodizhy u L'vovi," in Zenon Kuzelia and Mykola Chaikivs'kyi, eds., *1868–1908. "Sich". Al'manakh* (Lviv, 1908), p. 15. Kozakevych influenced the young Mykola Hankevych in the late 1880s.

113. There is an account of the Degen affair in V. I. Kalynovych, *Politychni protsesy Ivana Franka ta ioho tovaryshiv* (Lviv, 1967), pp. 120–34. Archival material relating to the affair can be found in HH, Informationsbüro, 2248, 2556, 2591–93, 2607, 2972, 3066, 3261, 3316, 3599/1889, and TsDIAL, 663/1/126–30.

114. HH, Informationsbüro, 2248/1889.

115. CA, 5/II-2, p. 9.

116. Danylovych to Franko, 10 December 1889, in IL, f. 3, od. zb. 1629, pp. 277–78. Danylovych to Pavlyk, 15 December 1889, IL, f. 3, od. zb. 1605, pp. 347–48.

117. Pavlyk, *Perepyska,* 6:7, 52. On 1 July 1890, Pavlyk analyzed the social composition of the 251 subscribers to *Narod*:

> 91 (36%) — secular intelligentsia. (41 lawyers, 28 medics, 16 teachers, 2 military officers, 5 Polish intellectuals.)
>
> 40 (16%) — priests, in spite of *Narod*'s anticlericalism. 12 additional copies were distributed gratis to Lviv seminarians.
>
> 25 (10%) — associations.
>
> 20 (8%) — gymnasium students.
>
> 16 (6%) — women.

15 (6%) — peasants. 30 additional copies were distributed gratis to peasants in Kolomyia district.

11 (4%) — burghers and merchants.

33 (13%) — subscribers outside Austria: America (14), Russia (11) and elsewhere in Europe (8).

On *Narod,* see M. L. Butryn, "Zhurnal 'Narod' pid obukhom reaktsii," *Ukrains'ke literaturoznavstvo* 13 (1971), pp. 37–41.

118. V. Budzynovs'kyi, "Ekshumatsyia i novyi pokhoron," *Dilo,* 13 April (31 March) 1912, no. 82, pp. 1–2. Budzynovs'kyi's memoir, the sole account of the summer meeting where the Ruthenians decided to found the Radical party, is partly corroborated in Pavlyk, *Perepyska,* 6:62, 192.

119. *Narod,* 22 October 1891, no. 20–21, p. 266, mentions that just under sixty delegates attended the party's second congress and that this was double the number that attended the first congress.

120. CA, 289/II — poz. 2, "Emil Haecker — spuścizna," p. 12. This seems to me correct, in spite of some contradictory evidence. Pavlyk himself does not mention his participation in composing the minimal program. Pavlyk, "Peredne slovo," *Perepyska Drahomanova z Okunevs'kymn,* p. xvi. Danylovych, however, remembers Pavlyk's input on the cultural section of the minimal program, but does not mention Franko in connection with the minimal program. Instead, he states that Franko worked with Levytsky on the maximal program. Danylovych, "Franko," in *Ivan Franko u spohadakh suchasnykiv* (1956), p. 231.

121. The program of the Ruthenian-Ukrainian Radical Party was published in *Narod,* 1890, no. 20.

122. S. M. Zlupko, *Ideina borot'ba navkolo ahrarno-selians'koho pytannia v Halychyni (kinets' XIX — pochatok XX stolit')* (Lviv, 1960), p. 66.

123. b + i, "Eine radikale ruthenisch-ukrainische Partei," *Arbeiter-Zeitung,* 7 November 1890, no. 45, p. 7.

124. "Ruska partya chłopska," *Robotnik,* 1890, no. 17, pp. 3–4. See also: "Nowa partja," *Praca,* 22 November 1890, no. 19, p. 2.

125. Letter of Okunevsky to Yakiv Nevestiuk, end of October 1890, in Pavlyk, *Perepyska Drahomanova z Okunevs'kym,* pp. 137–40.

126. Pavlyk to Drahomanov, 11 October 1890, in Pavlyk, *Perepyska,* 6:77.

127. Budzynovs'kyi, "Ekshumatsyia," *Dilo,* 1912, nos. 78 and 82. Budzynovs'kyi, "Avtobiografiia," p. 13. S. V. [= Viacheslav] Budzinovskii, *Kul'turnaia nuzhda avstriiskoi Rusi,* 2 parts (Lviv, 1891).

128. Daszyński, *Pamiętniki,* 1:67–68. Letter of Ignacy Daszyński to Wincenty Sikorski, 6 October 1890, CA, AM, 1248/8 II, no. 4.

129. "Towarzysze!" *Robotnik,* 15 November 1890, no. 18, p. 1. "Towarzysze!" *Praca,* 22 November 1890, no. 19, p. 1.

130. On the further history of the Polish social democrats and Ukrainian Radicals, see: Józef Buszko, *Ruch socjalistyczny w Krakowie 1890–1914 na tle ruchu robotniczego w Zachodniej Galicji* (Cracow, 1961); Julian Brunn, "Kwestia narodowa w rewolucji i kontrrewolucji. PPSD Galicji i Śląska," in *Pisma wybrane,* vol. 1 (Warsaw, 1955), pp. 133–50; V. Levyns'kyi, *Narys*

rozvytku ukrains'koho robitnychoho rukhu v Halychyni (Kiev, 1914); Himka, "Ukrains'kyi sotsiializm u Halychyni."

131. APKr, StGKr, 260, *passim* for 1891 and 1892. Józef Buszko, "Początki ruchu socjalistycznego w Galicji Zachodniej (1890–1892)," *Zeszyty Naukowe Uniwersytetu Jagiellońskiego,* no. 40 (1961), Prace Historyczne, z. 6, pp. 118, 120.

132. The statutes of Podgórze's Siła are in APKr, StGKr, 305.

133. Buszko, "Początki," p. 120.

134. V. Dmytruk, *Narys z istorii ukrains'koi zhurnalistyky XIX st.* (Lviv, 1969), p. 133.

135. For example, the Radicals sent a copy of *Hromads'kyi holos* (Voice of the Commune) to a reading club in Hadynkivtsi associated with Prosvita. In this particular case, however, the administration of the reading club wrote insulting (and anti-Semitic) remarks on the issue and sent the paper back to its editors. "Novynky. Nerozum," *Hromads'kyi holos,* 1900, no. 5, p. 43. And see above, p. 218, note 155.

136. At the turn of the century much debate centered around the relative merits of the Greek Catholic *Misionar'* (Missionary) and the radical *Hromads'kyi holos*; in one instance, a pastor allegedly stated that the devil himself wrote the Radical paper. "Novynky. Pip — voroh pros'vity," ibid., 1900, no. 16, p. 135.

137. For an account of radical peasant assemblies and other mass actions in the 1890s, see M. M. Kravets', "Masovi selians'ki vystupy u Skhidnii Halychyni v 90-kh rokakh XIX st.," *Z istorii Ukrains'koi RSR,* vyp. 8 (1963), pp. 3–27.

138. Huryk had made his debut speaking at the 1886 Stanyslaviv assembly, organized jointly by the Stanyslaviv group and the national populists.

139. W. Feldman, "Sprawa ukraińska," in Stefan Kieniewicz, ed., *Galicja w dobie autonomicznej (1850–1914). Wybór tekstów* (Wrocław, 1952), p. 321.

Select Bibliography

Archives

APKr	Archiwum Państwowe M. Krakowa i Woj. Krakowskiego. Cracow.
StGKr	Starostwo Grodzkie w Krakowie.
DPKr	Dyrekcja Policji w Krakowie.
SKKKr	Sąd Krajowy Karny w Krakowie.
CA	Centralne Archiwum Komitetu Centralnego PZPR. Warsaw.
HH	Haus-, Hof- und Staatsarchiv. Vienna.
Informationsbüro	Informationsbüro des k.k. Ministeriums des Äussern.
IL	Instytut literatury Akademii nauk URSR, Viddil rukopysiv. Kiev.
LODA	L'vivs'kyi oblasnyi derzhavnyi arkhiv. Lviv.
TsDIAL	Tsentral'nyi derzhavnyi istorychnyi arkhiv URSR u L'vovi. Lviv.
Verein	Verein für Geschichte der Arbeiterbewegung. Vienna.

Primary Sources

Baumgarten, Leon, ed. *Kółka socjalistyczne, gminy i Wielki Proletariat. Procesy polityczne 1878–1888. Źródła.* Warsaw, 1966.

Baumgarten, Leon, ed. *Krakowski komisarz policji na służbie carskiego wywiadu. Korespondencja komisarza Jana Kostrzewskiego z urzędnikiem do specjalnych poruczeń zagranicznego wywiadu departamentu policji w Petersburgu radcą stanu Fiodorem Sierakowskim w latach 1882–1884.* Cracow, 1967.

Bednarski, Szczęsny, trans. *Głosy robotników! Podług broszury F. Schönhofer'a. "Was wollen, was sollen die Arbeiter!"* Lviv, 1873.

Breiter, Ernest [J. L. Prawdzic]. *Krótki rys ruchu socyalistycznego we Lwowie w ostatnim 25–leciu.* Lviv, 1895.

Brzeziński, Edmund. "Wspomnienia z mojego życia." *Niepodległość,* IV (1931), z. 7, pp. 44–70; z. 2 (8), pp. 212–30.

Budzynovs'kyi, Viacheslav. "Avtobiografiia. (Fragment iz posmertnykh paperiv)." *Iak cholovik ziishov na pana.* Lviv, 1937.

Budzynovs'kyi, V. "Ekshumatsyia i novyi pokhoron." *Dilo,* 1912, nos. 78, 82.

Daszyński, Ignacy [Żegota]. *Krótka historya rozwoju partyi socyalistycznej w Galicyi*. Lviv, 1894.

Daszyński, Ignacy. *Pamiętniki*. 2 vols. Cracow, 1925–26.

Dei, O. I., and Korniienko, N. P., eds. *Ivan Franko u spohadakh suchasnykiv*. Lviv, 1956.

Dei, O. I., ed. *Ivan Franko u spohadakh suchasnykiv. Knyha druha*. Lviv, 1972.

Drahomanov, M. P. *Literaturno-publitsystychni pratsi*. 2 vols. Kiev, 1970.

Dragomanov, M. P. *Politicheskiia sochineniia*. Edited by I. M. Grevs and B. A. Kistiakovskii. Vol. I: *Tsentr i okrainy*. Moscow, 1908.

Dragomanov, M. P. *Sobranie politicheskikh sochinenii*. 2 vols. Paris, 1905–06.

Drahomanov, Mykhailo. *Vybrani tvory. Zbirka politychnykh tvoriv z prymitkamy*. Edited by Pavlo Bohats'kyi. Prague-New York, 1937.

Franko, Ivan. *Tvory*. 20 vols. Kiev, 1950–56.

Franko, Ivan. *V naimakh u susidiv*. Lviv, 1914.

Głodziński, Franciszek. *Odezwa do współkolegów Towarzystwa "Gwiazda" w dniu uroczystości poświęcenia jej chorągwi*. Lviv, 1871.

Kieniewicz, Stefan, ed. *Galicja w dobie autonomicznej (1850–1914). Wybór tekstów*. Wrocław, 1952.

Krzywicki, Ludwik. *Wspomnienia*. Vol. I: *1859–1885*. Cracow, 1947. 3 vols. Warsaw, 1957–59.

Limanowski, Bolesław. *O kwestji robotniczej*. Lviv, 1871.

Limanowski, Bolesław. *Pamiętniki. (1870–1907)*. Warsaw, 1958.

Limanowski, Bolesław. *Socyjalizm jako konieczny objaw dziejowego rozwoju*. Lviv, 1879. Actually published 1878.

Lystuvannia I. Franka i M. Drahomanova. Kiev, 1928.

Makovei, Osyp. *Istoriia odnoi studentskoi hromady*. Lviv, 1912.

Mikołajski, Szczepan. "Pierwszy posiew socjalizmu w Galicji. (Wspomnienia z procesu Ludwika Waryńskiego i 34 spólników w Krakowie 1878–1880 r.)." *Niepodległość*, XII (1935), pp. 342–63.

Molska, Alina, ed. *Pierwsze pokolenie marksistów polskich. Wybór pism i materiałów źródłowych z lat 1878–1886*. 2 vols. Warsaw, 1962.

Nechytaliuk, M. F. *Publitsystyka Ivana Franka (1875–1886 rr.) Seminarii*. Lviv, 1972.

Nowicki, Fr. "Pamiętniki." *Zjednoczenie* (Przemyśl), July 1906, no. 3, pp. 23–28.

O potrzebie stowarzyszeń przemysłowych czyli rzemieślniczych. Lviv, 1864.

Pavlyk, M. *Drukovanyi lyst Mykhaila Pavlyka do l'udei*. Geneva, 1880.

Pavlyk, M., ed. *Perepyska Mykhaila Drahomanova z drom Teofilem Okunevs'kym (1883, 1885–1891, 1893–1895)*. Lviv, 1905.

Pavlyk, M., ed. *Perepyska Mykhaila Drahomanova z Mykhailom Pavlykom. (1876–1895)*. 7 vols., numbered 2–8. Chernivtsi, 1910–12. Abbreviated in notes as Pavlyk, *Perepyska*.

Pavlyk, Mykhailo. *Tvory*. Kiev, 1957.

Piekarski, Witold. *Listy z więzienia (1879)*. Edited by Jerzy Zathey. Wrocław, 1953.

"Pochatky sotsiialistychnoho rukhu v Skhidnii Halychyni v dokumentakh avstriis'koi okhranky. I. Pershyi ukrains'kyi sotsiialistychnyi protses v Avstrii 1876 r." *Kul'tura*, 1929, no. 1, pp. 2–7.

"Pochatky sotsiialistychnoho rukhu v Skhidnii Halychyni v dokumentakh avstriis'skoi okhranky." *Kul'tura*, VII, no. 1 (January 1930), pp. 12–17.

"Pochatky revoliutsiinoho rukhu v Skhidnii Halychyni v dokumentakh avstriis'koi politsii. Vidozva 'do robitnyts'.'" *Kul'tura*, 1930, no. 6, pp. 23–28.

Podolinskii, S. *Sotsialisty Ukraintsy v Avstrii*. Geneva, [1881].

Przegląd Społeczny 1886–1887. Edited by Krzysztof Dunin-Wąsowicz. Wrocław, 1955.

Romanowicz, Tadeusz. *O stowarzyszeniach*. Lviv, 1867.

Skałkowski, Tadeusz. *Warsztaty i fabryki a postęp przemysłowy*. Lviv, 1869. Cover bears date: 1870.

Szczepański, Alfred. *Cechy i stowarzyszenia. Posłanie pierwsze*. Cracow, 1867.

Targalski, Jerzy, ed. "Krakowska sprawa socjalistów polskich. Materiały śledztwa z lat 1878–1880 (Wybór), Część I." *Z Pola Walki*, 1974, no. 4, pp. 133–86.

Terlets'kyi, Ostap. *Halyts'ko-rus'ke pys'menstvo 1848–1865 rr. na tli tohochasnykh suspil'no-politychnykh zmahan' halyts'ko-rus'koi inteligentsii. Nedokinchena pratsia*. Lviv, 1903.

Tych, Feliks, ed. *Polskie programy socjalistyczne 1878–1918*. Warsaw, 1975.

Z pola walki. Zbiór materyałów tyczących się polskiego ruchu socyalistycznego. London, 1904.

Źródła do dziejów klasy robotniczej na ziemiach polskich. Edited by Natalia Gąsiorowska-Grabowska. Vol. II: *Śląsk, Wielkopolska, Pomorze, Warmia, Mazury, Zachodnia Galicja 1850–1900*. Warsaw, 1962.

Secondary Literature

Assonova, N. T. *Sotsialistychni pohliady ukrains'kykh revoliutsioneriv-demokrativ (Kinets' XIX — pochatok XX st.)*. Kiev, 1977.

Bass, I. *Ivan Franko. Biografiia*. Moscow, 1957.

Baumgarten, Leon. *Dzieje Wielkiego Proletariatu*. Warsaw, 1966.

Blit, Lucjan. *The Origins of Polish Socialism: The History and Ideas of the First Polish Socialist Party 1878–1886*. Cambridge, 1971.

Bober, Adam Wiktor. *Historja drukarń i stowarzyszeń drukarskich we Lwowie*. Lviv, 1926.

Bujak, Fr. *Galicya*. 2 vols. Lviv, 1908–10.

Buszko, Józef. *Ruch socjalistyczny w Krakowie 1890–1914 na tle ruchu robotniczego w Zachodniej Galicji*. Cracow, 1961.

Buzek, Józef. *Stosunki zawodowe i socyalne ludności w Galicyi według wyznania i narodowości, na podstawie spisu ludności z 31. grudnia 1900 r*. Wiadomości statystyczne o stosunkach krajowych, tom XX, z. II. Lviv, 1905.

Chołodecki, Józef Białynia. *Półwiekowa przeszłość Stowarzyszenia katolickiej młodzieży rękodzielniczej "Skała" we Lwowie*. Lviv, 1906.

Cottam, Kazimiera. *Boleslaw Limanowski (1835–1935): A Study in Socialism and Nationalism.* Boulder, Colo., 1978.

Dei, O. I. *Ukrains'ka revoliutsiino-demokratychna zhurnalistyka. Problema vynykennia i stanovlennia.* Kiev, 1959.

Dei, O. I. "Zhurnal 'Tovarysh' (Epizod iz zhurnalistychnoi diial'nosti I. Franka)." *Doslidzhennia tvorchosti Ivana Franka,* vyp. 2 (Kiev, 1959), pp. 103–32.

Denysiuk, Ivan. *Mykhailo Pavlyk.* Kiev, 1960.

Feldman, Wilhelm. *Dzieje polskiej myśli politycznej 1864–1914.* 2nd ed. Warsaw, 1933.

Feldman, Wilhelm. *Stronnictwa i programy polityczne w Galicyi 1846–1906.* 2 vols. Cracow, 1907.

Grzybowski, Konstanty. *Galicja 1848–1914. Historia ustroju politycznego na tle historii ustroju Austrii.* Cracow, 1959.

Haecker, Emil. *Historja socjalizmu w Galicji i na Śląsku Cieszyńskim.* Vol. 1: *1846–1882.* Cracow, 1933. Only one volume appeared.

Harwood, William Lathrop. "Ignacy Daszynski: The Making of an Austro-Polish Statesman, 1866–1918." Ph. D. dissertation: The University of Illinois at Urbana-Champaign, 1977.

Himka, John-Paul. "Priests and Peasants: The Greek Catholic Pastor and the Ukrainian National Movement in Austria, 1867–1900." *Canadian Slavonic Papers,* 1979, no. 1, pp. 1–14.

Himka, John-Paul. "Ukrains'kyi sotsiializm u Halychyni (do rozkolu v radykal'nii partii, 1899 r.)." *Journal of Ukrainian Graduate Studies,* no. 7 (1979), pp. 33–51.

Himka, John-Paul. "Voluntary Artisan Associations and the Ukrainian National Movement in Galicia (the 1870s)." *Harvard Ukrainian Studies* 2 (1978): 235–50.

Hornowa, Elżbieta. *Ukraiński obóz postępowy i jego współpraca z polską lewicą społeczną w Galicji 1876–1895.* Wrocław, 1968.

Hrushevs'kyi, M. *Z pochyniv ukrains'koho sotsiialistychnoho rukhu. Mykh. Drahomanov i zhenevs'kyi sotsiialistychnyi hurtok.* Vienna, 1922.

Iashchuk, Pavlo. *Mykhailo Pavlyk. Literaturno-krytychnyi narys.* Lviv, 1959.

Iatskevych, Ie. A. *Stanovyshche robitnychoho klasu Halychyny v period kapitalizmu (1848–1900) (Narys).* Kiev, 1958.

Iavors'kyi, M. *Narysy z istorii revoliutsiinoi borot'by na Ukraini.* Vol. II, part 1. Kharkiv, 1928.

Kalynovych, Ivan. *Pokazchyk do ukrains'koi sotsiialistychnoi i komunistychnoi literatury.* Vienna, 1921.

Kalynovych, V. I. *Politychni protsesy Ivana Franka ta ioho tovaryshiv.* Lviv, 1967.

Kormanowa, Żanna. *Materiały do bibliografii druków socjalistycznych na ziemiach polskich w latach 1866–1918.* 2nd ed. Warsaw, 1949.

Kozik, Jan. "Moskalofilstwo w Galicji w latach 1848–1866 na tle odrodzenia narodowego Rusinów." M.A. dissertation: Jagellonian University, 1958.

Kozłowski, Józef. "Iwan Franko a polski ruch robotniczy w Galicji w latach siedemdziesiątych i osiemdziesiątych wieku XIX." *Kwartalnik Instytutu Polsko-Radzieckiego,* 1954, no. 1, pp. 93–108.

Kravets', M. M. "Pochatok robitnychoho rukhu v Skhidnii Halychyni." *Z istorii zakhidnoukrains'kykh zemel',* vyp. 2 (Kiev, 1958), pp. 23–59.

Kuzelia, Zenon, and Chaikivs'kyi, Mykola, eds. *1868–1908. "Sich". Al'manakh v pamiat' 40-ykh rokovyn osnovania tovarystva "Sich" u Vidni.* Lviv, 1908.

Levyns'kyi, V. *Narys rozvytku ukrains'koho robitnychoho rukhu v Halychyni.* Kiev, 1914.

Levyns'kyi, Volodymyr. *Pochatky ukrains'koho sotsiializmu v Halychyni.* Toronto, 1918.

Levyts'kyi, Ivan Em. *Halytsko-ruskaia bibliohrafiia XIX-ho stolitiia . . . (1801–1886).* 2 vols. Lviv, 1888–95.

Levyts'kyi, Kost'. *Istoriia politychnoi dumky halyts'kykh ukraintsiv 1848–1914.* 2 vols. Lviv, 1926–27.

Lozyns'kyi, Mykhailo. *Mykhailo Pavlyk. Ioho zhyttie i diial'nist'.* Vienna, 1917.

Makaiev, V. *Robitnychyi klas Halychyny v ostannii tretyni XIX st.* Lviv, 1968.

Moroz, M. O., ed. *Ivan Franko. Bibliohrafiia tvoriv 1874–1964.* Kiev, 1966.

Naimark, Norman M. *The History of the "Proletariat": The Emergence of Marxism in the Kingdom of Poland, 1870–1887.* Boulder, Colo., 1979.

Najdus, Walentyna. "Klasowe związki zawodowe w Galicji." *Przegląd Historyczny,* 51 (1960), z. 1, pp. 123–54.

Najdus, Walentyna. "Początki socjalistycznego ruchu robotniczego w Galicji (Lata siedemdziesiąte — osiemdziesiąte XIX w.)." *Z Pola Walki,* 1960, no. 1, pp. 3–34.

Najdus, Walentyna. *Powstanie związku zawodowego drukarzy w Galicji (Wyjątek z Księgi Pamiątkowej Związku Zawodowego Pracowników Poligrafii wydanej w 1960 roku z okazji jubileuszu 90-lecia Związku).* N.p., [1960], pp. 39–68.

Najdus, Walentyna. *Szkice z historii Galicji.* 2 vols. Warsaw, 1958–60.

Pavlyk, M., ed. *Mykhailo Petrovych Drahomanov 1841–1895. Ieho iubylei, smert', avtobiohrafiia i spys tvoriv.* Lviv, 1896.

Polska klasa robotnicza. Zarys dziejów. Vol. I, part 1: *Od przełomu XVIII i XIX w. do 1870 r.* Edited by Stanisław Kalabiński. Warsaw, 1974.

Rachwał, Stanisław. *Mieczysław Darowski. Czyny i słowa.* Lviv, 1923.

Rudnytsky, Ivan L., ed. *Mykhaylo Drahomanov: A Symposium and Selected Writings.* Annals of the Ukrainian Academy of Arts and Sciences in the U.S., II. New York, 1952.

Rudnytsky, Ivan L. "The Ukrainians in Galicia under Austrian Rule." *Austrian History Yearbook,* III, Part 2 (1967), pp. 394–429.

Styś, Wincenty. *Rozdrabnianie gruntów chłopskich w byłym zaborze austrjackim od roku 1787 do 1931.* Lviv, 1934.

Trusevych, S. M. *Suspil'no-politychnyi rukh u Skhidnii Halychyni v 50–70-kh rokakh XIX st.* Kiev, 1978.

Verves, H. D. *Ivan Franko i pytannia ukrains'ko-pol's'kykh literaturno–hromads'kykh vzaiemyn 70–90-kh rokiv XIX st.* Kiev, 1957.

Volianiuk, M. M. "Pershi nelehal'ni robitnychi hurtky u L'vovi." *L'vivs'kyi filial Tsentral'noho muzeiu V. I. Lenina. Naukovi zapysky,* vyp. 1 (1959), pp. 19–47.

Vozniak, Mykhailo. "Ivan Franko v dobi radykalizmu." *Ukraina,* 1926, kn. 6, pp. 115–63.

Wandycz, Piotr S. "The Poles in the Habsburg Monarchy." *Austrian History Yearbook,* III, part 2 (1967), pp. 261–86.

Wyka, Kazimierz. *Teka Stańczyka na tle historii Galicji w latach 1849–1869.* Wrocław, 1951.

Zlupko, S. M. *Ideina borot'ba navkolo ahrarno-selians'koho pytannia v Halychyni (Kinets' XIX — pochatok XX stolit').* Lviv, 1960.

Żychowski, Marian. *Bolesław Limanowski 1835–1935.* Warsaw, 1971.

Żychowski, Marian. "Społeczeństwo Galicji i Królestwa Polskiego wobec Pierwszej Międzynarodówki w latach 1864–1876." *Małopolskie Studia Historyczne,* 8 (1965), z. 1/2 (28/29), pp. 53–69.

Index

Austria...